Progress on safeguards for children living away from home

A review of actions since the *People Like Us* report

Marian Stuart and Catherine Baines

JR
JOSEPH
ROWNTREE
FOUNDATION
1904
2004

The **Joseph Rowntree Foundation** has supported this project as part of its programme of research and innovative development projects, which it hopes will be of value to policy makers, practitioners and service users. The facts presented and views expressed in this report are, however, those of the authors and not necessarily those of the Foundation.

Joseph Rowntree Foundation
The Homestead
40 Water End
York YO30 6WP
Website: www. jrf.org.uk

A CIP catalogue record for this report is available from the British Library.

ISBN 1 85935 255 3   (paperback)
ISBN 1 85935 256 1   (pdf: available at www.jrf.org.uk)

Cover design by Adkins Design

Prepared and printed by:
York Publishing Services Ltd
64 Hallfield Road
Layerthorpe
York YO31 7ZQ
Tel: 01904 430033; Fax: 01904 430868; Website: www.yps-publishing.co.uk

Further copies of this report, or any other JRF publication, can be obtained either from the JRF website (www.jrf.org.uk/bookshop/) or from our distributor, York Publishing Services Ltd, at the above address.

Contents

Foreword

'*People Like Us*' was widely welcomed when it appeared in 1997. Its central thesis was that safety was, in general, a function of overall competence: organisations that achieved their basic objectives for children were also likely to be the safest. Additional precautions were needed to guard against the neglect and exploitation of vulnerable groups.

The report caught the tide generated by a new administration's commitment to children. The Government's co-ordinated response accepted most of its recommendations about children living in children's homes, foster care, boarding-schools, and penal and health settings. The Quality Protects programme directed an additional £885 million over five years to services for children looked after by local authorities.

Several years on I thought it reasonable to ask how the promises made in 1998 had been fulfilled. I am grateful to my trustee colleagues of the Joseph Rowntree Foundation for funding the work required to answer that question, and to Marian Stuart for undertaking it with the help of Catherine Baines. Both Marian and Catherine worked with me on the original report.

This new report is a major piece of work in its own right. It provides critical evaluation of developments since 1997, and represents a significant case study of this area of social policy concerning children who live away from home. There is much reassuring news in, for example, the large sector of residential education. In some other areas progress is sluggish or stalled. Even sectors where much progress has been made – such as that for children looked after by local authorities – retain areas of weakness and policy neglect.

Indeed, the report exemplifies the condition of human services where centrally driven policies depend for their success on the motivation, skills and attitudes of thousands of front-line staff. Problems may arise in the policy itself, in resourcing it, in service management, or in the values and competence of the staff delivering services. Continuing failures of implementation point to weaknesses in managerial structures, and renewed efforts are needed through professional education and in-house training to improve the ability of individual staff to recognise and meet children's needs. At the policy level, too, it is plain that some obstacles remain to acknowledging and responding to the reality of some children's situations.

Credit must be given to government and its willing partners in statutory and independent services for the progress made. Much, nevertheless, remains to be done. The report confirms how difficult it is for disabled and disadvantaged children to have their needs recognised and met. It remains of enduring importance that they and their families continue to receive the support of committed champions within and beyond government.

Sir William Utting
August 2004

Acknowledgements

This study benefited from contributions from many people and organisations.

Our Advisory Group gave valuable support, advice and encouragement:
Sir William Utting, CB Chair
Professor Andrew Cooper, Professor of Social Work, Tavistock Clinic
Frances Crook, Howard League for Penal Reform
Maureen Eade, Education Consultant, former HMI
Michele Elliott, Kidscape
Donald Findlater, The Lucy Faithfull Foundation
Baroness Howarth of Breckland
Maggie Jones, Project Manager, Joseph Rowntree Foundation
Christine Lenehan, Council for Disabled Children
Gerri McAndrew, formerly of The Fostering Network
Professor Ian Sinclair, Social Work Research and Development Unit, University of York
Colin Turner, NSPCC

We wish to record our thanks to people working for different voluntary organisations and professional associations active in the field of children's services for giving us a lot of their time and knowledge.

We are grateful to officials in the Department for Education and Skills, the Department of Health, the Home Office, HM Customs and Excise and the Welsh Assembly Government for providing helpful responses and information.

1 Introduction

1.1 Background and scope of this study

Sir William Utting was commissioned in June 1996 by the Conservative Government to carry out a review of safeguards for children living away from home in the wake of allegations of widespread abuse in care homes and foster care in Wales. He presented his report *People Like Us: The Report of the Review of Safeguards for Children Living Away from Home* (1) in August 1997 to a new Labour administration which had tackling inequalities and social exclusion high on its agenda. Many children who live away from home fall into this category. The Report therefore coincided with the wider Government agenda.

People Like Us (1) made 20 Principal Recommendations which are 'both important in themselves and affect large numbers of children'. Other recommendations were made in the text of the Report. A year later the Government set out its response in the *Government Response to the Children's Safeguards Review* (2). This said what action it proposed to take on all 139 recommendations as well as the Principal ones – there were 139 in all.

This study has been funded by the Joseph Rowntree Foundation to establish what has happened since *People Like Us* (1) was published in 1997 and what the current state of play is on safeguards for children living away from home. It has looked at all the recommendations and concluded that action has been taken on all but a small number. All the significant recommendations are covered, including the few which were rejected by the Government. Appendix 1 gives a brief account of action on some recommendations not covered in the text.

Some areas have been looked at in more detail and will be covered in a separate report:

- abusers

- disabled children

- children and young people in prison settings.

People Like Us (1) did not claim to cover all situations in which children and young people live away from home, for example, it did not cover young people in the armed services. Since 1997 there have been new areas of major concern, notably the position of unaccompanied child refugees and children who are trafficked for the purposes of sexual abuse, slavery or even sacrifice. This report does not cover those groups but much of what is said will be applicable to them. They need the same level of safeguards as other children.

People Like Us (1) was a report to both the Department of Health and the Welsh Office. Since then responsibility for children's services in Wales has been devolved to the Welsh Assembly Government. While this report does cover some of the developments in Wales since devolution it cannot claim to be a comprehensive analysis of the position in Wales. The recommendations made are directed to English organisations but are likely to apply equally in Wales.

1.2 The Government response

The *Government Response* (2) provided an encouraging and positive set of proposals for tackling the problems identified. In a strongly worded Foreword the then Secretary of State, Frank Dobson, accepted that 'the whole system had failed' and 'there can be no more excuses' for failing to protect children. Importantly, the Government responded to the spirit of the whole Report – not just specific individual recommendations. For example, the creation of the Quality Protects programme in England and Children First programme in Wales used a holistic approach to the needs of children, and the pursuit of the concept of 'corporate parenting'.

The *Government Response* (2) was produced by a Ministerial Task Force consisting of ministers from ten Government departments and outside representatives from social services, education, the police and the voluntary sector. It therefore met the *People Like Us* (1) recommendation that 'Departments of State should respond to the recommendations of reports they have commissioned'. The Task Force also included a young woman with experience of the care system, thus making a promising start on one of the Principal Recommendations of the Report (1) that 'Local authorities should make direct use of the experience of the children they look after in developing policy, practice and training for services for children living away from home'.

Also in November 1998, the Department of Health (DH) published the White Paper, *Modernising Social Services* (3). The key themes and programme of action in the chapter on 'Services for children' was strongly influenced by *People Like Us* (1). The key themes were:

- new, stronger systems for protecting children

- Quality Protects – improving quality across all children's services

- better health and education for children in care homes, and more help for young people leaving care.

The action promised was:

- root and branch reform of the regulation system, introducing checks on the full range of children's care services, and strengthening safeguards;

- an extensive range of reforms, set out in the Government's response to the Children's Safeguards Review, to improve the protection of children living away from home;

- stronger systems for preventing unsuitable people from working with children;

- a thorough revision of the Government guidance on child protection.

It promised to commission and publish a single joint report on children's safeguards from all relevant Chief Inspectors at least every three years. The first of these, *Safeguarding Children* (4) was published in October 2002, although, unfortunately, it failed to cover children living away from home or particularly vulnerable children.

The Welsh Office issued a similar White Paper *Building for the Future* (5) in March 1999 and highlighted broadly the same themes.

1.3 Key changes since the publication of *People Like Us* (1)

There have been many changes in the central and local structures that deliver services relevant to safeguarding children since 1997 and more are planned. They include the following.

- Devolution of powers relating to social care, health and education of children in Wales to the Welsh Assembly Government.

- Creation of central units with cross-cutting responsibilities – e.g. Sure Start bringing health, social care and educational responsibilities together and the Children and Young Person's Unit.

- Transfer of responsibility for 'early years' from DH to the Department for Education and Skills (DfES).

- Transfer of children's social care to DfES and establishment of the Families and Children Division and the post of Minister for Children, Young People and Families.

This has been accompanied by changes in all the major services – social services, health, education and the prison and court systems – such as the following.

- More social service departments have combined with other services, education, housing, etc., in England and Wales.

- Creation of General Social Care Council in England (GSCC) and Care Council in Wales; Training Organisation for Personal Social Services (TOPSS); Social Care Institute of Excellence (SCIE); National Care Standards Commission (NCSC) (already replaced by the Commission for Social Care Inspection, CSCIE) in England and the Care Standards Inspectorate for Wales (CSIW).

- Care Trusts and Children's Trusts in England.

- *Shifting the Balance of Power within the NHS: Securing Delivery* (6) – to Primary Care Trusts (PCTs).

- Introduction of multidisciplinary Youth Offending Teams (YOTs).

- Establishment of the Youth Justice Board (YJB).

- Creation of the National Probation Service (NPS).

- Creation of the Connexions service.

There has been a welcome recognition that the needs of children should be looked at holistically. It is not enough for them to be securely attached to their parents/carers – they also need to have their health, educational and other needs met. Local authorities do now seem to recognise their responsibilities as 'corporate parents' for the children they look after.

An important development since 1997 which is very relevant has been the attempt to improve working across agency boundaries. Initially this focused in England on a range of initiatives such as Sure Start and Healthy Schools at the local level and the Sure Start and Children and Young Person's Units at central level to co-ordinate the relevant departmental interests. In other cases, local structures were introduced to bring the appropriate professionals together, such as Youth Offending Teams. More recently, attempts to get existing

services and professions to work together through joint initiatives, joint funding and new local structures have given way to a more radical attempt to break down service and professional boundaries through the introduction of new service delivery mechanisms – such as Children's Trusts in England – and the introduction of new ways of working and training. This, combined with the recognition of the difficulty of recruiting, retaining and training the staff needed in the different disciplines – nursing, social care, education – has led to attempts to address workforce and service needs in a different way. *Every Child Matters* (7) included workforce reform in the major areas for action, saying 'A Children's Workforce Unit, based in DfES, will develop the pay and workforce strategy for those who work with children. The Unit will work with the relevant employers, staff and Government Departments to establish a Sector Skills Council (SSC) for Children and Young People's Services to deliver key parts of the Strategy'.

In Wales, the Welsh Assembly Government set out its vision for children's services in *Children and Young People: A Framework for Partnership Consultation Document* (8). This required the setting up of local partnerships embracing all local agencies and interests. The partnerships cover 'Early Entitlement' up to age 10 and 'Extending Entitlement' for 11- to 25-year-olds with new grant funding streams for each. The partnerships are intended to operate at a strategic level and to drive planning of services for children.

In January 2004, the Welsh Assembly Government published *Children and Young People: Rights to Action* (9), which set out proposals for the next stage to transform the lives of children and young people in Wales. The focus in Wales is on strengthening local partnerships and enabling co-operation, pooling of budgets and closer working between agencies and professionals, rather than seeking to bring about improvement by structural change.

The recognition that professionals and others need to work effectively together to protect children and safeguard and promote their welfare is both welcome and necessary. However, it is important to retain essential expertise and experience at the same time as working to create new service structures and break down professional boundaries. This must be borne in mind should other structures and professional groups – such as education or health – with their different values and interests, come to dominate over social care whose ethos is based on safeguarding and promoting the welfare of children – the fundamental requirement of the main legislation (the Children Act 1989).

Many of these changes are – or could be – helpful in relation to safeguarding children living away from home but times of change and upheaval make it easy to lose sight of some of the fundamentals. This report seeks to identify areas of weakness that need to be addressed and remind people about the importance of maintaining consistent safeguards in all settings during the forthcoming changes.

1.4 Methodology

This was a two-year study, commencing in June 2002 and concluding in June 2004. The first year of the project involved finding out what had happened on the *People Like Us* (1) recommendations following its publication in 1997 and the *Government Response* (2) in 1998. This was done by consulting the Government departments involved – DH, DfES, the Home Office, HM Customs and Excise – and the Welsh Assembly Government. Relevant reports, research and other publications were identified and examined. Following an initial analysis of the information obtained, a wide range of organisations and individuals were consulted and their views were sought. At the same time we tried to keep track of as many as possible of the major developments in the areas covered by *People Like Us* (1) in the remaining year of the study up to the end of May 2004. Government departments and the Welsh Assembly Government were consulted, and provided comments, on the final draft of the report. Throughout we had the benefit of the help and support of our Advisory Group.

1.5 Structure of the report

The report is relevant to different audiences – central government, local authorities, both as commissioners and as providers of services, managers and practitioners in the public, voluntary and private sectors. It covers all types of service where children live away from home, not just those involving social services.

Chapter 2 provides a summary of the conclusions reached and brings together the recommendations in the report. Chapter 3 provides an overview of the state of safeguards today and the other chapters cover the specific areas dealt with in *People Like Us* (1).

Chapters 3–10 have the following structure.

- A brief summary of what *People Like Us* (1) said on the issue.

- *People Like Us* recommendations in bold type in boxes.[1]

- Bullets that set out the action promised in the Government's Resonse (2) to *People Like Us* in 1998.

- Bullets that set out the action taken by Government since then.

---

1 *People Like Us* only made 20 principal recommendations, however the *Government Response* covered 130 others that were in the text. This report covers all of those.

- A 'What happened' section that draws on evidence from reports, research and other sources, such as personal communications and provides the basis for our conclusions.

- An 'Analysis' section in green that gives our view of what has happened and the current state of play.

- Finally, there may be a shaded 'Recommendation' section that follows the numbering sequence in Chapter 2 Summary of conclusions and recommendations.

The Appendices are set out as follows:

- *People Like Us* (1) recommendations not covered in the text

- Bibliography

- Glossary

- Acronyms.

2 Summary of conclusions and recommendations

2.1 Overall

The Government responded fully and positively to *People Like Us* (1). It promised action on almost all the recommendations. Much has been done to amend legislation and develop policy and practice guidance to improve safeguards for children. The main challenge is to ensure that these are now fully implemented on the ground.

The spirit of *People Like Us* (1) was also responded to, not just its individual recommendations. The needs of children are now being looked at holistically, their views are being sought in developing policies and attempts made to ensure that professionals work effectively together.

Progress has been made, as part of the social inclusion agenda, in improving the life chances of looked after children and they are now less marginalised than previously. Progress is now needed in identifying and addressing the needs of the next groups of marginalised children who are particularly vulnerable to abuse of all kinds. This should include disabled children – particularly those in residential special schools with 52-week provision; children in hospital settings for long periods – including those with mental health problems; children with emotional and behavioural difficulties and very young children.

While the Government rejected only a few recommendations in *People Like Us* (1) some of these remain areas of real concern. Notably the need to:

- define parental rights and responsibilities;

- identify and respond to the needs of children with emotional and behavioural difficulties;

- register private foster carers.

A review of parental rights and responsibilities is now being undertaken. Children with emotional and behavioural difficulties and those in private foster care remain very vulnerable. It is disappointing that the review of children with emotional and behavioural difficulties has not yet progressed. The renewed attempts to enforce the current regulations on private foster care are unlikely to make any real impact and registration is essential to improving the protection of privately fostered children.

While some progress has been made in establishing a better framework for safeguarding children against sexual abuse, there has been less success in dealing with the main source of harm – those who seek to abuse them sexually. Much of the effort to protect children focuses on preventing people with convictions from working with them, yet only a fraction of those who sexually abuse children are convicted.

And, since *People Like Us* (1) was published new dangers to children have escalated – notably through the use of new technology, the internet, mobile phones, etc.

2.2 State of safeguards today

Departments of State

While efforts have been made to improve 'joined up' working in central government, this has not been applied successfully to safeguarding children. The level of commitment to this still varies between different departments. It is important that:

- DfES makes the safeguarding of children a top priority

- DH ensures it is a priority for health services

- the Home Office (HO) reviews its policies to reflect the need to protect children from adults.

The ministerial group

It is hoped that the Ministerial Committee on Social Exclusion and Sub-Committee on the Delivery of Services for Children, Young People and Families will be a permanent feature of government. They should ensure that services for children and young people get the attention and resources needed.

Review of guidance

The promised review of regulations and guidance and new Children's Services Guidance should ensure that safeguarding and promoting the welfare of children and young people is comprehensively covered and uniformly applied to all settings. The continuing gap between policy and practice needs to be bridged and practitioners must develop their understanding and ability to safeguard children and promote their welfare. Guidance should be in a form capable of being understood and used by staff who have to apply it and by managers with a responsibility for interpreting it.

Role of local authorities

Much has been done to improve the legislative framework, develop policies and produce guidance in response to the recommendations in *People Like Us* (1). Implementation at the local level has been more problematic. Attention now needs to focus on ensuring that policy aspirations are translated into improvements in the safeguards provided for individual children in all parts of the country.

Consistency of protection in all settings

Action has been taken to ensure consistency of safeguarding children in different settings in which they live away from home through regulation, inspection and the introduction of national minimum standards. Weaknesses remain in some areas, notably private foster care, prisons and some health-care settings. Further action should include groups not covered specifically by *People Like Us* (1) such as asylum seekers and young people in the armed services.

2.3 Children

Choice of placement

Efforts have been made to improve choice of placement for looked after children and reduce the number of moves that children experience. However, little progress appears to have been made and out of authority placements remain a problem. Policy seems to have been developed in a piecemeal fashion with insufficient attention being given to both foster care and residential care in recent years.

Health, education and transition to independent living

A strong policy framework is in place for improving the health, education and transition to independent living of looked after children. Some progress has been made on these fronts but it has been slow and more is needed.

Similar action is needed for children in the criminal justice system and children who spend long periods in health settings. There are welcome and much needed efforts by the Youth Justice Board to increase educational provision; however, children in prison settings should have the same statutory right to education as other children.

The Children (Leaving Care) Act 2000 is a major step forward but there are difficulties that need to be addressed and overcome, particularly for young disabled people.

Local authorities should not neglect the needs of other vulnerable children and young people who are not care leavers but who are living independently of their parents, including those leaving custody.

Disabled children

The vulnerability of disabled children to abuse is now recognised in policy documents and guidance, although this varies in different settings and is inadequately covered in health and penal settings. Disabled children remain vulnerable, particularly in health settings (where health authorities routinely fail to notify local authorities when children are in hospital for three months) and in residential schools with 52-week provision. And there is a shortfall of practical help and guidance on how to protect them.

There has been some progress in obtaining statistical information but much more is needed.

Better co-ordination and co-operation between services is still needed for disabled children in relation to health, education, welfare, residential provision and transition to adulthood.

Disabled children are considered in more detail in our companion report *Safeguards for Vulnerable Children*.

Children with emotional and behavioural difficulties

Policy for children with emotional and behavioural difficulties (EBD) appears to be a neglected area in England and it is disappointing that DfES has not yet started to review services for EBD children. This is urgently needed and it is hoped that work will start soon and be completed within a year.

The news about the Office for Standards in Education (OFSTED) investigation into the full range of provision for this group of children and young people is encouraging. It does not specifically cover the role of residential placements but should do so. Information supplied by the Welsh Assembly Government suggests that Wales may have done more about this group of children and young people.

Young children

Some helpful leaflets have been produced for the carers of under-fives to help to keep them safe but there is no evidence of any other specific action to protect young children. There needs to be further work on action that can be taken to protect very young children.

Lost children

The dangers to children who go missing from home have been recognised with guidance and an Action Plan issued. What is not clear is how far the Action Plan is being implemented. Children need safe places to stay while they are away from home and local provision should be increased. Provision is needed for those who leave their home area, yet the number of refuges has reduced to one since *People Like Us* (1) was published. A solution to the problem of how refuges are resourced is needed. More helplines are needed.

Views of children and young people

The need to involve children and young people in developing policy has been accepted and become the norm. However, there is still some way to go in ensuring that their views are properly taken into account – particularly in schools, Young Offender Institutions and health settings. There is also a need to improve the communication skills of staff, especially with disabled children and young people. Time and resources are needed to make communication meaningful.

Children and young people are still not properly consulted and listened to in relation to decisions about their lives. This needs to be addressed.

Right to treatment

The Government response on the need to give priority for treatment of abused children was weak and this is still a major problem. The recent investment in Child and Adolescent Mental Health Services (CAMHS) is much needed and very welcome but the services remain seriously inadequate and it will be a long time before the promised comprehensive service is uniformly available. In the programme of expansion, priority should be given to developing expertise and capacity to help abused children, particularly those who have been abused in public care. The quality, diversity and accessibility of the service need to be improved as well as the quantity. The NHS should implement vigorously the plans to improve the quality of CAMHS and provide a range of treatment methods accessible in all localities and available when needed.

Children's rights and complaints procedures

Complaints procedures are still not thought to be easily accessible. All authorities and organisations should give more help and encouragement to children wishing to make representations about services and ensure that their complaints and views are heard. This is particularly important for disabled children, young children and those from black and minority ethnic groups. Procedures need to be well publicised together with the support arrangements for those wishing to use them.

Independent visitors do not seem to be much used but advocacy services have grown. The roles of the two are different and there is still a need for independent visitors for particularly vulnerable children. Local authorities should ensure that all children entitled to independent visitors have one.

2.4 Places in which children live away from home

Children's homes

Policy on children's homes has been neglected and there has been no attempt to develop a national strategy for residential care which covers the number of places needed and for whom, and ensures that sufficient places are available. Small children's homes are now regulated and inspected.

Foster care

Children in foster care are not receiving the level of social work support they need, particularly in out of authority placements. Serious staff shortages play a part in this and should be addressed so that children get visits at the required intervals.

A Code of Practice on the recruitment, assessment, approval, training, management and support of foster carers (68) has been produced but some of the safeguards it proposed on checking applicants are not included in the subsequent Minimum Standards for Fostering Services. Local authorities and agencies need to ensure that *all* of the checks and enquiries in the Code of Practice on

Foster Care are applied consistently for all those having unsupervised access to children.

Independent fostering agencies are now regulated and inspected but teething problems in the first year of operation of the National Care Standards Commission (NCSC) give rise to fears that this may not have been as effective as it should have been in detecting the poorer agencies. Inspection in this area needs to be strengthened. It is hoped that the Commission for Social Care Inspection (CSCI) will develop expertise in foster care inspection, establish effective liaison arrangements with expert bodies and publish a list of registered foster care agencies with information about their date of registration, inspection and grading.

Foster care has also been neglected in policy terms and Choice Protects will not provide the overall strategy required. Fostering is a vital part of mainstream services for children unable to live with their families and its role should be defined as part of an overall strategy for children's services. Its true cost should be established and properly resourced plans made. Foster carers should be required to undertake training to improve their skills to meet the needs of children and should be properly recompensed, including tax and pension arrangements.

Private foster care

The Government rejected the recommendation that local authorities should register private foster carers. As a result unknown numbers of children have remained at risk. There have been only very limited attempts to improve compliance with the existing regulations and there is no evidence that they have had any real success. It is not likely that the measures being taken in the Children Bill will be any more effective. Action is needed to change the attitude of parents and carers and there should be clear incentives and disincentives. Private foster carers should be registered, like childminders, and it should be an offence to place a child with an unregistered private foster carer or to accept a child when unregistered – as *People Like Us* (1) recommended. Whichever course is adopted an accompanying publicity campaign is needed.

Research shows that children in language schools are at risk, yet there is still no evidence of the Code of Practice for language schools promised in response to *People Like Us* (1). It is needed quite independently of other action being taken on private fostering generally.

Schools

The state of safeguards in schools with boarding provision shows considerable improvement since 1997, although it is too early to judge the impact of changes made to the legal framework and registration system. Information produced by schools and professional associations should include details about how checks are made on teaching and other staff before appointment. More guardianship organisations should be accredited and parents advised to use only accredited agencies. It would be helpful if the Commission for Social Care Inspection included in its annual report separate comment on its inspections of the welfare arrangements in all schools with boarding provision.

It is not satisfactory that the governance clause for independent special schools was dropped from the Education Act 2002. Independent special schools should be required to have a governing body to provide some external oversight of each such institution. There should be an equivalent body to the National Association of Independent Schools and non-maintained Special Schools (NASS) for maintained special schools.

DfES and DH should take action to ensure that local education authorities and health authorities notify the responsible local authority when a child is resident in an educational or health setting for three months or more, as required by Sections 85 and 86 of the Children Act 1989.

Prisons

Prisons are the most worrying area in relation to safeguarding children. Children in prisons are not being safeguarded, although attempts are now being made to improve the situation. Instead of removing children from prison as *People Like Us* (1) recommended, more children are being imprisoned.

The policy for boys has been to put them in separate establishments and provide an appropriate regime – although implementation of the regime varies and some boys are still held on split sites with young offenders.

The numbers of girls in adult prison establishments has increased and they have not until more recently had an appropriate regime. During 2003 all 15- and 16-year-old girls were removed from prison establishments but a number of 17-year-olds remain and are not adequately separated from adults and young offenders.

Children in prisons should be separated from adults, including young offenders and the Government should remove the UK reservation to Article 37 C of the UN Convention on the Rights of the Child, which says 'Every child deprived of liberty shall be separated from adults unless it is considered in the child's best interest not to do so'.

Remands to prison are a serious problem and are increasing, with custodial remands extended to 12-year-olds. Also, 17-year-olds on remand are treated as adults for the purposes of remand and bail, in contravention of the UN Convention.

The welfare and protection of children has not been a priority for prison establishments, and their health and education needs are inadequately dealt with. Some progress is now being made but there is a very long way to go. Children in prison should have the same rights and access to universal services as other children and DH should give priority to addressing the health needs, particularly mental health needs, of children and young people in prison.

Children in prison are discussed in more detail in *Safeguards for Vulnerable Children*.

Health settings

There are a number of concerns about health settings.

There appear to be a significant number of children with disabilities and psychiatric conditions who are in health settings for long periods for whom the safeguards of the Children Act are not being applied. Hospitals are required to notify local authorities of children in hospital for three months or more but are not doing so. Nor does the recent *Standard for Hospital Services* (10) say that they should. DH needs to take action to ensure that hospitals notify local authorities so that children's welfare can be safeguarded.

It is not clear what action has been taken to ensure that CAMHS units have robust systems to prevent unsuitable people gaining access to children in them.

There are worries about the arrangements to check health staff with unsupervised access to children, particularly paediatricians in post for many years and GPs.

Education provision and transition to adult services and/or independent living need strengthening for children spending long periods in health settings.

Children in hospices should have the same level of protection as other vulnerable children.

The inspection and monitoring of children's wards should be improved, with the same expectation about rights and facilities accorded to looked after children.

2.5 Parents

Parental rights and responsibilities

The Government rejected the recommendation that parental rights and responsibilities should be defined in legislation but have recently agreed to a review of family policy.

Information for parents and others

There has been some action to increase the information available to people working with children and families about child abuse but much more needs to be done to increase public awareness of the risks to children and what measures can be taken to protect them. This needs to extend beyond police checks to other measures that should be taken. The Government needs to fund information programmes for parents. These should inform them of the risks to children and the range of measures that can be taken to safeguard them. Parents should be assisted to ask the right questions of organisations responsible for children living away from home. Programmes would need to be regularly repeated.

There has been a helpful increase in information for children and young people and an indication that they are seeking help earlier. This needs to be further developed so that abusive behaviour is recognised quickly. Help should be readily accessible in a variety of ways. The Government and children's organisations need to provide information for all ages of children and young people so that they can recognise abusive behaviour and know where to go to seek help.

2.6 Abuse and abusers

Abusers

Treatment arrangements for sex offenders fall well short of what is needed. Much more should be provided, including for users of child pornography. There is very little provision for female abusers. Better identification and treatment are required.

There is a long way to go to address the problem of young abusers, who account for about a third of abuse. More treatment for young offenders at an early stage is vital. Staff and foster carers should have training to help them identify warning signs that a child or young person may be being abused or abusing others. The Youth Justice Board should increase treatment for young offenders so that this can start on admission to custody. There should be continued supervision and treatment in the community after release.

Help and advice should be available to those who recognise that they are at risk of offending.

There should be more help for victims of abuse.

Abusers are covered in more detail in our companion report *Safeguards for Vulnerable Children*.

Child abuse images

The use of the internet in acquiring and spreading abusive images of children has emerged as a major problem that is thought likely to increase the abuse of children. The majority of people involved were previously unknown to police. The problem has been recognised and a new offence of 'grooming' created. It needs to be tackled urgently with adequate resources. Information is needed for children, parents and foster carers and staff who care for children living away from home. Government information campaigns need to provide staff as well as parents with information about the dangers of the internet and how they can be reduced.

Abuse of children through prostitution

It has been accepted that abuse of children through prostitution should be dealt with as a child protection issue and this is reflected in guidance and in the new sexual offence of commercial exploitation of a child. However, it is clear that there is a long way to go before the problem is properly recognised and effectively tackled at local level. Preventative strategies are needed and programmes of work with those involved. Local Safeguarding Children Boards (LSCBs) will need to ensure that there are mechanisms in place for addressing the needs of vulnerable children in their local area, including those being abused through prostitution.

It is regrettable that children involved in prostitution are still being prosecuted and cautioned, although it appears that the

Government does now have plans to rectify this. It is hoped that the law will be amended as soon as possible so that children involved in prostitution are not criminalised.

Bullying, racial abuse and sexual harassment

Bullying is recognised as an important problem. It remains a major concern to young people and needs to be systematically and continuously tackled, particularly in prison establishments and in relation to disabled children.

Racial abuse is a persistent problem but is not apparently always recognised as such or dealt with adequately. It remains a serious issue in prison establishments. The same appears to be true of sexual harassment.

2.7 People who work with children

Choosing the right people

The need to comply with *Choosing with Care* (11) arrangements when recruiting and assessing staff has been generally accepted, although implementation is inconsistent and application is more rigorous in some settings than others. There are also practical difficulties that need to be resolved. Guidance is needed on *how* to examine the attitudes and motivation of applicants and on retrospective checks on staff already in post.

All organisations responsible for looking after children should ensure that *all* of the checks and enquiries recommended in *Choosing with Care* (11) are applied consistently and that staff are trained on how to assess the attitudes and motivation of applicants.

It would be helpful if the Criminal Records Bureau (CRB) provided guidance to assist employers in checking ID, identifying forgeries and any other practical problems that have emerged.

Sources of background information

Following the establishment of the Protection of Children Act (PoCA) List and the setting up of the

CRB, it is now easier to get information about potential employees and volunteers. However, there are problems in ensuring that the right people are referred and employers make full use of the list. Consideration should be given to whether the PoCA List should be broadened to cover other people, such as those on social service lists of people suspected of abuse or known abusers, rather than limiting it to people in the work setting, and whether it should be mandatory for any organisation to refer staff or volunteers to the List. There should be publicity to ensure that human resources departments know that referral should be considered as part of the final stages of a relevant disciplinary case.

CRB checks have been subject to long delays and problems concerning accuracy, as well as increase in cost. CRB checks are only as good as the police data provided and the Ian Huntley case showed that important soft information is not being retained or collated and that there are long delays in recording convictions data. Clear guidance and monitoring are needed to ensure that all police forces handle data appropriately and meet targets for data entry. The scope of the PoCA List and of CRB checks should be reviewed to ensure that they include all relevant information and all situations in which children are vulnerable.

While police checks are important in preventing unsuitable people working with children and deterring those who have been convicted of a relevant offence, they are nowhere near sufficient. There is a danger that they will be seen as *the* means of safeguarding children, whereas they are just one element in this. There are many more abusers without convictions than there are with them. Rigorous checking of other information such as life histories, references and probing interviewing is also needed.

Dealing with unsuitable people

Appropriate sharing of information remains a problem. If the current legislation is too complicated to give staff the clear guidance they need it should be changed to ensure that information needed to protect children can be passed on. This should apply to people who may be a risk to children as well as to information about children who may be at risk. The *What to do if you're worried a child is being abused* (12) guidance covered information sharing and there are information sharing provisions in the Children Bill. It is hoped that in the wake of the Bichard Inquiry, the Government will issue definitive guidance on information sharing, covering both information about children who may be at risk *and* people who may pose a risk to children. If the Data Protection Act is unduly restrictive or unclear, it should be amended.

Measures have been taken to protect whistle-blowers and there is some evidence that people are becoming more willing to report concerns but there is still some way to go.

Training

There have been a number of developments in social work training since *People Like Us* (1) but little progress on a common approach across professional boundaries. However, the Government is planning to establish new types of social care professionals and there has been recent recognition of the need for all professionals to have training in child protection. This should include the medical and nursing professions and carers, such as foster carers, where necessary. Training needs to include the signs that a child may be being abused, how to deal with any disclosure, how and when to involve specialist staff who can undertake joint enquiries with the police and giving evidence in court. Training should also cover normal child development.

2.8 Maintaining standards: inspection

There has been disruption to inspection activity with the setting up of the National Care Standards

Commission and then the Commission of Social Care Inspection. The new Commission should give priority to safeguarding issues and inspect the new arrangements for private fostering.

The Joint Inspector's Report (4) is a very helpful document, although it is a pity that it did not cover children living away from home. The next triennial report should focus on the most vulnerable groups of children. Inspection programmes should cover these in the meantime. All inspectorates should cover and report on arrangements for recruiting, assessing and selecting staff to ensure consistency in safeguarding children from unsuitable people. It is hoped that the triennial safeguarding children reports will continue after the establishment of the joint inspection framework in 2005 and should cover those groups of children who are particularly vulnerable and neglected. The necessary inspection work should be programmed well in advance.

2.9 Criminal justice

Assisting children to give evidence

Efforts have been made to improve arrangements for child witnesses, although delays in implementation are unfortunate and it is uneven and under-resourced. The Home Office should ensure that the new arrangements for vulnerable witnesses are adequately resourced and carefully monitored and evaluated to ensure that they are fully and consistently implemented in all areas, so that lessons can be learnt and further improvements made. Particular attention should be given to arrangements for disabled and very young children.

More training on child development should be provided in the criminal justice system and judges should receive mandatory training before hearing cases involving child witnesses. There should be more help for non-abusive carers of children who are witnesses. A number of issues need to be resolved concerning support for child witnesses.

Prosecuting sex offenders

There has been no improvement in bringing perpetrators of child sexual abuse to justice. This undermines efforts to prevent unsuitable people working with children – particularly if too much reliance is placed on police checks which do not adequately cover 'soft' information. Research is needed on why the rate of convictions for offences against children is so low and action taken to remedy this. Statistics on the age of offenders against children should also be broken down by sex so that trends can be monitored.

2.10 Recommendations

1 Further information should be obtained about the needs of vulnerable groups of children, including:
   - disabled children – particularly those in residential special schools with 52-week provision
   - children in hospital settings for long periods – including those with mental health problems
   - children with emotional and behavioural difficulties
   - very young children.

   Safeguards should be an integral part of the policy developed to meet these needs. (DfES lead; DH and HO)

2 Attention now needs to focus on ensuring that policies to protect children are properly implemented in all parts of England and Wales. (All government departments, local authorities, health authorities and other organisations with responsibility for children living away from home. DfES lead)

3 Safeguards need to be strengthened in private foster care, prisons and health

(Continued)

settings. (DfES, DH and HO/Prison Service/YJB)

4 A strategic policy is needed to address holistically the needs of all children and young people in the public care and leaving custody without parental support. It should:
- take account of health, education, housing and leaving care needs
- cover the roles of all relevant services – foster care, adoption, children's homes, supported accommodation, residential schools, etc.
- address the standards and outcomes expected of services
- cover out of authority placements
- include residential care and foster care as important mainstream service provision, resourced accordingly.

Costed and resourced plans with appropriate timescales should then be made to develop provision. (DfES lead)

5 Strategic Health Authorities, Primary Care Trusts and other Health Trusts providing services for children should give priority to looked after children and children in custody, particularly those with mental health and emotional problems.

6 Local authorities should provide support to young care leavers *and* other vulnerable young people who do not have parental support, including those leaving custody.

7 DfES and DH should arrange the production and issue of practical guidance on the action that can be taken to safeguard disabled children in all settings, particularly in residential special schools and health settings.

(Continued)

8 Action is needed by DfES and DH to ensure that local education authorities and health authorities notify the responsible local authority when a child is resident in an educational or health setting for three months or more as required under Sections 85 and 86 of the Children Act 1989.

9 Children in Need Censuses should be held at regular intervals and DfES and DH should carry out the exercise to collate existing statistical information on disabled children in children's homes, residential special schools and health settings every three years.

10 All authorities and organisations need to ensure that children and young people are consulted and listened to in relation to decisions about their lives.

11 NHS needs to improve the quality of CAMHS and provide a range of treatment methods accessible in all localities and ensure treatment is available when needed. It should give priority to developing expertise and capacity to help abused children, particularly those who have been abused while in public care.

12 DfES and local authorities must address the serious staff shortages in social services so that regulations can be fully complied with. Where choices have to be made about the best use of limited resources it is recommended that local authorities give priority to increasing visits to the most vulnerable – the very young and disabled children.

13 The Government should introduce the registration of private foster carers as *People Like Us* (1) recommended. An

(Continued)

15

accompanying publicity campaign is needed for a registration scheme or for the 'enhanced scheme' being introduced in the Children Bill.

14 Local authorities should ensure that language schools comply with the private fostering regulations and are assisted where necessary to obtain CRB checks.

15 A Code of Practice for language schools should be produced and cover the arrangements for recruiting host families for the students attending the school. (DfES)

16 The Home Office should undertake a fundamental review of the use and place of custody in society and what the alternatives are, in line with the UN Convention on the Rights of the Child, i.e. that detention of children should be a measure of last resort and for the shortest possible time and that they should be separated from adults – including young adults. It should consider how far existing legislation helps or hinders this.

17 Children in custodial units should have the same rights and access to universal services such as health and education as all other children.

18 It would be helpful if the Youth Justice Board mounted a Quality Protects-style programme for children and young people in custody with a view to improving the quality of service they receive and improving their life chances.

19 DH should ensure that priority is given to safeguarding children in all health settings including hospices and CAMHS and other psychiatric units which admit children and young people and that the safeguards provided are consistent with

(Continued)

arrangements in other settings where children live away from home.

20 DH should collect and analyse statistics on children·in hospital for more than a month. It should fund research to identify the needs of these children, particularly those with a psychiatric diagnosis. This should include broader educational and welfare needs as well as child protection arrangements.

21 Children in health settings should, as elsewhere, be informed and consulted about decisions affecting their everyday lives and have access to independent advocacy and an accessible complaints procedure. (DH and health authorities)

22 The Government should fund a major expansion of treatment for those who abuse children – men, women and young abusers. Priority should be given to providing early treatment for both male and female young abusers. (Home Office and DH)

23 The Government should fund a national expansion of preventative schemes, on the lines of 'Stop it Now!', to provide information and advice for all adults, but especially for those who are abusing children, or fear that they may, and for those who suspect that others may be abusing or being abused. (Home Office to take lead responsibility)

24 Local authorities all need to have active prevention and rescue strategies in relation to children being abused through prostitution in their area. Local Safeguarding Children Boards should ensure that the needs of these children are addressed.

(Continued)

25 All inspectorates dealing with children living away from home should have the remit to cover the recruitment, assessment and selection of staff and should routinely cover and report on these arrangements.

26 DfES should review the scope of the PoCA List to see whether it should be widened to cover other sources of information and consider whether it should be made mandatory for organisations to refer staff and volunteers to the list. It should publicise the PoCA list and the process of making a referral.

27 The Home Office should review the coverage of CRB checks and ensure that they are affordable and available for *all* situations in which children are vulnerable.

28 The Home Office/Association of Chief Police Officers (ACPO) should issue guidance to all police forces to ensure that they have effective systems for recording and retaining 'soft' information and ensure that target times for entering criminal record information into the national computer are met.

29 The triennial safeguarding children reports should continue after the

(Continued)

establishment of the joint inspection framework in 2005 and should cover those groups of children who are particularly vulnerable and neglected. The necessary inspection work should be programmed well in advance. (All inspectorates)

30 The Home Office should commission research to establish the best methods of dealing with child witnesses. This will inform debate and policy-making so that fewer children are harmed by the process of giving evidence and more perpetrators can be brought to justice. Particular attention should be given to arrangements in relation to very young children and those who are disabled.

31 The Home Office should commission research to find out why alleged offences against children are not pursued/have a low rate of conviction and to suggest how conviction rates can be improved. The age and any disabilities the child has should be covered in the analysis.

32 The Home office should break down statistics on the age of offenders by sex as well as age so that any trend in the conviction of females for sexual offences can be monitored.

3 The state of safeguards today

What *People Like Us* said

Some chapters of *People Like Us* (1) dealt with the need to ensure that safeguarding children is given proper priority and that all children living away from home are protected.

Chapter 16 covered the role of local authorities and Departments of State in promoting and safeguarding the welfare of children.

Chapter 17 said that the quantity of current regulation and guidance detracts from its effectiveness and should be reviewed.

Chapter 10 said that arrangements for protecting children from abuse should be effective and consistent across all settings. There is no justification for different levels of protection against abuse or harm. 'Career' paedophiles would seek out the most vulnerable, where safeguards were weakest. This needs to be continually borne in mind as new threats to children emerge.

Chapter 20 accepted that some of the shortcomings in services stemmed from shortage of money or other resources but said that extra resources needed to be matched by managerial and professional efforts to improve general performance. It argued that in competition with other priorities for resources the needs of children should rank highly and that those who live away from home and are in need rank higher. It said that those with the strongest case for additional resources are children in the public care, disabled children, children with emotional and behavioural difficulties, and children in prison.

3.1 Departments of State

> **Principal Recommendation 18. Departments of State with responsibilities affecting children should adopt and actively pursue the aim of safeguarding and promoting their welfare.**

Government response

- To be included in Departmental Objectives from 1999 to 2000 and reported on in annual reports.

Government action

- Children and Young People's Unit (CYPU) established 2000 to take a cross-departmental view of children and young people in the way policy is formulated and a strategic view of children and young people's welfare across government.

- CYPU's consultation document, *Building a Strategy for Children and Young People*, March 2001, suggests 'protection' as the fourth of six key outcomes areas.

- Cabinet Committee on Children's Services, chaired by the Chancellor, with membership of every department with some responsibility for children and young people. They gave a commitment to support strategy to help ensure improvements to the well-being of children and young people across England by 2002.

- Statutory duty regarding child protection introduced in the Education Act 2002 – governing bodies or Local Education Authorities (LEAs) will have to have arrangements for ensuring their functions are carried out with a view to safeguarding and promoting the welfare of children.

- Home Office business plan included objectives on protection from paedophiles – the establishment of the Criminal Records Bureau and prevention of child pornography on the internet. There is nothing on safeguarding and promoting the welfare of children in general.

What happened

Getting the Right Start: National Service Framework (NSF) for Children. Emerging Findings (13), published for consultation in April 2003, had a welcome general statement of what is needed for 'safeguarding', including the recognition that disabled children are at higher risk of being abused. But the first draft of 'the aim for safeguarding and suggested actions' at Annex B is disappointing.

Safeguarding Children (4) said the following:

- Child protection and potentially dangerous offenders did not appear in police force or crime and disorder plans as priorities. We found little evidence of chief police officers' engagement with safeguarding work.

- Safeguarding children is not a stated priority for many agencies at national level, and so the commitment voiced by senior staff and leaders in organisations was often not reflected in local agency business plans or formal priorities.

- Government departments should ensure that the safeguarding of children is clearly identified as a priority at both national and local level.

- Only social services and education had relevant performance measures.

- GPs were not participating in the local safeguarding arrangements and were not perceived as being committed to the safeguarding agenda.

- Neither child protection work nor work in respect of dangerous offenders appeared as a priority in police business plans or local crime and disorder strategies.

The National Probation Service (NPS) reached similar conclusions in its Report *Safeguarding Children: Findings of the NPS role from three inspection reports* (14): 'Insufficient priority had been given to safeguarding children across all agencies in services planning and resource allocation nationally and locally'.

David Blunkett's Foreword to *Protecting the Public* (15) said 'Public protection, particularly of children and the most vulnerable, is this Government's priority'. The Overview says 'Sexual crime, and fear of sexual crime, has a profound effect on the social fabric of communities, and the fight against it is of the highest priority to the Government'.

Recommendation 106 in *The Victoria Climbie Report* (16) (the Laming Report) was that 'The Home Office must ensure that child protection policing is included in the list of ministerial priorities for the police' (implementation within 6 months).

In Wales, all Government departments with responsibility for children are to have objectives appropriate to those responsibilities and to report on performance in annual reports. There is a Cabinet Committee on Children and Young People to co-ordinate planning supported by an official level group bringing together all Assembly departments with responsibility for children and young people.

Every Child Matters (7) says that the Government will raise the priority given to safeguarding children in relevant organisations and the Home Office will review the National Policing Plan (November 2002) in which child protection was included but not as one of the four key priorities. It says that, subject to consultation, local bodies such as police and health organisations will have a new duty to safeguard children, promote their well-being and work together through partnership arrangements.

Keeping Children Safe: The Government's Response to the Victoria Climbie Inquiry Report and the *Joint Inspector's Report Safeguarding Children* (17) says that:

- child protection has been an explicit high priority for the Probation Service for many years

- the Education Act 2002, giving schools and further education institutions a duty to make arrangements to carry out their functions to safeguard and promote the welfare of children, comes into force on 1 June 2004

- letter to Primary Care Trusts of January 2002 set out their responsibilities for safeguarding children and the need to appoint a PCT director to take responsibility for child protection

- the full NSF framework, to be published in 2004, will set out common standards for child protection services against which health and social care organisations will be inspected.

Analysis

The commitment of individual Departments of State to safeguarding children has varied.

The Department of Health (DH) has included clear commitments in its priorities and guidance and in the targets set. But there are questions as to whether this applies as strongly in the NHS as in social services. DH and health authorities should ensure that it does.

DfES is now more active in this area, notably through the introduction of a statutory duty regarding child protection, and through units such as Sure Start. Given its new responsibility for children's services it is essential that safeguarding is a top priority.

The commitment of the Home Office and its agencies and services has been less clear-cut. Action is being taken in some specific areas – such as child pornography – but this is not underpinned by any general commitment to safeguarding and promoting the welfare of children. This is most notably lacking for children and young people in prison establishments. David Blunkett's Foreword to *Protecting the Public* (15) said 'Public protection, particularly of children and the most vulnerable, is

this Government's priority'. This is very welcome. Will this now be reflected clearly in Home Office priorities and objectives? The Home Office should review its policies to reflect the need to protect children from adults. And will child protection policing be included as one of the key priorities in the next version of the National Policing Plan?

The Government has been taking action to harmonise the working of different departments and improve working in areas of shared interest. Action has taken a variety of forms, including setting up task forces and units with cross-cutting responsibilities such as the Social Exclusion Unit (SEU) or relating to more than one department such as Sure Start, and the Children and Young People's Unit. However, little has so far been done to ensure a 'joined up' approach on safeguarding children at national level. The *Safeguarding Children* (4) recommendation that 'government departments should ensure that the safeguarding of children is clearly identified as a priority at both national and local level' echoed that made by *People Like Us* (1) five years earlier. Only social services and education had relevant performance measures. So there is still some way to go. The commitment of individual Departments of State with responsibilities for safeguarding and promoting children's welfare has been rather mixed, therefore the undertaking in *Every Child Matters* (7) to raise the priority given to this is welcome.

3.2 Ministerial group to safeguard and promote children's welfare

A ministerial group should be established to safeguard and promote children's welfare. It should secure a consistent government response to this report and other existing reports such as that of the National Commission in the Prevention of Child Abuse.

Government response

- Ministerial Task Force on the Children's Safeguards Review to draw up response.

- Task Force to continue to meet to monitor implementation of the response and consider linked policy initiatives.

Government action

- Ministerial Task Force established February 1998 to respond to *People Like Us* (1). This included ministers from 10 Government departments, devolved administrations of Scotland, Wales and Northern Ireland and representatives of social services, education and the voluntary sector and police.

What happened

The remit of the Ministerial Task Force was extended to include co-ordination of the Government's response to *Lost in Care* (18), the report of the Waterhouse inquiry into abuse of children in Wales. It identified five key areas as priorities which have clear overlaps with *People Like Us* (1):

- children's commissioner

- advocacy services for looked after children

- complaints procedures and whistle-blowing

- human resource issues; and

- the future role of children's residential care as a placement choice.

In 2003 the Government created a new Minister for Children, Young People and Families in DfES to co-ordinate policies across Government. This brings together responsibility for children's social services, family policy, teenage pregnancy, family law and the Children and Family Court Advisory Service (CAFCASS) within DfES. The Ministerial Committee on Social Exclusion and the Ministerial Sub-Committee on the Delivery of Services for

Children, Young People and Families appear to have taken on the role of the Ministerial Task Force in overseeing developments in this area.

Analysis

The Ministerial Task Force was effective in producing responses to *People Like Us* (1) and *Lost in Care* (18). It has now been replaced by the Ministerial Committee on Social Exclusion and the Ministerial Sub-Committee on the Delivery of Services for Children, Young People and Families. It is hoped that these will be a permanent feature of Government and proactive in ensuring that services for children and young people get the attention and resources needed.

3.3 Review of guidance

> **Principal Recommendation 19. Department of Health and the Welsh Office should in the medium term review and re-issue the Regulations and Guidance associated with the Children Act 1989.**

Government response

- Will be done once amending legislation enacted.

- Complete revision may be needed in longer term.

- Guidance on corporate parenting issued under Quality Protects programme to local authority members.

Government action

- Children Act Regulations amended in 2002 – Children Act (Miscellaneous Amendments) (England) Regulations 2002. They contain important changes in health requirements for looked after children.

- Disqualification from Caring for Children (England) Regulations also updated, 2002 – relating to private foster carers and residential social workers.

- National Assembly for Wales – key elements of legislation and guidance have been revised.

What happened

NCSC in exercising its statutory duty to advise Secretary of State made a report on the changes needed in *The Advisory Report Proposing Changes to Regulations and Minimum Standards* (19). This includes some standards which are problematic from the children's point of view – e.g. checks before overnight stays with friends. It covered a number of important safeguarding issues, including the following.

- CRB disclosure checks should be repeated every three years as recommended in the National Standards for Foster Care.

- CRB disclosure checks should be retained at least until the next inspection, not destroyed after six months as CRB guidance says.

- Children in hospices should have the same level of protection as elsewhere – e.g. child protection; statutory notifications and consultations with children/young people – current standards focus too much on clinical aspects.

- All independent hospital regulations should be amended to ensure they meet 'welfare, rights and safety needs'.

The Government is committed, following the Laming Report (16), to issuing shorter and clearer guidance to all those involved in safeguarding children and to revising the Children Act 1989 guidance to shorten it and bring it fully up to date. The revised Children's Services Guidance will consist of two core documents, one for people working directly with children and families, and their managers and one for organisations. *Keeping Children Safe* (17) said 'These two documents will bring together information from previous publications, and set out the processes for assessment, planning, intervention and review of all children who come into contact with social services, and the responsibilities of organisations to put in place systems that enable children to be safeguarded effectively, including the proper training and supervision of staff'. The core document for organisations will include, 'ensuring that staff are competent, including making checks when recruiting staff and training (including induction training) and supervision of all staff'. The core documents will be supplemented by short pieces of guidance on specific client groups or processes, or aimed at particular groups of staff. All to be completed within two years.

Analysis

There have been further amendments to the regulations but no thorough review or reissuing of guidance as was recommended. However, the Government is now committed to a comprehensive review of guidance and the issue of documents within two years (in 2005). DfES should ensure that new guidance is capable of being understood and used by staff who have to apply it and by managers with a responsibility for interpreting it and that it provides comprehensive coverage of arrangements needed to safeguard and promote the welfare of children and young people in all settings.

3.4 Role of local authorities

Social Services authorities should ensure that measures for safeguarding children who are looked after are given due priority by the council as a whole and that they review the

(Continued)

operation and monitoring of the relevant statutory requirements and central guidance.

Social services authorities should satisfy themselves that their managerial, professional and reporting systems are adequate for discharging their responsibility to these children.

Government response

- Guidance on roles and responsibilities of councillors issued in September 1998.

- Will be taken forward in Quality Protects with local authorities supported to improve performance and monitored through the performance management framework.

What happened

Lord Laming (16) commented on the lack of acceptance of responsibility by senior managers and members for service failures and the need for clear lines of accountability. He made 45 recommendations directed at social services, 27 of which were addressed to Chief Executives, lead members with social services responsibilities and Directors of Social Services, aimed at ensuring they established appropriate systems for delivering services and monitoring effectiveness.

Every Child Matters (7) set out plans for improving accountability and integration locally, regionally and nationally. These included:

- legislation to create the post of Director of Children's Services for local authority education and social services and a lead council member for children

- integration in the longer term of key services as part of Children's Trusts

- the creation of Local Safeguarding Children Boards (LSCBs)

- a new Minister for Children, Young People and Families

- a timetable for action on information sharing on children and young people.

Analysis

This study has found that much has been done to improve the legislative framework, develop policies and produce guidance in response to the recommendations in *People Like Us* (1). What is less clear is the extent to which these have been implemented. *The Victoria Climbie Inquiry Report* (16) demonstrates what a long way there is to go. Attention now needs to focus on ensuring that policy aspirations are translated into improvements in the safeguards provided for individual children in all parts of England and Wales.

3.5 Consistency of protection in all settings

Principal Recommendation 16. Government should ensure that legal protection against abuse and harm is consistent in all settings in which children live away from home.

Government response

- Principles of Children Act already apply to many and will be extended.

- Legislation will be taken to extend welfare inspections to all boarding schools and to require all children's homes to be registered.

- The new regime for juveniles in the Prison Service will reflect Children Act principles, regulations and guidance.

Government action

- Care Standards Act 2000 brought small children's homes and independent fostering agencies within the scope of inspection and regulation and extended Section 87 of the Children Act 1989 to all schools with boarding provision.

- The Education Act 2002 introduced a statutory duty regarding child protection. Governing bodies or LEAs will have to have satisfactory arrangements for ensuring their functions are carried out with a view to safeguarding and promoting the welfare of children. In setting these up they will have to have regard to DfES guidance.

- National Care Standards Commission started work in April 2002, to inspect and regulate public, private and voluntary care services along with private and voluntary health care services. The Commission also inspects the welfare aspects of all schools with boarding provision in England. Included among the inspection principles of the NCSC were that they stick to the standards, take the same approach whether inspecting a secure unit or a public school and that they are consistent. NCSC was replaced by Commission for Social Care Inspection in April 2004.

- National Minimum Standards issued 2002.

- Prison Order 4950 (2000), sets out regime for young sentenced prisoners.

What happened
The Committee on the Rights of the Child, 31st session (50), also recommended that the State party 'ensure consistent legislative safeguards for all children in alternative care, including those who are privately fostered'.

There has been progress in safeguarding children. *Your Shout* (20) – a survey of children and young people with experience of public care – found that four out of five said they felt safe in care. And a ChildLine leaflet (March 2003) said 'In 1987, a year after ChildLine began, only one in

fifteen children suffering sexual abuse called within the first month of it starting. Now half the children who call about abuse do so within one month'.

However, following consultation with adults from a wide range of professions, the NSPCC found that 'The majority of respondents considered the Children Act 1989 was broadly meeting its objectives and was a good piece of legislation which had been hampered in implementation by shortage of resources and the lack of an effective infrastructure of services to allow it to properly protect and secure children's futures'. (*NSPCC Review of Legislation Relating to Children in Family Proceedings Consultation Draft* (21) – the accompanying paper to *Your Shout* (20)). There was 'a high degree of consensus and concern' about the shortage of financial and human resources – within the court system and social services. The clear message was that shortages of resources mean that 'children in need become children at risk'.

The main sources of evidence on the state of safeguards today are:

- the Joint Inspector's Report *Safeguarding Children: A Joint Chief Inspector's Report on Arrangements to Safeguard Children* (4) and

- *Keeping Children Safe: The Government's response to The Victoria Climbie Inquiry Report and Joint Inspector's Report Safeguarding Children* (17).

Safeguarding Children (4) found that the safety of children is being compromised because of:

- insufficient priority being given to safeguarding of children

- lack of commitment to and inadequate resources for Area Child Protection Committees (ACPCs)

- severe difficulties in recruiting and retaining public sector professionals, particularly those working in the field of child protection and child welfare, which directly impacts on the effectiveness of measures to safeguard children.

Keeping Children Safe (17) said that 'the legislative framework for safeguarding children set out in the Children Act 1989 is basically sound. However, there are serious weaknesses in the way on which it is interpreted, resourced and implemented'. Particular problems include:

- organisations (and their staff) giving different levels of priority to safeguarding children, making working effectively together difficult

- weak and under-resourced ACPCs

- system does not always focus on the needs of the child but on the needs of the responsible adults

- senior managers do not know enough about and take enough responsibility for the actions of staff

- many staff are not adequately trained in safeguarding children – particularly those not considered to be 'child protection' specialists

- many staff do not know when to share information about a child and family and what information can be shared under what circumstances

- children in custody are not adequately safeguarded

- Multi-Agency Public Protection Arrangements (MAPPAs), although in very early stages of development, have already begun to develop very different practice across the country.

Every Child Matters (7) set out the following proposals for removing the barriers to effective child protection:

- clear practice standards across services

- shared responsibility across agencies through new statutory duties

- someone in charge locally with statutory responsibilities for child protection and co-ordinating the work of social services, police, housing, education and other key services

- an inspection system that assesses how well agencies work together

- workforce reform to ensure that all people working with children are trained in child protection.

Immediate steps are being taken to:

- revise and shorten the existing range of Children Act 1989 Regulations and Guidance

- audit the activities of local authorities with social services responsibilities, NHS bodies and police forces in safeguarding children

- raise the priority of safeguarding children among all relevant agencies/organisations.

Analysis

Efforts have been made to ensure consistency of safeguards in different settings, through making small children's homes and independent fostering agencies subject to statutory regulation and inspection and making *all* schools with boarding provision subject to welfare inspections. The National Minimum Standards for all these settings which cover arrangements for recruiting and selecting staff, including the checks recommended in *Choosing with Care* (11), has helped ensure consistency.

There has been good progress on schools with boarding provision. Since April 2002 all types of school and Further Education colleges providing accommodation for under-18s now have their welfare arrangements inspected by the NSCS

25

Commission for Social Care Inspection (from April 2004). The new National Minimum Standards for these educational institutions provide a national framework to achieve consistency of approach to welfare inspections. The Office for Standards in Education (OFSTED) and the Independent Schools Inspectorate (ISI) have to report on the pastoral care aspects of the school as part of their education inspections. However, co-ordination between social services departments and education authorities needs to be made more effective for children with special educational needs placed in out of area residential special schools. Some of this group of children do not benefit from the full protection of the Children Act.

Although progress has been made in improving the safeguards for children living away from home, the 2002 Joint Chief Inspectors' Report, *Safeguarding Children* (4) and *Every Child Matters* (7) recognise there is still a long way to go. There is still a lack of consistency, with some settings being better safeguarded than others. The main settings with poorer safeguards are:

- private foster care

- the prison service

- some hospital settings, particularly hospices.

On private foster care, the *Government Response* (2) rejected the *People Like Us* (1) recommendation to require private foster carers to register before they accept children. When reiterating the recommendation that legal protection against abuse and harm should be consistent in all settings, the UN Committee on the Rights of the Child (50) specifically mentioned private foster care. It is a serious disappointment that the Government has again, in *Every Child Matters* (7), and the Children Bill failed to introduce registration for private foster carers, as this is the measure most likely to protect the vulnerable children in private foster care and to extend to them the safeguards provided for children placed with childminders who are only

away from their parents for a few hours per day. (See Section 5.3 on private foster care.)

In the prison service, improvements have been made in the regime for sentenced male juveniles in the Prison Service, but the legal – and actual – protection against abuse and harm is considerably less than for other children and young people. Females under 18 have been placed in adult prisons with no appropriate regime until fairly recently. There has been no appropriate care and training regime for boys aged 15–16 who are remanded to prison custody. (Although the Prison Service and Youth Justice Board say that remanded juveniles are expected to receive the full PSO 4950 regimes in so far as their status as 'unconvicted' or 'unsentenced' allows.) The Howard League for Penal Reform case (82) ruling that local authorities have responsibilities to safeguard and protect children in prison as elsewhere may, in time, have some effect. There has been some useful progress during the last two years. A useful start has been made in improving the safeguarding and welfare of children and young people in prison, at least in policy terms. But there is still a very long way to go. The Home Office, the YJB and the Prison Service must be fully committed to achieving a change in culture, providing resources and ensuring that policies are implemented if the conditions and opportunities for these young people are to be improved. (See Section 5.5 on prisons.)

It also seems that the safeguards in the Children Act are not being applied to children in health settings because of a failure to notify local authorities about children being in hospital for three months or more. This affects children and young people with mental and behavioural difficulties in particular as they may stay in hospital for a long time.

People Like Us (1) noted that this group was particularly vulnerable. Children in hospices are vulnerable too, because these now also cater more for children with life-limiting conditions, as well as terminal illnesses. (See Section 5.6 on health settings.)

The proposals in *Every Child Matters* (7) for improving child protection arrangements across all agencies, in particular the appointment of a Children's Commissioner, are very welcome. It is encouraging that the Government has acknowledged that there are serious weaknesses in the way the legislation to safeguard children is interpreted, resourced and implemented. It is hoped that this report will help to identify the areas in which improvement is most needed for children living away from home.

People Like Us (1) did not cover all circumstances in which children live away from home – for example asylum seekers and children in the armed services – but the safeguards it proposed should be applied in *all* settings in which children and young people live away from home.

3.6 Resources

Government action

Since 1997 the Government has provided extra resources for personal social services education and the NHS. Targeted resources designed to improve services particularly relevant to *People Like Us* (1) recommendations have been provided, such as:

- the Quality Protects programme

- expansion of CAMHS

- health services in prisons

- Choice Protects.

Recommendations

1   Further information should be obtained about the needs of vulnerable groups of children, including:

- disabled children – particularly those in residential special schools with 52-week provision
- children in hospital settings for long periods – including those with mental health problems
- children with emotional and behavioural difficulties
- very young children.

Safeguards should be an integral part of the policy developed to meet these needs. (DfES lead; DH and HO)

2   Attention now needs to focus on ensuring that policies to protect children are properly implemented in all parts of England and Wales. (All government departments, local authorities, health authorities and other organisations with responsibility for children living away from home. DfES lead)

3   Safeguards need to be strengthened in private foster care, prisons and health settings. (DfES, DH and Home Office/ Prison Service/YJB)

4 Children

4.1 Choice of placement

What *People Like Us* said

Choice of placement for children looked after by local authorities – in children's homes, foster care or residential schools – is a fundamental safeguard.

Choice of placement is a vital factor in meeting the assessed needs of children. It is also important in keeping them safe. Shoehorning children into vacancies in unsuitable establishments exposes them, other children, and even the establishment itself to the danger of unforeseen harm … Choice is safety.

The high levels of placement breakdowns experienced by a significant proportion of looked after children is unacceptable. It takes a heavy toll on the children's future prospects and leads to long-term costs for society as a whole – through criminal and self-damaging behaviour, mental health problems, family breakdowns and parenting problems. It takes a heavy toll on those who try to care for them.

Placements outside the local authority may be necessary in the interests of an individual child, but special consideration is then needed for supervision and monitoring by the responsible authority. Local authorities should review their placement policies to ensure that the safety of each child remains a continuing priority.

> **Principal Recommendation 2. Local authorities should secure sufficient provision of residential and foster care to allow a realistic choice of placement for each child.**

Government response

- To be taken forward as part of Quality Protects.

- Some of the Children's Service Special Grant to be used to increase the range and choice of placement and to improve assessment and care planning to ensure that more children are appropriately placed when first looked after.

- Work with Local Government Association (LGA)/Welsh Local Government Association (WLGA)/Association of Directors of Social Services (ADSS) to improve quality and choice of placements.

- Support for national and local recruitment campaigns for foster carers and improved training and support.

- Code of Practice and National Standards for foster care commissioned.

- £500,000 Training Support Programme sub-programme for training foster carers and £2 million a year for three years from 1999/2000 onwards.

Government action

- Objective 1 of Quality Protects was 'to ensure stable, secure, safe and effective care for all children'. One of the six key priorities was to improve the supply and choice of placement, including adoption.

- National Priorities Guidance (1999) set a target to reduce to no more than 16 per cent in all authorities the number of children with three or more placements.

- £180 million provided over three years 'to expand and strengthen fostering services and to provide extra support for adoption so that more children get the chance of growing up as part of stable and loving families'. £70 million for adoption and special guardianship services and £113 million to fostering through the Choice Protects programme.

- The Fostering Network received a Section 64 grant to develop a recruitment good practice toolkit to be made available to all local authorities.

- Adoption given priority as a means of providing children with permanent families with targets set.

- The Adoption and Children Act (2003) provides for special guardianship orders to provide a legally secure placement for children who cannot live with their birth parents but where adoption is not appropriate.

The Welsh Assembly Government:

- Commissioned a study from Cardiff University on the placement of children looked after. The study provided a snapshot of placements and availability on 1 February 2000.

- A task group was set up subsequently to help develop a strategic framework for improving placement choice and stability for looked after children and an implementation group. The 2002 Placement Strategy considered fostering as one of a number of placement options.

What happened
The Choice Protects review seeks to build on the changes brought about by Quality Protects 'by focusing particularly on placement choice in fostering and the stability and effectiveness of placements'. The review has two main strands: the first focuses on the way in which services for looked after children are commissioned and the second concentrates particularly on fostering services.

The *Looking After Children* (22) materials:

- require that those responsible for children's care consider all aspects of their lives

- require plans to be made for looked after children and acted upon

- encourage partnerships between those responsible for a child's care

- promote continuities in the lives of children who are looked after.

However, the British Association for Adoption and Fostering (BAAF) said: 'We have seen evidence of a continuing difficulty with the quality and choice of placements. There is confusion about the role of the independent sector, who themselves complain of a poor service which is crisis driven from local authorities as including major slippage in the holding of statutory reviews, a lack of regular visits by children's social workers not meeting statutory requirements and placement moves which are ill considered and often without benefit of assessment. There continues to be an increase in the number of emergency placements of children who have not benefited from an assessment (despite foster care standards requiring assessments of children in need) and many local authorities tell us that on many days there are simply no in house placements available'.

'It doesn't happen to disabled children' – Child Protection and Disabled Children Report of the National Working Group on Child Protection and Disability (23) said: 'despite our knowledge of the importance of secure attachments for children's emotional and social development, young disabled children are still receiving service provision that involves them sleeping in several different places a week'.

Analysis

Priority has been given to increasing placement choice and reducing the number of placement moves that children have. However, despite policy acceptance of the importance of a proper range and choice of placements, relatively little progress has been made so far. Further action is planned as part of Choice Protects.

Much of the focus has been on adoption in recent years and this has stolen the spotlight from foster care despite the fact that far greater numbers of looked after children need, and will continue to need, short- and long-term foster care placements. Efforts to increase the number foster carers, notably through the recruitment campaign run in 2000–01, have not been successful and, despite being part of a Quality Protects objective, there remains a shortfall of some 8,000 foster care placements despite new demands for carers, for example, for intensive fostering for young people on the Intensive Surveillance and Supervision Programme.

The number of children being placed for adoption has increased. In all, 3,400 were adopted in the year ending 31 March 2002, up by 25 per cent in two years (*Every Child Matters* (7)) but these account for only a tiny proportion of looked after children. Older children are much more difficult to place for adoption and may prefer residential care in a children's home rather than a family placement, but little seems to have been done about increasing placement choice in this sector.

Placements needed in children's homes have not been properly addressed as part of a coherent strategy to provide the range of placements needed for all children. The needs of children may change over time and all needs should be catered for.

The wide range of carers required to provide a match for all the children and young people needing a family placement remains an aspiration and a concentrated and coherent effort is needed to turn this into a reality. A strategic approach is required to meet the needs of all children and young people who need, or may need, public care. It should cover *all* types of care – ranging from family support services to adoption and including residential, foster care, guardianship, etc. It should take a holistic approach to the needs of children and young people, covering their education (including higher and further education), health, leisure needs as well as their care needs, and ensuring that they are helped and supported in the transition to adulthood and independent living in the same way as children living in their own families. While there have been a number of very helpful Government initiatives in this area – including Sure Start, Quality Protects, the Adoption and Children Act, the Children (Leaving Care) Act, Choice Protects – these have provided a rather piecemeal approach. A coherent and comprehensive strategy is needed. Within this, residential care and the foster care service should be seen as important and mainstream ingredients in service provision – not expensive and undesirable adjuncts to it, as is the case with children's homes – or as a voluntary and cheap option, as is the case with foster care.

The strategy should encompass the roles of all relevant services, the standards and outcomes expected of them. It is hoped that now responsibilities have been concentrated in DfES and under the Minister for Families and Children, some real advances in this direction will be possible.

Out of area placements

> **Placing authorities should retain protective oversight of all children they are responsible for and children placed by social services, educational and health authorities some distance from their homes must not be overlooked.**

Government response
- To be picked up in Quality Protects.

Government action
- Objective 6 of Choice Protects is – 'develop strategic approach with health and education on 'out of authority placements', at both national and local level'.

- National Assembly for Wales. Revised guidelines on residency of looked after children and funding responsibilities of relevant agencies to be included in guidance on health of looked after children to be published 2003.

What happened

Safeguarding Children (4) reported that 'young people in residential and foster care were often unhappy about the lack of contact from their social worker, particularly those in out-of-area placements'.

Modern Social Services: A Commitment to Reform. The 11th Annual Report of the Chief Inspector of Social Services 2001–2002 (24) said that 'Placement and service choice was problematic'. The Social Services Inspectorate (SSI) estimates that an average 97 children per council are placed externally with half of them placed 20 miles or more away. This has implications for cost, efficiency and safety as well as making it more difficult to ensure that educational and health needs are met. Councils are developing strategies to manage this problem. Many have set up multi-agency family support and specialist leaving care and after care services.

The best place to be? Policy, practice and the experiences of residential school placements for disabled children (25) discussed the problems of disabled children placed far way from home and recommended that the following.

- DH and DfES should, through the Quality Protects programme, encourage LEAs to support educational psychologists to be closely involved with individual children placed out of authority, and to develop structures and resources for close working relationships between educational psychologists and relevant health and social services professionals.

- DfES should encourage all the Special Educational Needs (SEN) Regional Partnerships to establish systems to record out of authority placements of children with a statement of SEN, and to assign each school a Link LEA or similar system to monitor the standard of education and care provided and disseminate information to other LEAs.

- OFSTED should monitor the extent to which LEAs encourage parents to be involved in their child's education following a residential placement and also the provision of independent parental supporters in such situations.

Delivering Quality Children's Services: Inspection of Children's Services (26), a review of local authority children's services in 32 councils, found that:

- more than one in five looked after children are being placed in care outside the boundaries of the responsible council

- 22 per cent of children are placed externally, often inappropriately, potentially compromising the safety of the child and the financial stability of the council

- CAMHS was 'unresponsive', particularly failing disabled children and young carers

- 14 councils inspected between August 2000 and July 2001 had 'serious deficiencies' in staff recruitment procedures for safeguarding children.

In May 2004, *Community Care* reported that Peter Gilroy, the Social Services Director for Kent had written to the Children's Minister, Margaret Hodge, about the dozen local authorities in London and the South East that were using the county as a 'dumping ground' for looked after children. He said 'How can you place a vulnerable child who may have been abused in a poor setting three hours away from London?'. The situation was so acute that Kent has pledged to fund appeals against councils which refuse planning permission for residential care homes. The example from Kent illustrates the problems for all services in liaising with all partner agencies and authorities involved in out of authority placements.

Out of authority placements in Kent

In January 2003, over 1000 children were placed in Kent by other authorities. The problem is particularly concentrated in some parts of the county. In the East Kent Health Economy (which encompasses four PCTs) there were more children placed by other authorities (902 children) than were looked after by Kent (856 children) and there were 76 asylum seekers.

In November 2002, 85 different authorities had children placed in Kent. This gives rise to a number of problems for the children involved, for other children in Kent and for a range of public services:

- children have problems maintaining contact with home and friends, and access to services such as CAMHS may be disrupted
- for local children, access to services such as special educational needs and CAMHS may be made more difficult
- there are increased demands on a range of public services – health, education, Connexions, housing, police and social services.

For social services:

- placing authorities do not always follow the notification procedures
- more child protection investigations are needed and
- because of the preponderance of independent fostering providers (36 in Kent out of a total of 120 in England and 9 in Wales), it is difficult to recruit and retain foster carers for local children.

For education:

- there can be difficulty finding suitable school placements

(Continued)

- many looked after children have special educational needs and, if they do not already have Statements of Educational Needs, assessments need to be carried out and services provided.

For health:

- there is increased pressure on CAMHS.

And in May 2004 the Children's Rights Director, Roger Morgan, expressed his concerns to us about the vulnerability of children and young people who were placed a long way from their homes, friends and families (often contrary to Section 23(7)(a) of the Children Act 1989), where it was difficult for people, including their social workers, to visit them. Young people could not challenge the decision to make such placements, although they were nearly always completely disruptive to their lives, including schooling and treatment.

Analysis

There is clearly a problem in relation to children placed some way from home that needs to be addressed if they are to be properly protected. Again, disabled children living away from home are particularly vulnerable. As *'It doesn't happen to disabled children'* (23) says 'Their isolation from their placing authority and, for some children their parents, means that changes in behaviour and other indicators may not be noticed and questioned'.

4.2 Health, education and transition to independent living

What *People Like Us* said

The Review received vigorous representations about the inadequacies of both health and education services. Whatever the cause, it produces a scandalous situation in which the life prospects of these young people may be irretrievably damaged and their immediate safety put at risk. A corporate approach is needed by education and social services authorities to resolve it.

The health needs of looked after children seem … to be fundamental to keeping them safe. The Department of Health should facilitate the action needed by local and health authorities to identify and meet the health needs of looked after children.

> **Principal Recommendation 3. Local authorities must pay particular attention to the educational and health needs of the children they look after and ensure a better transition to independent living.**

Government response

- Inter-agency working to be enhanced and education and health outcomes improved.

- Significant improvements to after care provided to care leavers funded by the Children's Services Special Grant.

- Guidance to be issued in 1999 to ensure health assessment for every child/young person entering care.

- Survey of mental health of children and young people commissioned and being piloted

Government action

Quality Protects objective 4 is 'to ensure that children looked after gain maximum life chance benefits from educational opportunities, health care and social care' (objectives 3 and 4, sub-objective 4.4 are the same for children in need and for black and ethnic minority groups).

A 'major expansion in child and adolescent mental health services', announced in October 2002, £140 million over the next three years 'to build capacity, improve access and, together with new NHS investment, to help deliver for the first time a comprehensive CAMHS service in each and

every area'.

The Welsh Assembly Government response to this study provided an impressive list of what was happening and planned, including the following:

- All recent guidance, including that relating to Children First, Working Together, Children (Leaving Care) Act and education of looked after children says inter-agency working is essential to providing comprehensive and holistic care for children and young people.

- Framework for Assessment of Children in Need requires partner agencies to work together to assess and plan for the needs of children.

- New provision within the Standards Fund to help prevent exclusion and for special educational needs to support LEA initiatives to improve education of looked after children – covered by SEN Strategy and Code of Practice.

- Guidance on Education of Looked After Children requires individual Personal Education Plans for each child and will be statutory for social services and education. New measures to encourage carers and social workers to take an interest in and promote educational achievement of children in their care to be included.

- Meeting basic health needs of looked after children identified as a priority in National Priorities Guidance (NPG) for 1999–2000. Health of looked after children also a key priority area in Children First programme.

- Assembly Government Regulations and guidance on health of looked after children issued January 2003.

- New annual reporting mechanism to monitor improvements in child and adolescent mental health services at national level being taken forward by CAMHS Strategy Implementation Group.

- Children and Young People's Partnership Frameworks being established in Wales will further help to streamline/co-ordinate planning and delivery of services.

What happened

The 11th Annual Report of the Chief Inspector of the Social Services Inspectorate (24) says 'Progress in improving life chances for young people looked after has been disappointing. Performance indicators show that the educational attainment of care leavers in 2000–2001 was very low. 37 per cent of children achieved less than one GCSE grade A*-G compared with the target of 50 per cent. Councils have forecast a rise to 48 per cent in 2001–2002. Significant improvements are required if the target of 75 per cent is to be achieved for 2002–2003. On average only 69 per cent of children looked after continuously for at least a year at 30 September 2001 had all necessary health checks; one in eight was absent from school for at least 25 days in the year. They were three times more likely to receive a final warning or caution or conviction than young people generally'. However, 'links between education and social services were improving with most councils now using unique pupil reference numbers to collect data on educational attainment and to track individuals'.

A draft key objective in the Choice Protects National Partnership in Placement Forum (June 2003) is to 'improve multi-agency commissioning arrangements which take into account children's health and educational needs as well as their social care needs, including CAMHS provision and special educational needs provision for looked after children'. Relevant developments include Children's Trusts, the Integrated Children's System, etc.

The Social Exclusion Unit (SEU) report *A Better Education for Children in Care* (27) September 2003, which followed consultation with children, identified key problems:

- too much instability

- too much time out of school – exclusions, truancy, disruptions because of moves, etc.

- not enough help with their education if they get behind

- not enough support and encouragement from carers

- not enough support in school – to catch up, etc. Will be recommending bursaries when moving to a new school – to pay for additional help

- need more help with emotional, mental or physical needs.

Recommendations to tackle these problems include the following.

- Refining the legal framework and guidance in the longer term to improve placement planning, consulting on reducing the number of school moves due to changes in care placements, reducing long distance placements and improving regional commissioning of specialist services.

- LEAs to make immediate arrangements to provide full-time education for children who do not have a school place.

- Improving training and support for foster carers to prevent placement breakdowns so they can provide better support for schoolwork at home.

- Prioritising children in care in current and future policy developments in relation to pre-school children and children's emotional and mental health. [Interestingly this includes the suggestion that local authorities provide bursaries to facilitate admissions to schools of children in care but no equivalent recommendation for health authorities to provide any similar assistance for this group in relation for CAMHS treatment – as recommended by *People Like Us* (1)].

- Making better use of information and research to understand outcomes for children from ethnic minority groups and children with disabilities and by harmonising central government data requirements over the longer term.

The report also says the following.

- Children and young people should be consulted about matters relating to their education provision and their views acted upon.

- Leaving care services should work with colleges and universities to raise awareness of the specific needs of care leavers.

- A new project group will be established to take forward implementation of the report overseen by the Ministerial Committee on Social Exclusion and the Ministerial Sub-Committee on the Delivery of Services for Children, Young People and Families and an external advisory group on the education of children in care.

However, it acknowledges that this does not address the needs of some groups of children and young people such as those 'on remand in, or sentenced to, local authority secure units – as opposed to welfare cases' – nor does it deal with the needs of children in prison, who may also have been in care.

SEU also published a Practice Guide – *A Better Education for Children in Care* (27) in advance of its report, which was delayed to coincide with the publication of *Every Child Matters* (7).

Getting the Right Start: National Service Framework for Children: Emerging Findings (13) said

'There is evidence that some children in special circumstances have poorer access to mainstream services. For example … a third of looked after children do not have annual dental checks'.

Every Child Matters (7) says 'Our aim is to ensure that every child has the chance to fulfil their potential by reducing levels of educational failure, ill health, substance misuse, teenage pregnancy, abuse and neglect, crime and antisocial behaviour' and that LEAs will be given a duty to promote the educational achievement of children in care.

However, on Child and Adolescent Mental Health Services, it says there is 'currently poor or no provision' for some groups, 'including children with learning disabilities, autistic spectrum disorders, minority ethnic groups, children and young people who need in-patient care, children with behavioural problems, and those in the criminal justice system'.

Analysis

This recommendation has been responded to very positively. There is the right policy framework for progress – with targets being set and monitored. However, much remains to be done to ensure that a difference is made to individual children and young people.

Similar action is needed for children in the criminal justice system and children who spend long periods in health settings.

Education

The *Every Child Matters* (7) promise that local education authorities will be given a duty to promote the educational achievement of children in care is very welcome. The SEU report *A Better Education for Children in Care* (27) is a positive contribution to improving this key area and a good basis for taking forward constructive work. It tackles the main areas identified by *People Like Us* (1) such as choice of placement and stability, providing training and support to carers, improving the joint working of social services and school staff, tackling out of authority placements, etc. It is a shame that it does not deal with those children and young people with, perhaps, the greatest need of all – those in the criminal justice system – many of whom will have been in care. It is a shame too that health services have not been urged to give any priority to children in care with emotional and mental health problems, in the same way that local education authorities are asked to take action to prioritise the needs of looked after children for school places.

The modest improvements in educational attainment of looked after children fall well short of the targets set. New targets which focus on engagement in education as well as attainment and introduce a new focus on earlier attainment were introduced in 2003. While it is disappointing that the improvements have not been more marked as yet, it is recognised that it takes time for improvements in educational opportunities to translate into academic results. It is hoped that the effort will be maintained and show greater rewards in future. The inclusion of targets for younger children and the focus on keeping children in school is welcome, as exclusion can easily damage life chances.

Inadequate educational provision remains a major problem for children and young people in prison establishments, where special educational needs are often greatest. There are welcome and much needed efforts by the YJB to increase educational provision. However, children in prison settings ought to have the same statutory right to education as other children and responsibility for this should rest with DfES. There are also real problems for children and young people who spend lengthy periods of time in health settings which need to be addressed.

Health

More attention is now being paid to the basic health needs of looked after children –

vaccinations, dental checks, etc. – although there is clearly some way to go.

However, the real weakness remains the inadequacy of the Child and Adolescent Mental Health Service to meet the needs of the increasing numbers of children and young people with mental health problems and, in particular, of children who have been abused and/or who are looked after. The announcement of increased and improved services, together with extra resources, is very welcome. However, the gross inadequacy of the service should have been recognised much earlier. It will take years to reach appropriate levels of staffing and expertise. In the meantime many children will continue to suffer and their problems will become more intractable. CAMHS is considered in more detail in the section on right to treatment.

Transition to independence/leaving care

What *People Like Us* said
Chapter 8 was concerned about young people being compelled to live independently before they were ready. No responsible parent … turns a child away at 16 – or even 18 – unsupported financially, without hope of succour in distress.

> **Department of Health and the Welsh Office should amend Section 24 of the Children Act 1989 to convert into a duty the local authority's power to assist a child they have looked after, and to make clear that the looking after authority is responsible for after care.**

Government response
- Will be legislation to strengthen the powers and duties of local authorities to provide support and assistance, including a duty to assess and meet the needs of care leavers up to age 18.

- Also minded to extend to age 21 subject to affordability.

- Legislation to ensure there is a continuing responsibility to provide after care assistance.

Government action

Quality Protects objective 5 'to ensure that young people leaving care, as they enter adulthood, are not isolated and participate socially and economically as citizens'.

The Children (Leaving Care) Act 2000 came into force on 1 October 2001. Its principal aim is to improve the life chances of young people living in and leaving local authority care. It imposes new stronger duties upon local authorities to support care leavers until they reach at least 18. There are funds for qualifying children and young people in and leaving care to pay for a Pathway plan based on a needs assessment which includes:

- accommodation and maintenance for those aged 16 and 17

- general assistance and help with employment up to age 21

- help with education and training to the end of the agreed programme, even if that takes someone past 21

- provision of vacation accommodation (if needed) for someone in higher or further education which means living away from home

- provision of young people's advisors to the age of at least 21, or for as long as someone is being helped with education and training.

In Wales, objectives and targets for improving outcomes for care leavers are included as a priority in the Children First programme.

What happened

Transforming Children's Service: An Evaluation of Local Responses to the Quality Protects Programme Year 3 (28) reports significant movement in the right direction and an energetic commitment to implementing the legislation.

The Connexions service gives guidance and support to all 13–19-year-olds but targets most intensive help on those in greatest need. All children in care over the age of 12 will have an adviser to help them make a successful transition to adult and working life and must have a care plan which is reviewed regularly. This should consider the arrangements needed when the child will no longer be looked after/provided with accommodation. Caroline Abrahams, CYPU/NCH, said that there was some confusion about the role of Connexions and leaving care advisers. There was too much reliance being placed on Connexions to solve long-standing and intractable problems.

The best place to be? (25) said 'Our research confirms earlier findings that the transitional arrangements for young [disabled] people placed out of their local area are not working well … The new Connexions service is intended to include young disabled people placed at boarding schools within their remit but the responsibility will be shared between the Connexions Partnership in their home area and the Partnership where they are based in term time. It is uncertain how this will work and how the Connexions service will link in with existing responsibilities for supporting young disabled people in their transition to adulthood. The Supplementary Guidance issued by Connexions concerning young people with learning difficulties or disabilities makes no mention of young people placed outside their local area.

The *Children Act Report 2002* (29) said:

- the 2002 figures continue the trend for a greater proportion of young people remaining looked after until they are 18 years of age and a smaller proportion leaving at sixteen

- the Children In Need survey shows that the number of young people receiving active support having left care is a small proportion of those who were looked after when 16 or 17.

In September 2002 *Community Care* reported on the interim findings from a Social Exclusion Unit study of the first year of operation of the Leaving Care Act:

- in four out of the five authorities studied pupils failed to gain the target of one GCSE

- too many children were spending long periods of time out of school and being excluded; care placements remained unstable; and waiting times for therapy were too long – a 30-month delay for CAMHS in one council

- a Southampton University study showed that care leavers in post compulsory education had problems establishing relationships with peers and teachers, often had lower aspirations and were more likely to give up courses.

In its 17–23 October edition there was more positive news – Ealing was supporting 15 care leavers through university. Jane Sufian of First Key (and spokesperson for the Action on Aftercare Consortium group of charities) said that by providing ring-fenced money to fund care leavers through higher and further education courses, the Act was already improving educational opportunities. A clear theme of the First Key Conference to mark the Act's first year was that although some authorities have grasped the challenge, others have not.

In November 2002, the Roberts Centre seminar to review the Children (Leaving Care) Act 2000 (30) found that there have been some positive developments – e.g. a slight increase in the last two years of young people remaining in care until they are 18, a small but increasing number going on to higher education – but a number of difficulties were identified.

- Significant practical difficulties over financial arrangements – the Benefits Agency was unable to meet its obligations in some areas and care leavers have to turn to local authorities for help.

- Large variations in the level of funding between different areas and it was feared that this would become worse when ring-fenced budgets come to an end in April 2004. Older care leavers were thought likely to suffer most.

- The gap was widening between those covered by the Act and those who were not but whose needs may be similar – young refugees, those whose time in the criminal justice system became disqualified from entitlement to care leaver services and those with learning difficulties or mental health problems.

- Support to care leavers in higher education was inadequate – without parental support, the debt they faced was a significant disincentive. Accommodation during holiday periods was a problem – their financial position made it difficult to retain a home to return to and it was difficult to find short-term accommodation.

- Few authorities started preparation for independent living at an early enough stage. This needed to include social skills as well as practical ones.

- Accommodation was a key issue and source of difficulties if it went wrong.

In relation to disabled young people, the following were identifed.

- There was 'evidence that 'qualified' young disabled people are either by-passing the Act completely, or not receiving adequate services as a consequence of poor communication between specialist disabled transitions teams and leaving care services.

- Young people with mild to moderate learning disabilities living in foster care are falling between leaving care services and specialist disability teams. This becomes a major concern when these young people reach 18 and are expected to leave foster care services but are unable to manage on their own and are very vulnerable in hostel accommodation.

Some young people are excluded from the legislation altogether, including unaccompanied young asylum seekers who may have been defined as children in need rather than looked after children and young disabled people who have been resident in schools – or even in a succession of respite care placements – for long periods of time.

The *NSPCC Review of Legislation Relating to Children in Family Proceedings Consultation Draft* (21) commented on the lack of support for 16- and 17-year-olds. Although the Care Leavers Act 2000 had strengthened local authority responsibilities for care leavers, there was a problem of under-16s being placed in B&B accommodation when parents refuse to look after them and local authorities are reluctant to take on responsibility. In particular there is a lack of services for pregnant 16- and 17-year-olds who are passed to adult teams and placed in unsuitable B&B accommodation which has not been adequately checked. 'The paucity of services to teenagers, many of whom have become isolated from their families and denied services as children in need of family support services, including accommodation, is one of the most striking and worrying findings from the review. Local authorities have specific responsibilities under Section 24 of the Children Act 1989, strengthened

by the Leaving Care Act 2000, but many more young people apparently find themselves adrift in the community without adequate support or accommodation … It is a matter of regret that the concept of looking after young people on a voluntary basis under the Section 20 accommodation provisions appears to have gone into abeyance.' It recommended 'A recruitment drive to find suitable carers for teenagers as well as investment in supportive semi-independent accommodation is urgently needed'.

In February 2004 the National Children's Bureau (NCB) published the report of a study of eight London Boroughs which found that they were providing more services to meet the diverse needs of care leavers but that there was widespread concern about the removal of ring-fenced resources for leaving care services from March 2004.

Analysis

The importance of proper support for young people leaving care has been accepted and the Children (Leaving Care) Act 2000 is a major step forward. However, the findings of the Roberts Centre seminar to review the Act illustrate the difficulties that still have to be overcome before the aspirations of the Act become a reality, particularly for young disabled people.

While there is clearly some way to go to ensure that all young care leavers get the help and support they need, at least they now have the right to ask for this. This should, however, not be at the expense of other vulnerable young people, such as those identified by the NSPCC. Local authorities need the resources to fulfil their parental responsibilities to young care leavers *and* to provide help to other vulnerable young people who do not have parental support at the important and difficult transition to independent living. As in so many areas, the policy has moved forward but the practice lags behind, with resource constraints playing a major part in this.

4.3 Disabled children

What *People Like Us* said
Chapter 8 said that disabled children are both more likely to live away from their families than other children – sometimes for 52 weeks a year – and more likely to suffer abuse than other children living away from home.

Disabled children are extremely vulnerable to abuse of all kinds, including peer abuse, and high priority needs to be given to protecting them and ensuring that safeguards are rigorously applied.

Government response
- High priority should be given to protecting disabled children who make up a large proportion of children living away from home and are particularly vulnerable.

- Objective on disabled children included in new objectives for children's services.

- Government considering how to introduce Children Act principles into care of disabled children in residential care homes and nursing homes, to be developed with the new regulatory arrangements. Further details in 1999.

Government action
- Objective 6 of the Quality Protects programme says 'to ensure that children with specific social needs arising out of disability or a health condition are living in families or other appropriate settings in the community where their assessed needs are adequately met and reviewed'.

- Revised *Working Together*, September 2000, included advice and guidance in relation to disabled children.

- *Protecting the Public*, 2002 (15), recognises the vulnerability of children and those with a learning disability or mental disorder to abuse and proposed three new offences aimed at protecting vulnerable people.

What happened
The Children Act Report 1995–1999 (31) said 'clearly any child with a disability should benefit from all the Quality Protects objectives including being protected from abuse'.

Valuing People (32) proposed new objectives and sub-objectives for disabled children and young people building on Quality Protects. The main objective is 'to ensure that disabled children gain maximum life chance benefits from educational opportunities, health care and social care, while living with their families or other appropriate settings in the community where their assessed needs are adequately met and reviewed'. The six sub-objectives did not refer to safeguards or child protection. Its section on Residential Placements acknowledges that disabled children in these settings are particularly vulnerable to abuse.

Learning the Lessons (33) says 'when we talk of children we mean all children, including disabled children. We recognise that disabled children are particularly vulnerable to abuse of all kinds and that high priority needs to be given to protecting them and ensuring that safeguards are rigorously applied' (with a footnote referring to Chapter 8 of *People Like Us* (1)).

Assessing Children in Need and their Families: Practice Guidance (34) includes a chapter on disabled children. It says the following.

- Disabled children are more likely to live away from home: to be accommodated on a short-term or long-term basis and/or to be in state-funded residential education.

- Some 46,000 disabled children are thought to be living away from home, with over 4,000 of them '… isolated from their families, and with little or no contact with people outside their schools, foster or residential homes and a circle of busy professionals'.

- Disabled children are 'particularly vulnerable and face an increased risk of suffering abuse in many settings'.

- They ought to be over-represented in our child protection systems, yet research suggests they may be significantly under-represented.

- There is some evidence that institutional care should be considered a risk factor in itself.

The Council for Disabled Children (CDC) and NSPCC set up a National Working Group in 2001 in response to concern among many groups that there was no learning about why things kept going wrong. The first report *'It doesn't happen to disabled children'* – *Child Protection and Disabled Children: Report of the National Working Group on Child Protection and Disability* (23) identifies the key issues concerning safeguarding disabled children and says that recognition of the vulnerability of disabled children has increased and principles of good practice are included in government guidance. However, there is only limited guidance on what local agencies should do and applying the principles in practice presents a challenge to practitioners, particularly where the child's impairment affects their communication. It makes two main recommendations:

- that DfES should review the current child protection system in respect of disabled children and

- develop a national strategy for the safeguarding of disabled children.

> **Statistics should be collected to enable policy makers and planners to assess need, establish trends and develop services accordingly.**

Government response
- Considering the data that could and should be collected – further information in consultation on performance assessment framework for social services.

Government action
- First Children in Need Census in February 2000 provided much new information on disabled children and the services they were receiving. This was used for the *Children Act Reports* in 2000

and 2001 (35, 36). Two further Censuses held in September/October 2001 and February 2003.

- There is now a disability identifier on LAC returns – these show 1,215 in residential settings – 595 in residential schools and 620 in children's homes.

- A joint DH/DfES working group established early 2002 to look at the needs of disabled children in residential care and consider how to progress with data collection.

What happened

Modern Social Services – A Commitment to the Future, the 12th annual report of the Chief Inspector of Social Services 2002–03 (37) said 'In general, information about services for disabled children from data collected during the year was limited and patchy, but overall suggests the need for development'.

'It doesn't happen to disabled children' (23) says 'adequate statistics of disabled children in residential care do not exist' and recommended the collection, analysis and publication of statistical information on a regular basis.

DfES/DH published *Disabled Children in Residential Placements* (38) in spring 2004. This was the outcome of the joint working group mentioned above and drew together available information collected by social services, education and health authorities about the numbers, circumstances and outcomes for disabled children in residential settings. We discuss this report in more detail in our companion report (*Safeguards for vulnerable children*). Here we note that the data on looked after disabled children is more comprehensive than that on disabled children in residential special schools or health settings who are not looked after.

> The Review discusses the need for co-operation between education, social services and health authorities and for a specific commitment to work together to protect disabled children.

Government response

- Co-operation being improved generally.

- New objective provides an incentive for agencies to work together to provide good quality care.

- Revision of *Working Together* to cover child protection in relation to disabled children.

- Regulatory changes to ensure protection in all settings being considered.

What happened

The joint working group described at the beginning of the previous section began to consider this issue and what needed to be done.

Revised *Special Educational Needs Codes of Practice* (39, 40) were issued in England and Wales and include paragraphs on:

- placing a child in a residential school or other residential setting

- the duty of the LEA to help social services if a child is suffering or at risk of suffering significant harm

- relationships between schools, LEAs and social services.

The 11th Annual Report of the Chief Inspector of Social Services 2001–02 (24) said 'In the autumn position statements 95 per cent of councils claimed to have achieved at least some level of integration of services for children with disabilities across health, social care, education and the voluntary sector. However, only 19 per cent rated themselves as having good integration and only one council stated that services were fully integrated. Inspection findings indicated that partnership working with health particularly in the Child and Adolescent Mental Health Services (CAMHS) needed development. Inspectors found services for disabled children and work with young carers to be less well developed, lacking co-ordination and integration'.

The best place to be? Policy, practice and the experiences of residential school placements for disabled children (25) said the following.

- Placements funded solely by the education authority received little monitoring of care standards and children's welfare. Social services departments followed a variety of practices, but very few children received the full protection of the Children Act. Both education and social services professionals admitted they would rarely know if children were safe and happy, given the difficulties that they had in spending any time with disabled children and young people at boarding school.

- There was confusion about statutory duties towards children at residential schools. 'Our research has demonstrated that, in practice, the current legislative framework is not adequately protecting and promoting the interests of disabled children at boarding schools'.

- Parents were rarely supported to maintain contact with their children. It recommended DH and DfES should … encourage local education and social services authorities to jointly take responsibility for protecting and promoting the welfare of disabled children placed at residential schools and for supporting parents in maintaining contact with their children. Monitoring of whether the placement is meeting a child's educational, care, cultural and emotional needs should take place at six-monthly intervals and should involve someone from the placing authority spending time with the child.

The *NSPCC Review of Legislation Relating to Children in Family Proceedings Consultation Draft* (21) said 'There is a general feeling that resources are simply not there to meet the needs of disabled children, who are described as hugely under-

provided for. Multi-agency packages are apparently not forthcoming'.

Kirsten Stalker in *Supporting Children with Complex Needs* (41) refers to work by Noyes (1999) on children in hospital – the families experienced 3 main areas of difficulty:

- following referral, social services did not comply with the Children Act requirements about meetings, etc., children were not assigned social workers

- some children had little or no access to suitable education

- discharge was not even raised as an option for some – health authorities and social services could not agree on funding, etc.

- many difficulties were reported in joint working for children with complex support needs including different views about when 'childhood' ended; difficulties about education in health-care settings and when they left and when children spent more time at home, social services expected to have more input but were not given additional resources to meet this responsibility.

The introduction to *Disabled Children in Residential Placements* (38) sets the policy context describing the work of the NCSC, discussions about the definition of 'looked after' and its implications for disabled children, Sections 85 and 86 of the Children Act 1989, and the Quality Protects and Choice Protects programmes.

Analysis

As far as policy is concerned, a range of policy documents and guidance (on Quality Protects, in *Assessing Children in Need and their Families: Practice Guidance* (34), *Valuing People* (32) and *Learning the Lessons* (33)) do now recognise the vulnerability to abuse of disabled children. However, the degree of recognition varies between settings and is inadequately covered in, for example, health and penal settings.

But, while there is now more general recognition of the vulnerability of disabled children there is less evidence of clear practical help and guidance on how to protect them. The quality and coverage about the needs of disabled children and their vulnerability to abuse and harm is variable – the National Minimum Standards for residential special schools are best, because, by definition, they are dealing with special needs. They cover providing intimate personal care and how to do this professionally, while this is not mentioned in the fostering services, boarding schools or college standards. The coverage is least good in the foster care National Minimum Standards; for example, the standard on respite care, which is predominantly used for disabled children, does not mention disability.

Despite this recognition, disabled children remain vulnerable and many continue to have grounds for concern about how effectively disabled children are protected. In practice, the needs of disabled children are not being given priority so they are not being adequately safeguarded. There are particular problems in residential care, health provision and schools – especially those with 52-week provision. Research has discovered that significant numbers of children and young people have been resident in health settings for long periods and that local.authorities have not been notified of this as they should have been under Sections 85 and 86 of the Children Act 1989.

There has been some progress in obtaining statistical information about the numbers, locations, and needs of disabled children and the services provided for them but much more is needed. Children in Need Censuses need to be carried out at regular intervals so that trends can be established. The report *Disabled Children in Residential Placements* (38) provides a useful analysis of the current situation, its gaps and weaknesses. This is discussed in more detail in our companion report *Safeguards for vulnerable children*.

There are, undoubtedly, efforts to encourage more co-operation between different services but there is still a very long way to go, particularly for disabled children whose needs span several services and whose quality of life depends upon seamless health, education, welfare and residential provision. They also need to be assured of a planned and positive transition to adulthood. This is unlikely to be the case for many without far better co-operation between the relevant services. It is hoped that lessons can be learned from pathfinder Children's Trusts such as Gateshead, which focus on the needs of disabled children and CAMHS and which have strong user involvement.

Recommendations

7   DfES and DH should arrange the production and issue of practical guidance on the action that can be taken to safeguard disabled children in all settings, particularly in residential special schools and health settings.

8   Action is needed by DfES and DH to ensure that local education authorities and health authorities notify the responsible local authority when a child is resident in an educational or health setting for three months or more as required by Sections 85 and 86 of the Children Act 1989.

9   Children in Need Censuses should be held at regular intervals and DfES and DH should carry out the exercise to collate existing statistical information on disabled children in children's homes, residential special schools and health settings every three years.

4.4 Children with emotional and behavioural difficulties (EBD)

What *People Like Us* said

The emotional needs of children with emotional and behavioural difficulties makes them susceptible and their behaviour means that they are less likely to be believed. Agencies responsible for them may not be too disposed to ask too many questions of institutions that seem to be successfully containing particularly difficult children. And they may be exposed to abuse under the guise of innovatory treatment.

> **Principal Recommendation 8. Local authorities should unify their educational and social arrangements for assessing and supporting children with emotional and behavioural difficulties and their families.**
>
> **Children with emotional and behavioural difficulties who are placed in residential schools for social and educational reasons should also be assessed as potential children in need.**
>
> **The protection for emotionally and behaviourally disturbed children should be extended and improved.**

Government response

- *Rejected*. No obstacle to this being taken forward in Children's Services.

- Current procedures appropriate if properly followed.

- Quality Protects will improve assessment and placement procedures by SSDs.

- Procedures for making educational placements in residential schools and for considering allegations to be looked at further.

What happened

OFSTED's *Effective Education for Pupils with Emotional and Behavioural Difficulties* (42) discussed key features of effective schools for these children, focusing on educational attainment not safeguards. It used evidence from inspections of 40 schools (day and residential) judged to be good or very good; four schools that had emerged successfully from special measures; interviews with parents, pupils, teachers and professionals. The brief reference to residential care said 'residential provision could be used more flexibly than at present'. Staff in both day and residential EBD schools told OFSTED that few LEAs had encouraged them to develop close liaison with parents, although headteachers were 'generally convinced, sometimes quoting research, of the greater success of special schools, in relation to residential homes or foster care, in building bridges between pupils and their families'.

The policy guidance *Framework for the Assessment of Children in Need and their Families* (43) refers briefly to this group in the section on Special Education Needs Code of Practice saying '[SEN] cover a wide spectrum of needs/difficulties including emotional and behavioural difficulties' and summarises what the code (since revised) said about such children. The practice guidance *Assessing Children in Need and their Families* (34) does not mention this group as a specific category.

The revised *SEN Code of Practice for England* and the one for Wales (39, 40) include references throughout identifying a child presenting 'persistent emotional and/or behavioural difficulties' that are 'not ameliorated by the behaviour management techniques usually employed in the setting' as having special educational needs that need additional or different interventions.

Some EBD children could be sent to school a long way from their families, usually because they were thought to need highly specialist education not available locally (source: DfES). The *SEN Codes of Practice* (39, 40) say that the LEA and the parent 'should also agree the arrangements for the child's contact with their family and for any special help … which may be needed to maintain home/school contact'. DfES had no information about whether parents were helped to keep in contact.

The Welsh Assembly Government has taken action over this group of children. Welsh Office Circular 56/94 deals specifically with 'The Education of Children with Emotional and Behavioral Difficulties' and National Assembly Circular 3/99 'Pupil Support and Social Inclusion' includes practical advice for schools in addressing emotional and behavioural difficulties.

In Wales there is guidance on assessment and planning of services for children with emotional and behavioral difficulties in the comprehensive *Framework for Assessment of Children in Need and their Families*, published in 2001. This has also been included in the Carlile Report (44) as recommendation 84. Further guidance will be published by the Assembly Government's NHS Department.

In their article *The Development of Provision for Young People with Emotional and Behavioural Difficulties: An Activity Analysis* (45) Harry Daniels and Ted Cole analyse how services for these children have evolved over time and explore ways of making things better in the future. While much of the article is for an academic audience, it makes these general points about services for these children.

- They should be, but often are not, clients of many services. Their problems that are in practice rounded ones are 'sliced into segments for treatment by different services. This often reflects the historical happenstance of which agency "picks up" which child. This may be juvenile justice, or welfare or health or education'.

- 'Cross sector collaboration and support is inhibited by current regulation, systems of accountability, rules and the focus on narrow performance indicators. Teachers rarely

appreciated the difficulties under which social services departments operated.'

In *Patterns of Provision for Pupils with Behavioural Difficulties in England: A study of government statistics and behaviour support plan data* (46) Ted Cole *et al.* found that in 1998 around 4,500 pupils with EBD were in schools with boarding provision – around 30 per cent of all pupils with EBD being educated in special schools. Some placements are jointly funded by social services and education and occasionally the NHS. Schools with boarding provision for children with EBD are 'expensive, difficult to staff and challenging to run effectively … There has been a move away from seven nightly boarding to young people typically spending only four or five nights a week in the boarding schools or returning home every second weekend'. The authors argue that placements in residential special schools are socially rather than educationally driven. This may be because social services departments now have limited placement options available after closing children's homes and Community Homes with Education over the last 20 years. *Disabled Children in Residential Placements* (38), which analysed available information about numbers, circumstances and outcomes for disabled children, noted that the biggest single group of children placed in special schools was teenage boys with EBD.

DfES with DH are proposing to review policy on children with EBD, but work on this was held up while DfES prepared its 10 Year Action Plan for SEN. There is no information yet available about the scope of the review or its timetable. The 10-year plan in *Removing Barriers to Achievement: The Government's Strategy for SEN* (47) includes the following proposals that are relevant to children with EBD.

- Over one-third of special schools are approved for children with emotional and behavioural difficulties and autistic spectrum disorder (Source: Pupil Level Annual Schools Census, PLASC). In 2001/02 27 per cent of looked after children had statements of SEN and schools' admissions and exclusions policies can be unfavourable to this group. Local authorities tend to find it difficult to find suitable places for [these] children, … or because schools assume looked after children are likely to have behavioural difficulties.

- There is a current OFSTED investigation into the full range of provision for young people with behavioural, emotional and social difficulties (BESD).

- Findings from this investigation will be used as the basis for improving the quality of education for those with more severe and complex behavioural, emotional and social difficulties, by better partnership working especially with CAMHS, etc.

- The section on specialist provision for children with 'low incidence' needs refers to the small number of children with 'extremely severe and complex needs [who] require more support than can ordinarily be made available within the local community of schools' and goes on to discuss residential special schools.

NASS, which represents non-maintained and independent special schools and the staff working in them, says that special schools for children with emotional and behavioural difficulties, in common with other special schools, often feel isolated, especially if they are residential. They may be isolated from mainstream schools and from local education authorities. Non-maintained and independent special schools may also be isolated from other special schools. This feeling can be lessened through networks to share good practice. Nevertheless NASS says inspection reports show that many schools provide high quality services for this group of children with good child protection procedures in place.

NASS comments that there are a lot of sources for conflict in the current system for deciding

whether to send a child to a non-maintained or independent special school, especially a residential one. Most places are funded out of the public purse, and some local authorities may have philosophical objections to using such places. NASS and the LGA have produced a model contract for the placement of children and young people in day and residential independent and non-maintained special schools. DfES, DH, the SEN Regional Partnerships and ADSS support the contract.

SEBDA, the Social, Emotional and Behavioural Difficulties Association, formerly called the Association of Workers for Children with Emotional and Behavioural Difficulties, is a UK body founded in 1952 with a multi-professional membership including staff working in Pupil Referral Units, mental health service workers, educational psychologists, teachers and parents. It changed its name in January 2003. Its website says '[it] supports parents, who, unlike parents in other special needs groups, feel that they evoke very little public sympathy and do not form pressure groups'. SEBDA produces an international journal and a newsletter, puts on conferences and workshops and provides a distance education course.

Analysis

The Government rejected the recommendations in *People Like Us* (1) for this group of children. This included categorising children with emotional and behavioural difficulties sent to residential special schools as potential children in need. They said this group would be covered in the different programmes being set up to improve services for all children. There is little information available about how the programmes listed in the Government's response have helped this particular group, so it is impossible to assess whether they have benefited.

The information available suggests that more attention has been focused on the educational needs of children with emotional and behavioural difficulties than on safeguards. In England children with emotional and behavioural difficulties make up a significant proportion of children with SEN, and it is welcome that the revised Code of Practice gives due weight to the importance of identifying and addressing their special educational needs at each stage of their education. As said elsewhere in this report, it is also helpful that the Code has clear guidance about helping any child sent to a residential special school keep in touch with his or her family. It is also welcome that the NASS/LGA model contract explicitly covers this. These children need a good education, but they are also vulnerable and the importance of effective safeguards in residential settings must not be overlooked. Enabling them to keep in touch with their families should help with this.

This remains a somewhat neglected area in England and it is disappointing that DfES have not yet started to review services for EBD children. This is urgently needed. It should start as soon as possible and be completed within a year.

It is encouraging that *Removing Barriers to Achievement* (47) refers to action now in train to improve information about this group of children. The news about the OFSTED investigation into the full range of provision for this group of children and young people is welcome. It does not specifically cover the role of residential placements but should do so. Information supplied by the Welsh Assembly Government suggests that Wales seem to have done more about this group of children/young people.

4.5 Young children

What *People Like Us* said

> Young children are less able to protect themselves and to complain. Regulatory bodies need greater awareness of this in considering the position of younger children in foster care, preparatory schools and hospitals.

Government response

- Quality Protects will give children a greater role in service planning and development, which should give them a more effective voice.

- Work underway on facilitating greater participation for younger children.

- Issue will be considered in legislation for independent regulatory arrangements.

What happened

National Minimum Standards require an appropriate response to complaints.

Leaflets for the carers of under-fives – *'Protecting your children'* and *'Keeping young children safe'* (48) – have been produced by Kidscape with funding from Sure Start and *Feeling happy feeling safe. A safety guide for young children* (49), published by the Home Office.

Analysis

The production of information for carers is a helpful development and the leaflets should be widely available to all parents and carers of young children.

This study has found no other evidence of specific action being taken to improve the protection of young children. This is an area where further work is needed to establish what further safeguards are appropriate to protect very young children and to ensure these are put in place.

4.6 Lost children

What *People Like Us* said

Homeless children – lost children – are most vulnerable of all. Physical and sexual abuse is common. The reasons why children run away should be established. There should be an analysis of the information available and a viable strategy developed for tackling the interlocking problems.

> Local authorities should take all steps that responsible parents take when children run away. Returning children should be interviewed by somebody independent.
>
> Refuges play a useful role and there is a case for recognising them in service plans, and for extending – perhaps as a regional resource to other centres of population. Ideally this should be as part of a more strategic approach to the problem of homeless, 'missing' and disturbed youth.
>
> DH should commission a project to assemble and analyse information about the adequacy and co-ordination of local services for troubled young people with a view to producing a national strategy.

Government response
- Further guidelines to be developed and statutory guidance issued by April 1999.
- Implementation to be monitored through SSI and SSIW inspections.
- Plans on refuges being drawn up with voluntary sector and local government.

Government action
- Minimum Standards cover absence without authority: Standard 19 for Children's Homes.
- *Working Together* deals with unauthorised absence from foster care.
- Social Exclusion Report *Young Runaways* published, 2002.

What happened
In 1998 ACPO and the LGA issued guidelines to all police forces and chief executives of local authorities and directors of social services setting out best practice in dealing with children who abscond from care.

Safeguarding Children (4) said 'information about children going missing from specific children's homes was not being captured to identify that there were particular problems at some homes that warranted investigation'.

The *Report of the 31st session of the Committee on the Rights of the Child* (50) recommends that the state party – 44b) 'better co-ordinate and reinforce its efforts to address the causes of youth homelessness and its consequences; and c) review its legislation and policies concerning benefits and social security allowances for 16 to 18 year olds'.

In *It's someone taking a part of you. A study of young women and sexual exploitation.* Jenny Pearce *et al.* (51) describe the vulnerability of children who run away to sexual exploitation. Approximately 100,000 children have run away from home or care in one year – more than 100 children each day. 'Refuge provision for children running away from home is sparse.' There is one refuge for children under 16, in London, run by the NSPCC. It has eight beds and provides accommodation for two weeks. This requires complicated negotiations to be done in a short period. Between April 2001 and February 2002 there were 387 referrals with 122 admissions involving 97 young people; 57 of the non-admissions were because there were no beds available at the time of referral.

Young Runaways (52) says running away affects approximately one in nine young people under the age of 16 and that about a quarter (20,000) of runaways are under the age of 11. The Social Exclusion Unit review was in response to the concern in *People Like Us* (1) about children who go missing and the suggestion that services for these children should be planned for, and the reasons that they go missing identified, so that they can be properly safeguarded. It provides a thorough analysis of the problem and proposes an Action Plan for services for runaways which would provide 'a coherent, long-term approach' and covers arrangements at central and local level.

In response to *People Like Us* (1), DH

commissioned research from the University of York to provide the evidence base. This was delivered in 1999 and drew on two major studies, *Still Running* (53), a UK wide survey of young people who run away and *Going Missing,* a detailed examination of young people missing from care in four local authorities. This showed that those missing from home had similar needs to those missing from care. DH's *Children Missing from Care and from Home – A Guide to Good Practice* (54) summarises messages from the York University research and details good practice that agencies need to follow to respond effectively. Said to be published 'alongside' the Social Exclusion Unit report.

Community Care, 5–11 December 2002, reported that 'Barnardo's slates runaways study for failing to tackle sexual exploitation'. It 'broadly welcomed' the report but said specialist expertise was needed to move vulnerable children away from adults who exploit them. It criticised the decision not to implement the proposals until 2004.

Research report received in June 2002 on runaways in Wales. Draft guidance in course of preparation.

Recommendation 17 of the Laming Report (16) was that a national database for children should be piloted 'to explore its usefulness in strengthening the safeguards for children'. The table annexed to *Keeping Children Safe* (17) said that better information sharing was crucial and the Identification, Referral and Tracking Project is exploring how information about children can be shared appropriately within and between agencies, and more easily transferred across local authority boundaries. Such a database would be very useful in identifying children who go missing.

Lost from View: Missing Persons in the UK, a study by the University of York for the National Missing Persons Helpline, which was reported in *Community Care* 6–12 March 2003, confirmed the dangers faced by young people who go missing – almost one in nine are sexually assaulted while they are away.

Thrown Away (55) a report of a survey by the Children's Society and the University of York, said that in the UK one in 50 children (15,000) are forced to leave home by parents or carers before they are 16 and 20 per cent end up sleeping rough. 100,000 children run away overnight each year. It found that:

- only a third of local authorities had policies in place for young runaways

- only seven of the sample of 150 had fully implemented the 2002 Government recommendation to draw up a plan, appoint a 'runaways' manager and monitor and evaluate this work.

It recommended:

- all local authorities put in place guidance on young runaways as recommended by Government

- a national network of safe emergency accommodation for under-16s

- better access to benefits for 16–17-year-olds.

Analysis

The recognition of the dangers to children and young people who go missing from care and from their homes is very welcome. Guidance has been issued. The Social Exclusion Unit's analysis in *Young Runaways* (52) is very useful, as is the Action Plan it recommends. The Report, quite rightly, placed emphasis on prevention and early action on the reasons why children run away with recommendations for 'ensuring immediate safety' (including community-based refuges) and 'providing longer term support' (including providing interviews following return). However, it seems that the Action Plan is not being implemented in the majority of local authorities. Further work is needed to follow up the *Young Runaways* (52) Action Plan and DH *Guidance on*

Children Missing from Care and from Home (54) to ensure that progress is made.

Only one of the refuges that *People Like Us* (1) regarded as valuable and in need of extension on a regional basis has survived. *Young Runaways* (52) said that DH was developing a programme from 2003 to develop and test options for community-based refuge provision. What has happened on this? Children will continue to run away and to need safe refuge. Refuges are a high cost, low volume provision which is frequently out of area and local authorities have found it hard to pay for children they were often not aware of. But, while more provision is needed on a local basis, there will always be a number of children who leave their local area and are in need of a safe place to stay. A solution to how this should be paid for needs to be found – whether by grant from central government or by individual local authorities or a combination of the two. DfES, in consultation with the LGA, should find a solution to the problem of funding a small number of local refuges or a national network of emergency accommodation. It may be necessary to consider an amendment to the legislation if this is unduly restrictive in the time children and young people can be accommodated or in other respects.

As recommended in *Young Runaways* (51), more helplines are needed, which are staffed 24 hours a day and can give advice to children and young people on where they can go and be safe while their immediate problems are addressed.

4.7 Views of children and young people

What *People Like Us* said

The voice of authentic experience of young people spoke more clearly than any other. Their comments about being looked after were not as negative overall as their suggestions for improvement suggest.

The danger most often referred to was from other children: particularly bullying, physical abuse and theft. 'Generally, foster care was experienced as safer than residential care on this score'. For some, foster care was worse than being in a residential home; they found none of the benefits of being in a family, and lost any of the advantages of communal living. Abusive families continued to be a danger. Confidence in the complaints procedure is low.

The common theme … was their very reasonable desire to be treated as people and as individuals … and the reality that local authorities needed much more than avowed good intentions to achieve this.

These young people had the potential to contribute to overcoming the difficulties they and their contemporaries face … their ability gives us a great deal of confidence that looked after children can not only share decisions about their own future as individuals but also contribute to the better working of the systems that govern their lives. Children who are or have been looked after by local authorities can offer advice on policy and service developments and assist in the training and selection of staff.

> **Principal recommendation 15. Local authorities should make direct use of the experience of the children they look after in developing the policy, practice and training for services for children living away from home.**

Government response

- Quality Protects programme to promote involvement of young people in local planning and Government to involve young people in developing policy, practice and staff training on a national basis. One of the themes of Quality Protects.

- Young person on Ministerial Task Force for response.

Government action

- Involving children and carers has been included in developing policy, practice and staff training in the objectives for Quality Protects (objective 8) and in commissioning processes in Choice Protects (objective 2).

- The Interim Good Practice Guidance on children's services planning said that the planning process should involve 'children, young people and their families' and made it clear that views must be obtained, in a representative way at the outset of the planning cycle.

- Central to the new Integrated Children's System (ICS) is ensuring that children understand them, know what part they can play in them and are given the tools to make their voices heard.

- DH has commissioned Barnardo's to produce information for children about assessment processes and formats to help children participate in them (January 2003) and the Council for Disabled Children and Triangle to provide a list of the resources available to help practitioners communicate more effectively with disabled children.

- CYPU's *'Learning to Listen – Core Principles on the Involvement and Engagement of Children and Young People* (November 2001) required Government departments to produce action plans to implement the principles and publish them on the CYPU website in June 2002. DH action plan – *'Listening, Hearing and Responding'* published 20 June 2002.

- The Care Standards Act 2000 requires the Children's Rights Director to give proper consideration to the views of children and their parents. He must ascertain the views of children and their parents about regulated services they receive and report findings to the Commission.

- SSI have experimented with the use of care-experienced young people as inspectors (aged 18–25) in 'Listening and Responding' Teams obtaining the views of children and young people in SSI inspections on how well local authorities listen and respond to them. An evaluation of this – *Voices and Choice: young people participating in inspections. Learning from the Listening and Responding component of SSI inspections of Local authority children's services.* Barnardo's *et al.* 2002 found that the involvement of young inspectors was valuable and enhanced both the quality and quantity of information acquired. There were teething problems to be sorted out for future inspections. SSI needed to learn lessons from the experience and use them to for future work. Barnardo's and the Children's Society have been commissioned to further develop the models in *Voices and Choice* with a view to establishing something permanent during 2004.

What happened

The *Children Act Report 2000* (35) said that 'there was clear evidence from the Children Act research studies that there has been a substantial shift in culture to include children in planning and decision-making that affects their lives'.

The *Children Act Report 2001* (36) says 'Although there is a great deal of policy development work across Government concerned with engaging children and young people in the decisions that affect their lives, there is as yet no quantitative information from which the extent of the penetration of these policies can be assessed. Consideration is being given to how this can be addressed in the review of the Performance Assessment Framework for Social Care'.

In his *Annual Report and Accounts 2001–2002* the Children's Commissioner for Wales (56) said 'The National Assembly for Wales has made significant progress in advocating and supporting children and young people's participation in civic life in general, and the services provided for them in particular. It has stimulated and funded "Funky Dragon", an organisation of and for young people to inform the Assembly itself. The Framework for Partnership requires the establishment of youth forums in each and every local authority in Wales and Extending Entitlement proposed the establishment of schools councils in every school … but, despite some genuine attempts at partnership, progress to date can only be described as patchy and inconsistent. In others, there has been very little progress, or the young people report only tokenistic relationships, with their views being at best listened to – never acted upon … There is still not a sufficient number of adults confident and skilled in this way of working to make the cultural change we want to achieve'. The involvement of young people in the formulation and implementation of 'Children First' is cited as an example of good practice but too many other policy documents are emerging with no involvement.

Safeguarding Children (4) says:

- agencies recognise that they have much to learn in listening to the views and experiences of people, including children and young people, who use their services, often involuntarily

- local authorities had taken steps to engage with the experiences and views of young people who have been in their care

- all agencies recognised they could, and should, do more to involve young people in services and their development

- the systematic involvement of users and carers in the planning and development of services was still very patchy but there was some evidence that councils recognised the importance of participation and were slowly improving, particularly in relation to parents of disabled children and looked after children.

NCH's *Factfile* (57) says 'progress [has been] made in the last five years, nationally and locally, in encouraging children and young people's participation. However, practice remains patchy: although children who are looked after are increasingly asked, for example, to help with the recruitment of social services staff, they are less likely to feel that their views are listened to and acted on in terms of the choices they are offered in their own lives'.

Developing Quality to Protect Children – Inspection of Children's Services SSI (58) said 'In general, the involvement of children and young people in commenting on and helping to plan and develop services was not sufficiently consistent to make a long term difference. Young people, when consulted, need to be supported and also needed to be given timely feedback about the results of the consultation process. Few councils had permanent channels of communication from young people to senior managers and councillors'.

The *Chief Inspection of Social Services' 12th Annual Report for 2002–2003* (37) says that 'we have come a long way' since the first Quality Protects Management Action Plans (MAPs), which showed that listening to children was a new area of work for councils. Although 'techniques for working with younger children are under-developed and direct consultation with individual children is still a challenge for many social workers. We still have to find better ways of involving children in decisions about themselves and their own futures'. Nonetheless, in fourth year MAPs 'a substantial number of MAPs showed improved participation and consultation with children and young people both on a strategic and individual level'.

Published in March 2003, the first report of the Children's Rights Director, *Children's Views on Complaints and Advocacy* (59), was based on three forms of consultation: visits to children's establishments, schools, college and services to consult with groups of children and young people; children's workshops on selected topics and national children's rights conferences. Two further forms of consultation are being established – sample surveys of children and their parents and a children's website for children to submit views on a variety of welfare topics.

In May 2004, the Children's Rights Director, Roger Morgan, said that, although it was now well-established practice to consult children, they felt that authorities and organisations still took little notice of their views. Consultation was very much an agenda set by adults with children not being expected to put items on it – for example, children were given a limited range of points they could respond to on the key Green Paper, *Every Child Matters* (7). They are given little opportunity to raise other matters that concern them. There was one chink of light – for many years looked after young people have been saying that they wanted the requirement for checks to be made when they were to stay overnight with friends removed and at last this has been done. Really taking account of the views of children and young people was the next big challenge.

The most definitive evidence on the views of children and young people comes from the NSPCC's *Your Shout! A Survey of the Views of 706 Children and Young People in Public Care* (20). This is an analysis of responses to a questionnaire designed to explore how far services have incorporated the key principles of the Children Act 1989 and the extent to which Quality Protects has transformed children's services. The key themes were experience of decision-making in court and participation in own care plans; contact issues; and safety – both feeling safe and being free from violence and abuse.

On participation in decision-making and children's rights it found that 43 per cent considered they were listened to, 27 per cent did not know. There was no difference in respect of disability. 'It is clear from the responses that not being listened to is a problem for some whilst in care and that this is exacerbated by lack of

knowledge about the way in which young people can influence the decisions taken about them.'

On contact with family and friends – 'A substantial proportion did not see enough of the friends they cared about and over half did not see enough of a previous carer. It appears that either children's opinions were not sought or their views over-ruled'.

On children's verdict on the Children Act 1989 – 'There is much in the responses from the young people to indicate that the principles on which the Children Act is based are in line with what they want for themselves'. There are mixed messages about children being enabled to express their views with the expectation that they will have an impact on decisions taken in court and in respect of their care planning. Overall the evidence points to a 'could and indeed must do better' verdict. The following areas where children's wishes are frequently being disregarded need specific attention.

- Whether, how often and where they have contact with family and friends.

- The neglect of fathers and previous foster carers as people with whom children want more contact.

- The distress caused by separation from, and inadequate contact with, much-loved siblings should increase the priority given to maintaining sibling contact.

One of the recommendations was the exploration of effective avenues of communication for children who are subjects of court proceedings, with the aim of facilitating their participation in decisions made about their lives.

Clear views on what children and young people want also emerged from consultation carried out for the NHS Children's National Service Framework (NSF). This found 'The main message was the importance of having someone who would listen to them. Children and young people wanted services that were inclusive rather than making them feel different from their peers, that had clear policies on confidentiality, and were based in attractive welcoming places where they could have fun and not just focus on their difficulties. There was a general dissatisfaction with the service provided by GPs, and the comments of these young people suggested their needs would best be met by a one-stop shop for health, advice, counselling and social services'.

There is also evidence that there are some groups of children and young people whose views are not being sought to the same extent as others.

The Committee on the Rights of the Child, 31st Session, quoted by the Children's Rights Alliance for England in *State of Children's Rights in England. A Report on the Implementation of the Convention on the Rights of the Child in England* (60), November 2002, while welcoming 'the increasing encouragement of participation of and consultation with children in government, local authorities and civil society throughout the State party, the establishment of consultative processes with children in local authorities' services planning, the establishment of a youth advisory forum in the CYPU and other platforms' was 'concerned that, there has been no consistent incorporation of the obligations of article 12 in legislation for example in private law procedures concerning divorce, in adoption, in education, and in protection throughout the State party … in schools children are not systematically consulted in matters which affect them'. And recommended that 'the State party … takes further steps to promote, facilitate and monitor systematic, meaningful and effective participation of all groups of children in society, including in schools, like school councils'.

State of Children's Rights in England (60) pointed out that the Children Act 1989 requires local authorities to take account of the views of children in certain respects but that there is no legal requirement on education authorities, schools, health and local authorities, parents or national government to give consideration to the 'ascertainable wishes and feelings of children'. In the Education Act 2002 LEAs and schools must 'have regard to any guidance issued from time to time by the Secretary of State about consultation with pupils in connection with decisions affecting them'. Guidance can be ignored where reasonable to do so. In contrast, Scotland has given pupils the legal right to be heard (and a right to be consulted by parents on 'major decisions' affecting them). 'There has been no review of the legal changes required to give effect to article 12.' (Right to express views and have them taken seriously.)

Research by the Children's Society indicates that the views of young people in foster care are being ignored – only 13 per cent of social workers felt that the children's views influenced services (*Community Care* 26 September –2 October 2002).

Rethinking Child Imprisonment (61) points out that 'Children in Youth Offender Institutions do not have the right to be heard or involved in decision-making or the development of policy and practice' but inspectors have found 'occasional examples of good practice'.

Kirsten Stalker in her study of children with complex support needs in health-care settings (41), said 'A number of young people were apparently not being consulted about aspects of their care and treatment either because professionals believed they were unable to contribute and/or because agreed processes for doing so were not in place'. This is not unusual, other research has shown that in practice many authorities fail to meet their duties in this regard, particularly in relation to young people with communication impairments and/or complex needs.

There are other, more general impediments to effective consultation with children and young people.

The British Association for Adoption and Fostering (BAAF) say they are 'concerned that the skills base for social workers both in pre and post qualification training for developing their skills in communicating with children are very poor. This is not helped by the enormous turnover in social workers, leading to vulnerable children that are unable to trust'.

In March 2003, the NSPCC *Review of Legislation Relating to Children in Family Proceedings Consultation Draft* (21) said 'In general, the professional expertise and time needed to gather children's views is currently not available'.

Analysis

A number of sources indicate that the need to involve children and young people has really been picked up and become the norm. It is also clear that there is still some way to go in ensuring that this is done consistently and effectively before it can be said that children's and young people's views are properly taken into account.

There has been a large shift in attitudes to involving children and young people – starting with the inclusion of a young woman who had recent experience of the care system in the Ministerial Task Force which developed the Government Response to the Review. It is now accepted that children and young people should be consulted about developments which affect their lives and it has become much more common practice to produce children's versions of consultation documents and arrange consultation meetings on key policy changes and developments, such as the National Standards for Adoption, the SEU Report on education for looked after children, the Children and Young People's Unit strategy and *Every Child Matters*. Clearly *People Like Us* played an important part in this.

But children and young people are still not listened to and involved in decision-making and policy development in:

- Young Offenders Institutions

- schools, where there is also no legislative requirement for LEAs/schools to take

account of children's views, although there is guidance that they should

- health settings, particularly where there are complex needs or where long in-patient stays are involved.

These areas must be brought into line.

There is scope for improvement in training staff and carers in the communication skills needed, including with disabled children and young people. It is also clear, from a number of reports, that there is some way to go in ensuring that consultation is meaningful and takes proper account of the views expressed so that young people are convinced that their voices matter and are heard. This involves finding time to do this among other pressures on time and resources. All authorities and organisations need to ensure that their staff have the time to communicate properly with children and young people, particularly those who are disabled, and that they have time to make communication meaningful.

It is very disappointing that there is less evidence that children and young people are consulted and listened to in relation to everyday decisions about their lives. It is hoped that work on the Integrated Children's System will help to address this.

Recommendation

10   All authorities and organisations need to ensure that children and young people are consulted and listened to in relation to decisions about their lives.

4.8   Right to treatment

What *People Like Us* said
Chapter 10 said that more information had been received on treatment for abusers than for abused children.

Principal Recommendation 17. Local and health authorities should assess and meet the need for treatment of children who have been abused.

Abused children should attract high priority for treatment from public funds – especially children ... abused while in public care. Local and health authorities should ensure that it is provided.

Government response

- Children's Services Plans should cover joint working to ensure that needs are assessed and met.

- Programme of improvement of CAMHS, ensuring more equitable availability of effective treatment. Priority determined by clinical need.

Government action

- £90 million programme over three years (1999/2000 to 2001/2002) to improve mental health services for children and young people. HSC 1999/126:LAC(99)22, directs Health Authorities and Local Authority Social Services Departments to work together to produce joint three-year development plans to deliver CAMHS objectives set out in NHS Priorities Guidance.

- The Secretary of State for Health announcement of a major expansion in child and adolescent mental health services. £140 million over the next three years 'to build capacity, improve access and, together with new NHS investment, to help deliver for the first time a comprehensive CAMHS service in each and every area' (October 2002).

What happened

The Committee on the Rights of the Child, 31st session (50), recommends that the State party 'provide for the care, recovery and integration of victims'.

Mental health

In August 2002 *Community Care* launched its 'Changing Minds' campaign following a survey of professionals, conducted by NSM Research, which found a severe crisis in mental health services. The number of children with mental health problems was said to have increased over the last five years. One-fifth were said to have been turned down for a service and two-thirds of those did not access alternative services. Two-thirds of social care professionals believe that health care professionals are under-diagnosing the problem with 80 per cent citing lack of services as the reason.

Chapter 7 of *Getting the Right Start: NSF for Children. Emerging Findings* (13) has as its aim 'to meet the needs and views of children and young people with mental health problems, together with those of their families and carers, in order to improve their life chances within family, social and educational settings'. It says:

- several studies suggest that up to two million under-16-year-olds in England may require help at some time, of whom about half suffer from mental health disorders and a smaller number have severe mental illness

- recently there has been a concerted effort, nationally and locally, to improve service provision. Significant progress has been made through the establishment of multi-agency CAMHS Development Strategies

- the challenge now is for commissioners and providers to respond to *Improvement, Expansion and Reform* (62) which says CAMHS should provide comprehensive services by 2006.

It gives examples of where multi-agency partnership within CAMHS is essential, including:

- child protection and post-protection services; contributing to the assessment of complex child abuse cases, to the assessment and provision of post-abuse therapeutic services and to services for looked after and adopted children

- specialist residential provision when required for children and young people with complex, severe and persistent behavioural and mental health needs

- assessment and provision of the educational needs of children and young people with mental health problems ... whether they are living in the community, in hospital or in residential settings.

It also said that the age range for CAMHS would be extended 'over the period of the implementation of the NSF' to cover from 0 to 18 years. 'In the meantime, further attention needs to be paid to the safety of young people cared for in adult psychiatric beds until sufficient adolescent beds become available. We strongly recommend the adoption of one of the existing sets of standards for in-patient units. (Quality Network for In-patient CAMHS)'

Other treatment
National Plan for Safeguarding Children from Commercial Sexual Exploitation (63) refers to 'the centrally funded child abuse treatment initiative ... to support a number of projects by voluntary organisations providing different types and ranges of treatment'.

The Welsh Assembly Government in *Practice Guide to Investigate Allegations of Abuse against a Professional or Carer in relation to Looked After Children* (64) says one of the tasks of the Investigation Outcomes Review meeting is to 'ensure therapeutic support is available where it is needed'.

Rethinking Child Imprisonment (61) recommended: 'children in custody shall have a right to treatment and other measures to secure that they recover from any psychological hurt ... Social

services should be charged with full responsibility for acting as a good parent for all children it is looking after who are locked up'.

At the Stop It Now! conference in March 2003, Hilary Eldridge, Director of the Lucy Faithfull Foundation (LFF), described the provision for child victims and their families as 'highly variable; the statutory and voluntary sectors are over-stretched and under-funded'. It was 'a scandal' and provision for adult victims was 'horrendously poor'.

Analysis

The Government's response to this recommendation was weak. It is clear this is still a major problem. The *Community Care* 'Changing Minds' campaign illustrated the shortfall in provision for children with mental health problems and the service's lack of responsiveness. Against the background of grossly inadequate service provision, there is no evidence that the Government has sought to provide priority for abused children. However, it has now promised 'a major expansion' in CAMHS. It will take time to build the capacity needed and in the meantime children will continue to suffer without recourse to help. It is hoped that, in the programme of expansion, priority can be given to developing expertise and capacity to help abused children, and to treatment for those who have been abused while in public care.

This is not just a question of capacity, it is also the quality and fundamental approach of the service. It requires a range of methods, including clinical, community-based and others and which reflects diversity. Children who have suffered significant harm have suffered developmental delay and should be offered the opportunity to recover and regain their potential. This should be accessible locally and at times when it is required, particularly at key stages of development.

Recommendation

11 The National Health Service needs to improve the quality of CAMHS and provide a range of treatment methods accessible in all localities and ensure treatment is available when needed. It should give priority to developing expertise and capacity to help abused children, particularly those who have been abused while in public care.

4.9 Children's rights and complaints procedures

What *People Like Us* said

Chapter 10 said implementation of the Children Act in respect of rights has been patchy. It considered a range of related issues including children's rights services and Independent Visitors. Chapter 18 covered complaints procedures.

Local authorities should offer children's rights services to all children they look after. Children's rights training should be included in training for all staff … in residential settings. Children wishing to use formal complaints procedure should be entitled to the services of an advocate.

Children wishing to use statutory complaints procedure should be offered the help of an independent adult or children's rights officer.

Local authorities should ensure that independent sector providers have effective formal complaints procedures and should enable children to use their own procedures.

There should be faster and less formal procedures for airing grievances. Local and departmental managers should establish a

(Continued)

culture in which minor problems can be sorted out on the spot.

Local authorities should satisfy themselves that adequate formal procedures for dealing with complaints exist in all residential schools for which they are responsible. Disabled children and others with special needs are likely to need help in making use of formal systems.

Government response

- Concept of children's rights officers supported.

- Government will consider the outcome of a Children's Society research project before making plans.

- Children's rights issues will be taken forward in the NVQ training initiative, not separately.

- Welsh Office (WO) funding research on advocacy for children and will develop policy in the light of that.

- Part of Quality Protects and DH carrying out a review of complaints procedures.

- Governing bodies of all organisations responsible for care of children and young people to be reminded of need to have procedures for staff to raise significant concerns outside their normal line management when the manager is unresponsive or the subject of concern.

- Governing bodies should inform staff of the established procedures for making complaints, in line with *Choosing with Care*.

Government action in England

- Care Standards Act requires all establishments regulated under Part II to set up and maintain in-house complaints procedures.

- National Minimum Standards require all schools with boarding provision to have a formal complaints procedure and mechanisms to secure the views of boarders.

- *National Standards for the Provision of Children's Advocacy Services* (November 2002) issued under Section 7 of the Local Authority Social Services Act 1970 apply to councils providing, or paying others to provide, independent advocacy for looked after children and those in need – including care leavers and disabled children.

- The Adoption and Children Act 2002 places a duty on local authorities to make arrangements for the provision of advocacy for children and young people who want to make a complaint under Children Act procedures. It applies to children in care and care leavers.

What happened

The Government issued a consultation document in June 2000 – *Listening to People: A Consultation on Improving Social Services Complaints Procedures* (65). Proposals included:

- speeding up the complaints process

- making it more user-friendly

- giving a right of advocacy to looked after children who wish to make a complaint

- introducing an informal or local resolution stage without an independent person but with an advocate.

Developing Quality to Protect Children – Inspection of Children's Services (57) said 'Listening and Responding Inspectors expressed concerns about the unrealistically low numbers of formal complaints made by young people being looked after. Disabled children had little chance of accessing the complaints process. Only 1.4 per cent of children being looked after had an independent visitor. A number of councils had children's rights services which, at their best, included an independent visitors service, advocacy about complaints, the facilitation of effective communication for disabled children and a brief to increase children's participation, both in individual care planning and in issues around service development'.

The Council for Disabled Children say that services are still being developed in lots of places and that they are not embedded in the system. The numbers of people involved with looked after children was confusing for the child and they may well not understand the differences between advocates, mentors, key workers, inspectors, etc. Disabled children who were not 'looked after' had no such problem!

In *State of Children's Rights in England* (60), the Children's Rights Alliance in England (CRAE) says the statutory complaints and representation procedure for children in need established in 1991 has been 'poorly implemented and is generally inaccessible and ineffective in resolving children's concerns. The Government has still not implemented the recommendations of the Waterhouse Tribunal in relation to complaints. Access to independent advocacy is now an entitlement to care leavers wishing to make a complaint but there is still no legal right to such provision for those in state care and for other vulnerable children'.

The Committee on the Rights of the Child, 31st session (50) calls for 'systematic and ongoing training programmes on human rights, including children's rights, for all professional groups working for and with children (e.g. judges, lawyers, law enforcement officials, civil servants, local government officials, personnel working in institutions and places of detention for children, teachers and health personnel)' (Rec 21b). It welcomed the establishment of CYPU 'but remains concerned that the absence of a central mechanism to co-ordinate the implementation of the Convention across the State party makes it difficult to achieve a comprehensive and coherent children's rights policy'. Rec 17a is that the State party should 'establish independent human rights institutions … to monitor, protect and promote all the rights of the Convention for all children'. And d) 'ensure that children and children's organisations are effectively involved in their establishment and activities'.

CRAE also notes this serious flaw in the child protection system: 'Children are not systematically provided with information on their right to protection, through schools or in other settings such as children's homes, custody or residential schools'.

Safeguarding Children (4) said that, in relation to social services, there were variable practices in care planning, reviews, visits by social workers and independent visitors, access to complaints procedures and independent advocates for children looked after. It found that 'young people still experience serious barriers to making complaints about services'. and 'one of the key findings of the [Commission for Health Improvement (CHI)] investigation was that there was an NHS culture that did not listen to, or treat, complaints inquisitively. Patients who had tried to raise their concerns were left powerless in their discussions with professionals and managers. The NHS complaints system failed to detect issues of professional misconduct or criminal activity'. It also said 'Most social services now have staff dedicated to the welfare of children looked after: children's rights officers or advocacy services, etc'.

Rethinking Child Imprisonment (61) quoted from the Prison Ombudsman's March 2001 report – *Listening to Young Prisoners* – 'that the under-representation of young prisoners [in making complaints] is a particular personal anxiety … Is it a paradox or actually part of the explanation that the worst institutions seem to generate the fewest formal complaints?'

The *NSPCC Review of Legislation Relating to Children in Family Proceedings Consultation Draft* (21) said 'Section 26 complaints procedures are also seen as a problematic area. A common feeling is that they are too complicated and inaccessible for children to use and that they, too, need review in the light of experience'.

Kirsten Stalker, in her report on children in health-care settings (41) said 'Although all the agencies had complaints procedures, parents and sometimes care staff appeared unaware of them. Organisations need to ensure that complaints procedures are well publicised: they may need to refresh families' memories about them from time to time. Children and young people should also know whom to approach and how, if they are unhappy about any aspect of their care, and be reassured that this will not lead to any unpleasant repercussions for them'.

Roger Morgan, May 2003, pointed out that the Adoption and Children Act does not introduce advocacy for *all*, only for those to whom the local authority decision-making process applies. It only applies to the Children Act 1989 complaints procedure. It is a big gap that it does not cover non-local authority situations. He thinks it should cover all children living away from home in regulated settings and not be limited to the making of complaints. There was more now in regulations and standards about access to complaints procedures and whistle-blowing and more on consulting children at critical points, such as after absconding; he was still not satisfied that children were able to use the complaints procedure appropriately.

In May 2004 he said that children have little confidence in the complaints procedure and that, in the light of this, the procedures could not be seen as a significant contribution to safeguarding children. They often saw little point in making a complaint since this was unlikely to change a decision that had already been made. The local authority complaints procedure did little to encourage the making of representations but this might be more productive – so that, for example, children would have a chance to make representations about proposals that affect them, such as the closure of a children's home, before a decision was taken. He pointed out that, from April 2005, the Commission for Social Care Inspection (CSCI) would have a statutory role in this procedure when, under provisions in the Health and Social Care Act 2003, it would take over responsibility for the review stage from local authorities. This would introduce a truly independent element into the process.

Government action in Wales

- Broader complaints procedures under consideration. Proposals likely to go out to consultation 2002/early 2003.

- National Minimum Standards for Children Homes require homes to have written complaints procedures which enable children to make minor or major representations or complaints.

- National Minimum Standards for boarding schools, residential special schools, FE colleges and residential family centres, will have a similar requirement for written policy and procedures. It is planned to introduce these by April 2003.

- *Practice Guide to Investigate Allegations of Abuse against a Professional or Carer in relation to Looked After Children* (64) says that 'in all cases, an advocate will be appointed for the child'.

- Research report on advocacy services for children published December 1999. Comprehensive review of advocacy services for vulnerable children to be undertaken in 2002–03.

- Children's Commissioner appointed 2001.

What happened

The Committee on the Rights of the Child, 31st session (50), welcomed use of the Convention in the Strategy for Children and Young People in Wales but 'remains concerned at the lack of a rights-based approach to policy development' and lack of 'a global vision of children's rights and its translation into a national plan of action'.

In his *Annual Report and Accounts 2001–2002* (55) the Children's Commissioner for Wales said 'Systems that enable children and young people to make complaints, and for concerned adults to blow the whistle when employers are acting against children's interests, are a critically important element of safeguarding their rights and welfare. Most young people I have listened to do not have a clear picture of how they can complain, or of where they might get support to do so. What young people told me suggests that we have some way to go before we can say that we have systems that are adequate'. He was undertaking a thorough review of such systems. The results reported in *Community Care* 6–12 March 2003 showed 'worrying inadequacies' in Welsh social services departments systems for safeguarding vulnerable children. One of the key recommendations of the Waterhouse report was the appointment of specialist children's complaints officers, yet, three years on, only eight out of 22 councils had done so. The survey looked at children's advocacy, complaints procedures, whistle-blowing and arrangements to safeguard and promote the rights and welfare of young people. Local authorities were failing to appreciate the importance of whistle-blowing policies and no specific attempt had been made to ensure that children from the most marginalized groups had access to these services. It calls for the Welsh Assembly Government to set up a unit to co-ordinate the provision of advocacy services and for its proposals for reform of the complaints procedures to be shelved as they are not child-centred enough. Whistle-blowing should be more directly linked to child protection and failure to report malpractice made a disciplinary offence. There were only nine instances of staff raising concerns during one year.

Sir Ronald Waterhouse was appalled at the findings and said financial pressures were no excuse for not appointing specialist complaints officers. 'We called our report *'Lost in Care'* (18) because children feel isolated if they do not have access to a complaints procedure they understand and are prepared to use, and without that the sense of isolation will continue'. He called for advocacy services for vulnerable children to be publicised, arguing that many children are still unaware of how to complain or where to obtain support to do so. (*Community Care* 17–23 July 2003.)

> **Department of Health and the Welsh Office should support a project to test the feasibility of providing independent visitors to all children looked after by local authorities who might benefit from them.**
>
> **Disabled people should be involved in policy-making and helping children to protect themselves and have means of gaining help from others when needed. There may also be a need for a specialist advocacy/best friend service for disabled children independent of service providers.**

Government response
- Action will be taken to ensure all children statutorily entitled to independent visitors have one and to encourage befriending and mentoring schemes.

- Existing schemes and research to provide evidence of current range of services and their benefits, costs and feasibility.

- Consideration on how to take further work forward, to be linked with Quality Protects.

What happened
Safeguarding Children (4) said many councils have set up independent visitor and advocacy schemes.

NSPCC Review of Legislation Relating to Children in Family Proceedings Consultation Draft (21) said 'There is a strong body of opinion to support the right of looked after children to have a statutory right of access to independent advocacy services'.

The growth of advocacy services seems to have replaced independent visitors.

Analysis

Complaints procedures are not thought to be easily accessible, particularly for disabled children. There seems to be general concern that complaints procedures are not well understood and they should be better publicised, along with the support arrangements, including advocacy, that are available for children and young people who wish to make complaints. There is particular concern about how some of the most vulnerable groups – those in health and penal settings, disabled children and young people – can access and use complaints procedures. Black and ethnic minority children may be under-represented too. It is important that all authorities and organisations should give more help and encouragement to children wishing to make representations about services and ensure that their complaints and representations procedures are accessible, particularly for disabled children, young children and those from black and ethnic minorities; that they are well publicised and that there are support arrangements for those wishing to use them.

The Children's Rights Director reports that children are themselves reluctant to use complaints procedures and that it would be more helpful to assist them to make representations about matters that affect them before decisions are taken. He would like to see the right to advocacy extended and not limited only to children while in the process of making a complaint under the Children Act. There should be more scope, and encouragement, for children to make representations about changes that affect them.

Independent visitors do not appear to be much used but there has been a growth in advocacy services with national standards being published for them. However, the roles of independent visitors and advocates are different and the growth of advocacy does not compensate for the lack of independent visitors. Local authorities should

ensure that independent visitors are provided for all children entitled to have one and who wish to do so.

5 Places in which children live away from home

5.1 Children's homes

What *People Like Us* said

Chapter 2 said children's homes were the area of greatest current anxiety.

There is little doubt that the 'best' homes (or schools, or hospitals) are also the safest. Safety is a function of overall effectiveness. If the child is not safe, the home is achieving objectives neither for the child nor for itself as an institution. Quality protects.

The persistent deficiencies in children's homes are symptoms of a lack of commitment by political and service managers to unpopular, expensive but necessary provision.

What is needed is a national strategy which should extend to the volume and nature of service needed, with plans for securing provision to the standards required.

Staffing is a chronic problem and should be addressed in a national strategy.

There are problems of out of authority placements.

Children are at risk in small unregistered homes.

The Report concluded that 'residential care is an important option for looked after children ... it feels that residential child care has shrunk to below that which provides a realistic choice of placement for each child'. Urgent action was needed to raise standards, but the sector now lacks enough providers of sufficient size to organise and achieve this from within. Government action is needed to implement a strategy to drive up standards all round.

Principal Recommendation 1. Department of Health and the Welsh Office should establish and resource a dedicated group to develop and maintain a comprehensive strategy for residential child care.

Government response

- Three-year Quality Protects programme to be led by focused DH team.

- DH will work with the Local Government Association and Association of Directors of Social Services to design strategic arrangements for residential and foster care services and review arrangements for specialist services.

- The Government will encourage regional groupings to review provision available and commission better specialist facilities, facilitating specialist placements in residential and foster care.

- Welsh Office to work with Welsh Local Government Association on a Children's Strategy for Wales, including services for children in need and residential and foster care services. From May 1999 National Assembly for Wales is responsible for this.

What happened

Others have commented on the shortage of places in children's homes as follows.

- In 1998 in their *Second Report: Children Looked After by Local Authorities* (66) the House of Commons Select Committee on Health said 'There is a clear need for an increase in the number of children's homes countrywide, to enable local authorities to make appropriate placements, to reduce the problems arising within homes from an inappropriate "mix" of children, and to relieve pressure on the fostering service'.

- *Learning the Lessons: The Government's Response to Lost in Care* (33), the Waterhouse Inquiry (18), said 'We recognise that the number of residential placements has reached such a low level that there is insufficient choice to meet all children's needs'.

- *The NSPCC Review of Legislation Relating to Children in Family Proceedings Consultation Draft* (21) said 'Local authorities have cut back on the provision of residential care and there is a group of needy and demanding children, who cannot cope with family life, for whom there is little provision'.

There has been no progress on strategic arrangements. Regional groupings were not established, although most regions have 'contracting consortia'.

More recently, the Choice Protects review, announced in March 2002, mentioned residential care as a component, albeit a clearly subsidiary one. A meeting with key stakeholders held in October 2002 echoed the main points made in *People Like Us* (1):

- residential care makes a unique contribution in providing placements for certain groups of children

- local authorities should develop a proper strategic plan for the residential care element in services provided for looked after children

- regional commissioning strategies should be encouraged.

Analysis

Since *People Like Us* (1) was published policy on the residential childcare sector has been relatively neglected. It appears to have taken a back seat to attempts to increase adoption and fostering placements. There is no indication that politicians' and service managers' lack of commitment to the residential childcare sector, noted in the Report, has been reversed. Despite the further fragmentation and realignment of local authority social services, there seems to have been no attempt to develop a

national strategy for residential child care in order to ensure sufficient places to meet the needs and wishes of children and young people, for whom this is the most appropriate option, and avoid the risk involved in inappropriate mixes.

However, Choice Protects does bring together key stakeholders in its National Partnership in Placement Forum. Its draft objectives cover commissioning of children's services generally, with the aim of promoting 'greater partnership working at strategic and implementation levels between local authorities and providers'. It is hoped that this group will give residential care the place in their considerations that it needs and deserves and go some way to providing the comprehensive strategy that *People Like Us* (1) recommended.

Regulation and registration

The Burgner recommendation that small children's homes be brought within the regulatory framework should be implemented as soon as possible.

Local authorities should register and inspect voluntary children's homes.

Local authorities should have powers to take over management of a registered children's home in an emergency. The appeals process to a Registered Homes Tribunal should be speeded up.

Government response
- To be covered in Social Services White Paper and in legislation when parliamentary time available.

Government action
- The Care Standards Act 2000 brought small children's homes within the scope of regulation.

- In April 2002 the National Care Standards Commission took over regulation of social and health care services previously regulated by local councils and health authorities (and the Secretary of State for Health for voluntary children's homes) and other services not previously requiring registration.

- National Minimum Standards for children's homes issued in March 2002.

- In Wales, small homes were made subject to regulation from February 2001. All other homes, including those previously referred to as community homes, were made subject to regulation from April 2002.

What happened

The Training Organisation for Personal Social Services *National Occupational Standards for Managers in Residential Child Care* (66) provides a management tool and 'will assist the implementation of changes to residential child care recommended in the Waterhouse enquiry ... as well as helping compliance with each country's regulatory requirements'.

The National Children's Bureau's Children's Residential Standards Implementation Project is producing guides to assist providers in implementing the minimum standards, translating the legislation into daily practice, following consultation with a range of providers and children and young people.

Analysis

Some important recommendations in *People Like Us* (1) on children's homes have been acted upon, such as the regulation and inspection of small children's homes. There are now National Minimum Standards. We need to see what effect the introduction of standards will have on the sector – will it raise standards or will it put too much pressure on the weaker areas and put them out of business? There seems to have been no concerted effort to raise the standards in this sector. The National Care Standards Commission (NCSC) got off to rather a slow start – and has since merged with SSI in April 2004 to become the Commission for Social Care Inspection.

DfES should ensure, through Choice Protects or other means, that residential care is included as an integral part of an overall strategy for children's services.

5.2 Foster care

What *People Like Us* said

About two-thirds of looked after children are in foster care and their needs are more complex than hitherto. The current policy interest in foster care, which had previously been neglected, was welcomed. Given the relative isolation of foster care and the young age of many of the children, it urged priority be given to safeguards. It suggested a number of steps to improve safeguards, increase the support given to foster carers and provide information to children in foster care.

The Report discussed wider welfare issues relevant for fostered children – including the need for an adequate choice of placement, importance of good education and health care, and priority to be given to proper after care.

Regulations

Principal Recommendation 4. Local authorities must observe the Regulations governing the placement and supervision of children in foster care.

Local authorities should keep records of allegations of abuse and have a clear policy on when carers would be removed from the foster care register. Records should be taken

(Continued)

67

into account in further allegations, during regular reviews and in deciding what to put in references.

Placing authorities should notify approving authorities of any allegations and their outcomes; foster carers whose approval is terminated as a result of investigations should be put on DH Consultancy Index.

Government response

- Quality Protects programme makes this clear and statutory powers will be used where they are not.

- Part of Quality Protects to ensure procedures followed and records correctly kept.

- Will be in National Standards and Code of Practice.

- Local authorities to improve quality of assessments, care planning, placement and supervision by 2002.

- Local Government White Paper proposed new powers of intervention where regulations are not observed and Social Services White Paper to build on this.

Government action

- Objective 9 in Quality Protects says 'to ensure through regulatory powers and duties that children in regulated services are protected from harm and poor care standards'.

- Allegations covered in National Standards, Minimum Standards and Code of Practice.

What happened

The 11th Annual Report of the Chief Inspector of Social Services 2001–2002 (24) said 'Policies and procedures were generally in place to safeguard children in foster care but not applied consistently. Checks in two councils were considered inadequate

and there were serious deficits in others with respect to the quality of supervision for carers, investigation of complaints against carers and the quality of statutory visits, care planning and reviews'.

Safeguarding Children (4) said 'Services for children in public care are probably subject to greater regulation than any other social service ... inspections found that young people in residential and foster care were often unhappy about the lack of contact from their social worker, particularly those in out-of-authority placements. Some councils were not meeting the minimum requirements for visits by social workers of children looked after'. Practice is said to have been improving in recent years in relation to independent and unannounced monthly monitoring visits to children's homes and the availability of independent advocates but 'there remains a lack of consistency'.

Because of potential isolation in foster care, it is recommended that social workers should be required to see the child alone during each visit made under Regulation 6(3) of the Foster Placement Regulations.

Government response

- Already the case for proportion of visits, may not always be possible/child may not want it.

- Promoted in Quality Protects and in National Standards.

What happened

Covered in National Standards, *Code of Practice* (68), Regulation 35 accompanying the Minimum Standards, and *Working Together* (69).

Robert Tapsfield of the Fostering Network (May 2004) says that one impact of the inspection process has been to increase the likelihood of children placed by independent agencies being seen alone, as agencies are now ensuring that the fostering worker sees the child on their own as they cannot always rely on the local authority social worker to do this.

> **Foster Placement Regulations should be amended to reduce maximum period between visits to a child in a foster home after the first year of placement from three months to eight weeks.**

Government response

- Phasing in of this to be considered as part of work to improve quality and choice of placements through extra support and training for foster carers.

What happened

Regulation 35 accompanying the Minimum Standards retains the intervals of three months.

Learning the Lessons (33) in responding to Recommendation 11 of *Lost in Care* (18) (looked after children to be visited by field social workers not less than every eight weeks and they should be required to see older children alone) explained the regulations, including the Review of Children's Cases Regulations which requires reviews within four weeks of placement, after three months and then at six-monthly intervals. It says 'We are conscious that there is considerable evidence both in *Lost in Care* (18) and elsewhere of inadequate supervision of placements, particularly where children are placed out of authority. At the same time requiring visits … at set intervals could have significant cost and staffing implications. A better approach may be to ensure that children's placements are regularly reviewed in accordance with the Review of Children's Cases Regulations. Further thought will be given to this'. This would be *less* frequent than under existing Regulations.

Analysis

There has been some action on compliance with the regulations but the situation is still unsatisfactory. Choice Protects is unlikely to make any impact on these issues, being more concerned with commissioning than service delivery and compliance with regulations.

There is now a much greater awareness of the need to investigate allegations but *how* they are handled is still causing a lot of problems. Practice is very inconsistent and the situation has remained unresolved for too long. Choice Protects is to cover this.

It is understood that staffing shortages may make it difficult to reduce the maximum periods between visits – or even to undertake these at the prescribed intervals. Where choices have to be made about the best use of limited resources, it is recommended that priority be given to increasing visits to the most vulnerable – the very young and disabled children.

Here, as elsewhere, the serious staffing shortages in social services play an important part. These issues must be addressed if children are to have the safeguards they both need and deserve.

Code of Practice

> **Principal Recommendation 5. Department of Health and the Welsh Office should commission a Code of Practice for recruiting, selecting, training and supporting foster carers.**
>
> **Foster carers should be treated as full partners who are entitled to all relevant information.**
>
> **There should be more emphasis on authorities' obligations for support and training in foster care agreements.**
>
> *(Continued)*

> Awareness training should be provided for all staff involved in assessment about both male and female offenders who abuse in a family context.

Government response

- Code of Practice commissioned. A consultation document to be issued later in 1998 and the final document in May 1999.

- Training Support Programme project on training materials on profiles and methods of child abusers by end 1999. Plans to improve in-service training should also help.

Government action

- Code of Practice (67) published June 1999 in England, November 1999 in Wales.

- National Minimum Standards published March 2002 in England, November 1999 in Wales.

What happened

There is confusion around the difference in legal status and content between the National Standards, Code of Practice (68) and Minimum Standards. The latter are the standards that agencies are inspected against and therefore carry more weight but fail to incorporate many of the recommendations in the Code of Practice (68). Some examples of the differences are as follows.

- Section 5 of Minimum Standards sets out requirements for agencies to check references on prospective foster carers and keep a record of the checks and references obtained. Schedule 1 of the Regulations does not require an employer's reference, even where the employment is child-related, nor previous spouses and adult children of the applicant to be interviewed.

- Schedule 3 of Regulations says members of household aged 18 and over should be subject to criminal records checks while the Code of Practice said children over 10 should be checked.

- A number of other enquiries are recommended in the Code but not covered – e.g. adult children living away from home, previous partners, any voluntary or leisure pursuit, etc.

- The Code of Practice says 'Those assessing potential foster carers, and supervising those who have been approved, need to be well informed both of the risks and of the sort of warning signs to which they should be alert'. And 'all staff involved in the assessment and supervision of foster carers should be informed about the risks posed by those who abuse children, particularly sex offenders; all those involved in interviewing should be trained in how to ask questions about adult relationships to elicit attitudes to child sex abuse and interpret responses'. This is reduced in Minimum Standards to considering 'sexual boundaries and attitudes; awareness of issues around child abuse' of applicants. Training for assessing staff is not mentioned.

The British Association for Adoption and Fostering (BAAF) say that the requirements for training of foster carers are of a much higher standard than hitherto. Minimum Standards now require a programme of ongoing training to be provided to all carers, both at preparation and post approval stage, and also require all carers in the household to undertake training in key areas such as safe caring. Carers are also required to keep a portfolio of training they have undertaken. This suggests a move towards acknowledging that foster care is no longer a service staffed by volunteers, of whom few demands can be made. The introduction of National Vocational Qualifications (NVQs) for foster carers has helped change the climate, although relatively few foster carers undertake the NVQ. It is still not clear how fostering agencies will react to carers who are not prepared to participate in ongoing training. They are also concerned that foster carers are often not given access to training provided by outside trainers, and the use of joint social worker/foster carer training is not maximised.

Awareness training about abuser behaviour does not seem to be being provided systematically to all staff involved in the assessment and supervision of foster carers. Recently qualified staff may have received training on their initial qualification course, but many family placement workers qualified at a time when this would not have been standard content on courses.

There is a long way to go before most foster carers feel treated as partners; the level of support is patchy and not normally of sufficient depth.

The Training Support Programme for foster care has now finished and there is no ring-fenced money for training for foster carers. The Fostering Network say that, as a result, there is now less demand for its training service. The Choice Protects review is to examine the current framework for training foster carers, looking in particular at the role of NVQ level 3.

Analysis

The Government took prompt action on this recommendation with helpful UK National Standards and a Code of Practice on Foster Care (68) produced. However, the subsequent production of the Minimum Standards seems to have caused some confusion and undermined some of the safeguards in the Code of Practice – as explained above.

The UK National Standards were based on a holistic approach to children's needs including social work input and planning, whereas the Minimum Standards are based on a more limited approach geared to regulation of providers.

However, there can be no acceptable 'minimum' when it comes to checking the suitability of staff and prospective carers. While the extension of criminal record checks to children under 18 may need to wait until Criminal Records Bureau resources permit, all the other checks and enquiries in the Code of Practice (68) can and should be applied consistently for all those with unsupervised access to children.

Training for foster carers needs to be addressed. Some carers who have been fostering for a long time may never have received any training. Consideration should be given to making training mandatory, as independent providers do as part of the contract. Along with this there should be consideration of a proper reward system for carers, including tax and pension arrangements.

Regulation of independent fostering agencies

> **The Burgner recommendation that Independent Fostering Agencies should be brought within the regulatory and inspection framework should be implemented as soon as possible.**

Government response
- Plans to be in Social Services White Paper and legislation sought as soon as possible.

What happened
Achieved by Care Standards Act.

Independent Fostering Agencies are subject to Minimum Standards and inspection by National Commission for Social Care.

Analysis

The NCSC had teething problems in its first year of operation which were most marked in establishing inspection arrangements for foster care. Its staff had less experience on foster care than in other areas and there were big inconsistencies in approach, although the methodology used was the same. It was feared that it had not been as effective as it should have been at detecting the poorer agencies. In 2003 the Fostering Network believed local authorities were not well enough informed about agency status when making a placement and may, unknowingly, have placed children with unregistered providers. A year later progress has been made, and the Fostering Network feels that local authorities are now well enough informed and that the independent sector had welcomed inspections while being concerned about inconsistencies.

It would be helpful if the Commission for Social Care Inspection (CSCI) published a list of registered agencies with information about their date of registration, inspection status and NCSC/CSCI grading. It is important that CSCI develop good links with expert bodies in this field such as the Fostering Network and BAAF, so that it can receive feedback and advice to help develop and strengthen its inspection and regulation of these areas. Effective liaison arrangements should be established to do so.

On foster care in general, some action has been taken in policy terms: the Quality Protects programme, UK National Standards, the Code of Practice (68) and Minimum Standards, regulation and inspection of independent fostering providers and changes to the tax and pension arrangements for foster carers.

But how much has found its way into practice on the ground? Local authorities are still not complying with important regulations such as visits by social workers. The Minimum Standards undermine some of the safeguards recommended in the Code of Practice (68) and this sector has probably suffered most as a result in the change in inspection arrangements.

Some areas of concern remain.

- The continuing shortage of family placements means matching children's needs

to available carers is not possible and the dangers of peer abuse are not being adequately dealt with.

- The lack of a central drive for an audit of long-term foster carers means the position is likely to differ between those local authorities that have done one and those that have not, with consequent variability in safeguards.

- The failure to reduce the period between visits after the first year is to be regretted.

- It is not known whether councils are providing more support to single foster carers, or to the children with them but we are told that this is unlikely.

Since *People Like Us* (1) was published, the number, and proportion, of children in foster care has continued to increase yet foster care has not received the policy attention it needs and deserves. After an initial period during which important progress was made – in the production of National Standards and the Code of Practice (68) – it again stepped into the policy shadows with adoption taking centre stage following publication of *Lost in Care* (18) in 2000. Interest surfaced again in *Every Child Matters* (7) but the Fostering Network says that progress on many of the issues highlighted is still awaited.

People Like Us (1) said 'Despite the predominance of foster care for looked after children, there is relatively little data on it. It has had a lower profile than residential care and less media and policy attention'. 'Adoption' could be now substituted for 'residential care' in this sentence. It is hoped that 'Choice Protects' will, at last, correct the balance.

However, Choice Protects is driven by commissioning issues rather than strategy and with an operational focus on a national blueprint that can be replicated regionally. It is taking place in a policy vacuum with no overarching strategy for children's services to set out the role that is expected of foster care. There is no strategic oversight of foster care to show where it fits with other services for children and how it should meet their needs. Foster care has not had the fundamental policy review given to adoption. It remains on the sidelines of service provision with no real understanding of its true cost or the action needed to drive up quality and ensure that children in foster care get the same chances in life as other children. It needs to be accepted that foster care cannot any more be regarded as a largely voluntary and altruistic service but as a vital part of mainstream services for children unable to live with their families. Its true costs need to be established and properly resourced plans made for ensuring a safer, better quality and more consistent service for the two-thirds of looked after children who benefit from foster care. This will undoubtedly involve paying foster carers more and ensuring that they have appropriate pension and tax arrangements and that, in return, they are obliged to undertake training to improve their skills in relation to the competencies required. As part of the strategic policy for children's services which we recommend is produced, DfES should establish the true cost of foster care and make properly resourced plans for a better quality and more consistent service. It should consider making training mandatory for foster carers along with a proper reward system, including tax and pension arrangements.

Recommendation

12 DfES and local authorities must address the serious staff shortages in social services so that regulations can be fully complied with. Where choices have to be made about the best use of limited resources it is recommended that local authorities give priority to increasing visits to the most vulnerable – the very young and disabled children.

5.3 Private foster care

What *People Like Us* said

Little was known about the extent of private fostering since central collection of statistics was discontinued in 1991. Private fostering took many different forms – West African and Chinese children placed for varying lengths of time, foreign language students, children attending independent schools for whom arrangements are made during school holidays, those who stay with friends or relatives when their parents move, etc. West African children caused the greatest concern.

Private fostering is clearly an area where children are not being safeguarded properly, indeed an unknown number are likely to be seriously at risk. The legal framework should provide some protection but it was not generally known about, complied with or enforced. 'This is a situation that cannot be tolerated. These must surely be the most vulnerable of children living away from home'.

It said that the current arrangements for private foster care clearly do not work, that attempts to improve the level of notifications appear to have little effect and that the situation should not be allowed to continue. There are three options: 'to leave things as they are; to de-regulate on the grounds that current legislation is unenforceable; or to enforce regulation on the basis of the risk to the children'. Children in private foster care should have the same level of protection as other children living away from home and since the present arrangements do not seem workable.

Principal Recommendation 6. Department of Health and the Welsh Office should secure legislation requiring local authorities to register private foster carers and making unregistered foster care a criminal offence.

It should be an offence for parents to place children with unregistered foster carers.

(Continued)

> Public notification of the proposed changes in the law should be given in a public awareness campaign.

Government response

- *Rejected*. A new system of regulation is unnecessary. Compliance to be improved within existing regulations.

- Steps to be taken in 1999 to enforce the current regulations more effectively, including an awareness campaign targeted at the most vulnerable groups of children.

- When Parliamentary time allows, legislation will be introduced to target placements lasting more than 42 days.

- A Code of Practice for language schools to be drawn up.

- Public information campaign to promote compliance with existing regulations and inform parents of proposed Code of Practice for language schools.

What happened

Awareness campaign in 2002 – 2 years late. It consisted only of a leaflet aimed at professional staff.

Parliamentary time not found for 42-day legislation.

The Code of Practice on language schools was never published.

Efforts to improve compliance with existing regulations seem to have failed. When producing *By Private Arrangement: Inspection of Arrangements for Supervising Children in Private Foster Care* (70) SSI found it difficult to find councils with enough privately fostered children to inspect.

Concern about privately fostered children has continued and the recommendations made in *People Like Us* (1) have been reiterated by others, as follows.

- BAAF wrote to peers urging them to back an amendment to the Adoption and Children Bill to include measures to protect privately fostered children, including a registration system to approve private foster parents.

- *The UN Committee on the Rights of the Child*, 31st session (50), recommends that the State party 'ensure consistent legislative safeguards for all children in alternative care, including those who are privately fostered'.

- In the *Victoria Climbie Inquiry Report* (16) Lord Laming contrasted the situation of private foster care with that of childminding saying 'this inconsistency in the law should be removed' and recommending 'The Government should review the law regarding the registration of private foster carers'.

- The NSPCC *Review of Legislation Relating to Children in Family Proceedings Consultation Draft* (21) said many respondents raised concerns about current arrangements for private fostering and the loopholes created by lack of consistency between private and public fostering arrangements. It said 'Private fostering is based on self-report and is basically an "unplumbed depth"' and 'Despite the presence of Section 66 of the Children Act 1989 …, it was a common perception that … private foster care is outside the regulatory framework'. It recommended the law be amended to require all private foster carers to be registered in the same way as childminders.

- In March 2003 Shadow Health Minister, Tim Laughton introduced a Private Members Bill to regulate private fostering in line with the *People Like Us* (1) recommendations plus a tracking system for unaccompanied children entering the country.

The Social Care Institute of Excellence (SCIE), commissioned by DH/WA, published *Effectiveness of Childminding Registration and its Implications for Private Fostering* (71) in January 2003. It concluded that two groups of children were involved, one of which 'would be more likely to define themselves as entering into or providing private foster care arrangements' (largely West African families placing their children with white foster carers) and another, more miscellaneous group (language schools, arrangements with friends, children trafficked as servants, etc.). The former were thought likely to be 'more responsive to participation in a registration system based on supervision and support', but for the second group 'Registration may not offer the most appropriate or effective safeguard to children in these categories'. A legal requirement to register would provide a significant incentive, particularly if combined with support. Little is said about how to protect the children in the second group although reference is made to the Avon and Somerset police study which identified 550 incidents of neglect, emotional and sexual abuse among language school students within a 15-month period – of which just three had been reported to them. It recommends, rather vaguely 'A range of solutions to safeguard the welfare of all vulnerable children living away from parents or close relatives should be considered'.

Every Child Matters (7) and *Keeping Children Safe* (17) say the Government has undertaken a review of private fostering 'which found that the critical factor in whether or not children in private fostering arrangements are safeguarded is that councils with social services responsibilities take a proactive approach to discharging their existing duties under the Children Act 1989 and the Children (Private Arrangements for Fostering) Regulations 1991. The standards and monitoring of council activity on fostering will therefore be strengthened'. National Minimum Standards are to be introduced (in 2004), enforced through inspection by the Commission for Social Care

Inspection. They will require a more proactive approach to identifying private fostering arrangements. Councils will be required to provide information about the numbers of notifications they have of arrangements. These measures are included in the Children Bill. The 1991 Regulations will be reviewed at the same time.

During debates on the Children Bill the Government resisted calls to introduce a registration scheme, preferring to rely on an 'enhanced scheme' which places the onus on local authorities rather than on parents and individuals and a 'sunset clause' which would enable a registration scheme to be introduced. A short timescale applies to this clause and the Government has promised an early evaluation and published report on the impact of the new measures during the lifetime of the registration provisions with an indication of whether it is minded to move to a registration scheme. This will be based on results of the new annual data collection exercise which came into effect in April 2004, monitoring and inspection and the National Minimum Standards.

Analysis

As a result of the rejection of this important recommendation, which others, including the UN Committee on the Rights of the Child (50) and Lord Laming (16), have reiterated, unknown numbers of children who could have been given at least the degree of protection afforded to children living with their parents, who stay with a childminder for a few hours during the day, have remained at risk for a number of years.

Since *People Like Us* (1) was published there have only been very limited attempts to improve compliance with the current regulations with little chance that they have improved the situation.

SCIE is right that private fostering covers disparate groups of children and different arrangements may be needed for different groups.

But they are all vulnerable children. Soon after the publication of *People Like Us* (1) the Avon and Somerset police study showed the risks of abuse of children attending language schools both in this country and abroad. A Code of Practice for language schools was promised but has not been delivered. Children attending language schools for a relatively limited period of time (although some courses deal with young children and can last for up to a year) may require a slightly different approach than, say, West African children who may be fostered for many years with little contact with their family. But children living in homes in which CRB checks have not been carried out are, necessarily, very vulnerable and need protection. It should be easier to enforce the regulations in this sector as language schools are much easier to identify than private fostering arrangements between parents and individuals. They can also be expected to comply if they can obtain the necessary checks and if local authorities are able to undertake home visits to check host families for them. A Code of Practice would help schools know what is expected of them and parents would be able to check whether a particular school complied with the Code before placing a child in the school. It is needed quite independently of other action being taken on private fostering generally. DfES should arrange for the production of a Code of Practice for language schools. Authorities should ensure that language schools comply with the private fostering regulations and are assisted where necessary to obtain CRB checks.

Legislation has not been introduced to increase the defined period for private foster care to 42 days instead of 28, but this is welcome as the effect would have been to reduce the number of children who are at least theoretically entitled to some protection under the current arrangements.

It is extremely disappointing that the response on private fostering in *Every Child Matters* (7) was so weak. It is unlikely that the 'enhanced scheme' will make much impact or identify those private fostering situations of most concern. Despite estimates of several thousand children being privately fostered, the Social Services Inspectorate has so far been unable to identify enough councils with enough notified cases for a meaningful inspection. Why should the new Commission be any more successful? What good will new minimum standards and revised regulations be when there has been such a signal failure to apply the existing regulations in anything other than a handful of cases? What good will initiating the collection of numbers of notifications do? Statistical collections were abandoned previously because they were an extremely inadequate reflection of the real situation. What will have changed to elicit the missing several thousand notifications this time? The Government proposals say nothing about a publicity campaign to make parents and carers aware of the more proactive approach, thus leaving local councils with the whole burden.

Action is needed to change the attitude of parents and private foster carers alike. There should be clear incentives and disincentives for parents who want to have a child privately fostered and for carers who wish to privately foster. The recommendation made in *People Like Us* (1) provided this. Incentives for parents would include the fact that the prospective carer has been checked and is registered and, for carers, the prospect of help, support and availability of training. The disincentive for both would be if it were an offence to place a child with an unregistered carer or to accept a child when unregistered (offences are already involved in failure to notify arrangements under the current regulations under Section 70 of the Children Act 1989).

Recommendations

13 The Government should introduce the registration of private foster carers as *People Like Us* (1) recommended. An accompanying publicity campaign is

(Continued)

needed both for a registration scheme or for the 'enhanced scheme' being introduced in the Children Bill.

14 Local authorities should ensure that language schools comply with the private fostering regulations and are assisted where necessary to obtain CRB checks.

15 A Code of Practice for language schools should be produced and cover the arrangements for recruiting host families for the students attending the school. (DfES)

5.4 Schools

What *People Like Us* said

Chapter 4 covered boarding and residential schools and found more reports on abuse in maintained residential special schools than in independent boarding schools. It looked at safeguards for 'ordinary' children and for children with special educational needs. Some types of school might be associated with greater risk – those with no external oversight from a board of trustees, governing body or advisory group; those catering for EBD children; special interest schools. The independent sector had responded positively to the new duty in the Children Act 1989 requiring schools to promote and safeguard children's welfare and giving local authorities a duty to inspect the arrangements. Maintained residential schools and non-maintained special schools were outside its scope.

Children who are far away from home, such as those with families in the Armed Forces and foreign children who come to this country to be educated may be more at risk. There needs to be continuing care to ensure these children are not targeted by abusers or otherwise harmed. Children placed by social services, educational and health authorities some distance from their homes must not be overlooked.

Welfare inspections and publication of reports

> **Principal Recommendation 7. Department of Health and the Welsh Office should extend Section 87 of the Children Act 1989 (which requires independent boarding schools to safeguard and promote the welfare of children, and opens their arrangements for doing so to inspection) to all schools with boarding provision.**
>
> **Section 87 inspection reports to be publicly available and written to a common format in simple language.**

Government response
- Social Services White Paper to set out plans to extend Section 87 when Parliamentary time allows.

Government action
- Care Standards Act 2000 included provisions to extend Section 87 of the Children Act to all schools with boarding provision in England and Wales.

- The National Care Standards Commission was set up in April 2001 and from April 2002 took over responsibility for carrying out Section 87 inspections from local authorities in England.

- The Education Act 2002, which came into force on 1 September 2003, requires all schools, day and boarding, to comply with Section 87 of the Children Act.

- The Care Standards Inspectorate for Wales (CSIW) carries out Section 87 inspections in Wales.

- Consideration being given on how to make reports publicly available and reader-friendly.

What happened

All schools with boarding provisions and Further Education (FE) colleges now have their welfare arrangements inspected by the National Care Standards Commission (CSCI from April 2004) or the Care Standards Inspectorate for Wales. The NCSC issued National Minimum Standards to accompany the Regulations for independent boarding schools, residential special schools and FE colleges accommodating students under 18 in March 2002. In Wales the CSIW introduced standards by April 2003.

The NCSC's first Annual Report and Accounts, *Protecting People Improving Lives* (72), said it does not have the power to publish reports of inspections of schools and colleges. It does not comment on findings from any of these inspections. The Children's Rights Director issues a separate report on services used by children, but his first report (58) did not cover findings from inspections. At present reports can only be published if the school agrees. The Health and Social Care (Community Health and Standards) Act 2003 includes a provision giving the NCSC power to publish reports of inspections of all schools with boarding provision and FE colleges.

The Independent Schools Inspectorate (ISI) (see below) – the operationally independent arm of the Independent Schools Council (ISC) – has an agreement with the NCSC to co-ordinate inspections wherever possible with summaries of NCSC reports being included with ISI reports.

Protecting People Improving Lives (72), says one of the NCSC's goals is to achieve consistency of inspection with a quality board set up to sample inspection reports to see whether decisions are made consistently. The NCSC's Children's Rights Director (Roger Morgan) said that the Commission strived to ensure reports were written in plain English for a lay readership. Its business plan for 2003–04 says one of its key objectives is 'to publish inspection results in full and in public summary to enable user choice based on quality'.

In 2002 the Welsh Assembly Government said that the arrangements for reporting on welfare inspections had yet to be finalised, but the CSIW intended to make these reports accessible to a wide range of potential interests. The language used and the format chosen will reflect this intention. The CSIW will also liaise closely with Estyn (Office of Her Majesty's Chief Inspector of Education and Training in Wales) and the Registrar of Independent Schools in the Assembly to ensure action is taken quickly to follow up reports.

Registration of Independent Schools and Inspection of Educational Arrangements

> The Review of Registration of Independent Schools should be based on the principle that boarding schools should not accommodate children without preliminary examination of the welfare aspects and any new Notice of Complaint procedure should allow for immediate cancellation where children are in danger.

Government response

- Review being carried out by DfEE and Welsh Office – consultation in Autumn 1998.

Government action

The Education Act 2002 introduced a new system for regulating all independent schools, which came into force on 1 September 2003. No independent school can open before being registered by the Secretary of State. New independent boarding schools cannot now be granted registration until the NCSC (from April 2004 the Commission for Social Care Inspection) has inspected the boarding standards and reported on these to the Secretary of State. Schools failing to meet standards can now be removed from the register immediately after a statutory 28-day period for appeal, where it is considered that there is a risk of serious harm to the welfare of pupils.

What happened
There are two systems for inspecting the educational arrangements in schools:

- since 1999 OFSTED inspects maintained and non-maintained schools and independent schools that are not members of the ISC

- the ISI inspects schools that are members of the ISC.

Both Inspectorates publish all their inspection reports. OFSTED monitors ISI performance.

OFSTED's *Inspecting Independent Schools: A Framework for use by Her Majesty's Inspectors of Schools* (73) says inspectors must evaluate and report on 'the steps taken to ensure pupils' welfare, health and safety, including the school's arrangements for child protection and effective liaison between care and teaching staff, and procedures for vetting new staff'. Inspectors should consider the extent to which the school '… has care arrangements for boarding pupils that take account of the Children Act 1989'. Its *A Handbook for Inspecting Special Schools and Pupil Referral Units* (for inspections from September 2003) (74) says that inspectors must evaluate and report on how well the school 'ensures pupils' care, welfare, health and safety, assessing as appropriate the extent to which the school has effective procedures for the protection of pupils in line with agreed child protection arrangements'.

OFSTED's *Annual Report of Her Majesty's Chief Inspector of Schools* for 2001/02 (75) said it had inspected 364 independent schools for registration purposes plus full inspections of 10 more schools 'including 2 in receipt of public funding'. It does not say how many were boarding schools. The report said 'of mainstream independent schools … only 60 per cent complied with all statutory requirements. Two common problems were the

employment of staff before checks on their suitability had been carried out and failure to complete registers in line with the requirements'. But it said 'Most schools had child protection policies in place' and 'the number of schools where boarding accommodation is unsatisfactory is diminishing; those that remain are mostly provisionally registered schools'.

The ISI inspects schools which are members of associations affiliated to the Independent Schools Council every six years. Each year they inspect about 200 independent schools, but they do not say how many are boarding schools. Their *All Round Education in ISC Schools – A Digest of Reports 2000–1* (76) comments that 'The overwhelming majority … carried out the required checks to ensure that staff having unsupervised access to minors are carried out [sic]. In one school twenty members of staff had been overlooked, in most cases non-teaching or occasional staff'.

OFSTED publishes annual reports on its monitoring of the ISI performance. There have been three such reports – in 1999, 2000–01 and 2001–02 (77). These show that the ISI is improving its performance. The *Independent Schools Council Inspections 2001–02* report (77) commented '… this area has improved and writing on boarding provision now generally matches the quality of the report as a whole. ISI inspections now follow the National Standards for Boarding, and under an agreement between DfES, the ISC and the National Care Standards Commission, it is anticipated that ISI and NCSC inspections will be carried out jointly'.

The Boarding Schools Association (BSA) – an associate member of the Independent Schools Council – aims to improve boarding practice. Some 550 boarding schools belong to the BSA. About 110 do not. The BSA appointed a Director of Training in 1997. It has had grants from DfES since 1998 to expand its publications and develop and subsidise the cost of training courses for boarding staff. Training courses leading to qualifications for boarding staff were introduced in 1998 covering such subjects as legislation, child protection, National Minimum Standards for Boarding Schools, conflict resolution and counselling skills, and structures for managing crises and stress (bullying, homesickness and relationships.) The first students completed their course in 2001. This development has been well received with 4,000 people going on BSA training courses annually and it has already done a lot to make boarding staff more professional in their approach. Publications include briefing papers on 'Safer staff recruitment', 'Effective welfare policies', 'Policies for partnership with boarding parents' and booklets for parents and new boarders. Chapters in its manual *Good Practice in Boarding Schools* cover 'Boarding welfare and the law', 'Confidentiality', 'Reducing bullying' and 'Ensuring a safe environment'.

Information for parents

Independent schools should include information on safeguards in their brochures and there should be a section on this in ISC's guide to choosing an independent school.

Government response

- The DfEE are working with relevant interests to ensure that schools tell parents about arrangements for safeguarding children.

- The Independent Schools Information Service includes this in their guide to choosing a school.

What happened

The Independent Schools Council's information service (ISCIS) guide to parents choosing an independent school was amended to include a section on safeguards in 2000.

The BSA's *Choosing a Boarding School: A Guide for Parents* (78) refers to welfare and bullying and the list of questions for parents to ask include 'what are

the arrangements for pupils and parents to raise concerns'.

The ISI's briefing paper *Information about ISI for Parents* includes sections on 'What if I have concerns about my child's school' and 'Will ISI ensure that the school is safe for my child?'. These refer to the requirement to have a complaints procedure, child abuse and the local authority SSD's welfare responsibility.

The Right Place? (79) – a booklet by parents of children in residential special schools has advice to help parents choose a school and covers:

- how to find out about the availability of residential special schools

- how to get information about a school

- what to look for and ask about when deciding which school would be best for your child

- what should ring alarm bells for you when looking at a school.

The education of service children

The Boarding School Allowance should be conditional on parents seeking advice from the Service Children's Educational Authority about choosing a school.

Government response

- Advisory role of the Service Children's Education Agency to be enhanced with claimants being required to certify that they are aware advice is available, or has been obtained.

- Changes to be made to the Accredited Schools Database (ASD).

What happened

From September 1999 schools wanting to be on the Accredited Schools Database have to be:

- either affiliated to the Independent Schools Council, or

- in the maintained sector, or

- governed by an appropriate professional or vocational organisation.

Schools and colleges must agree to their inspection report being in the public domain.

Revised arrangements for taking schools off the list mean that this will be done if they fail to meet criteria or when Notice of Complaint is issued. Parents choosing to keep children in a school taken off or not on the list will jeopardise their entitlement to the Boarding School allowance.

Service parents are encouraged to seek advice from the Service Children's Education (SCE)'s UK Office before choosing a boarding school. SCE and the Ministry of Defence (MOD) are introducing a system under which parents will be required to produce a certificate saying that they have sought advice and present this to their pay office before the Boarding School Allowance is made available. This is because there was evidence that not all pay units were applying the current 'strong encouragement' policy to contact SCE's UK Office.

From August 2004 SCE (UK) will separate from Service Children's Education and will be called Services Education Advisory Service (EAS).

There are now a small number of pupils in non-accredited schools – those close to completing their education and at their parents' request.

Guardianship

> **Parents should always appoint guardians from an agency accredited by the umbrella body for guardianship agencies and conforming to their Code of Practice.**
>
> **Children who live far away from home may be more at risk. Schools with more than 10**
>
> *(Continued)*

> **per cent of pupils from abroad might revert to annual welfare inspections. The accreditation of 'guardianship' schemes should be accelerated and their use by parents and schools encouraged. Arrangements for a foreign child aged under 16 to live with a private family for 28 days or more comes within the scope of private fostering regulations, which should be applied.**

Government response

AEGIS (the Association for the Education and Guardianship of International Students) and Code of Practice were launched in November 1997. Government agrees it is desirable for parents always to appoint guardians from an agency accredited by AEGIS.

The Government rejected the recommendation about children living far from home for the following reasons.

- Numbers fluctuate from year to year, not necessarily correlated to risk and not good use of additional resources.

- Further consideration of how to respond to spirit of the recommendation.

- It intends to improve enforcement of private fostering arrangements, targeting the most vulnerable groups.

What happened

AEGIS awards accreditation to all reputable guardianship organisations after a rigorous inspection process carried out by trained OFSTED and/or ISI inspectors. Its leaflet quotes DfES as saying 'Desirable that parents from overseas appoint a guardian from an AEGIS accredited agency'. AEGIS has developed links with the NCSC and the ISI. It is now a registered charity and is working closely with schools in developing its policies.

AEGIS estimates there are around 50–100 guardianship organisations in the UK of which 10 are accredited with a few more going through the accreditation process each year. Some will be very small, catering for three or four guardians looking after a few children, and some very large with an extensive network of guardian families. The accreditation process is thorough. It involves two inspectors visiting the organisation to check administration procedures, then talking to schools, host families and children to gather information about standards. All guardians are subject to CRB checks.

Each year around 8,000 foreign children come to the UK to be educated and many more come to language schools for shorter stays. Most children coming here to be educated go to boarding schools, but some may go to day schools and be placed with private foster parents. AEGIS said it was important for the protection of foreign children that schools do more to encourage parents to choose guardians from an accredited agency. Some schools make every effort to ensure that foreign children leaving their care at half-term, etc. are given into the care of responsible adults (aged over 25) – either someone known to and trusted by the parents or someone from an AEGIS-accredited agency. Some schools make less effort to protect the welfare of foreign children. They may be allowed to go off with a very young adult or stay on their own in university student accommodation or bed and breakfast establishments.

The Boarding Schools National Minimum Standard 22 refers to the appointment of guardians, but does not mention AEGIS or accreditation.

Language schools

Section 5.3 on private foster care refers to language schools. The Government response said that a Code of Practice for these schools should be drawn up.

What happened

The Code of Practice for Language Schools has never been published.

There are no precise figures about the number of foreign children attending language schools, but, as noted above, it is likely to be many more than 8,000 a year. Typically schools recruit host families for children to stay with. There is little information about how schools recruit families or the checks they make before placing a child. A study by Avon and Somerset Police – reported in *Effectiveness of childminding registration and its implications for private fostering* (71) identified 550 incidents of neglect, emotional and sexual abuse among language school students in a 15-month period, of which just three had been reported to the police.

Analysis

The state of safeguards in schools with boarding provision has been transformed since 1997. Extending Section 87 of the Children Act and introducing the new system for registering independent schools in the Education Act 2002 have strengthened the legal framework. The Government is to be congratulated on introducing these changes.

The Section 87 changes have been in force since April 2002 so it is too soon to assess the impact on residential special schools. The new registration system is even more recent. The National Minimum Standards are comprehensive, but, as the NCSC's first annual report does not comment on the results of its inspections of schools with boarding provision, no judgement can be made about consistency of approach. CSCI took over the NCSC's functions for inspecting schools in April 2004. The subsequent period of settling down may slow down or hinder progress in developing the new inspection regime. CSCI should include separate comment about its inspections of the welfare arrangements in all schools with boarding provision in its reports.

The BSA represents the majority of independent boarding schools and they benefit from its publications, conferences and training. It has been greatly helped by the grants given by DfES to enable it to expand its work of fostering good boarding practice. This is most welcome. The 110 or so schools that do not belong to the BSA or one of the other bodies on the ISC may be more isolated and have fewer opportunities to share ideas and good practice.

There is quite a lot of information available for parents, most of which refers to safety and what to do if there are concerns. It is disappointing that this does not include details about what checks are made on teaching or other staff before appointment. This should be included.

The changes made for payment of the Boarding School Allowance are most welcome.

AEGIS has achieved a lot in helping guardianship organisations to improve their practice. But more needs to be done to encourage:

- more guardianship organisations to become accredited by AEGIS and

- schools to recommend parents to appoint guardians from accredited agencies.

Children attending language schools are vulnerable because they are in a foreign country and may not speak or understand English very well. Language schools must have rigorous and effective systems for recruiting host families so that children are safe and well cared for. In Section 5.3 on private foster care we argue that it would be easier to enforce regulations in this sector because they are easier to identify than arrangements between parents and individuals. A Code of Practice would mean that such schools would know what is expected of them and importantly parents could check whether a school complied with its conditions before placing a child there.

Special schools

> Independent special schools should be required to have a governing body to make arrangements for safeguarding and promoting the welfare of pupils.

Government response
- Consultation early in 1999 on plans for doing so in relation to approved independent special schools.

What happened
In May 2000 DfES consulted in *Proposals for the Placement of Children with Statements of SEN in Independent Schools* (80) on whether such schools attended by children with statements of SEN or in public care should have to have a governing body and whether this body should be set up along similar lines to those for non-maintained special schools. Requiring independent special schools to have a governing body or similar was intended to be in the Education Act 2002. However, the clause was dropped because it was decided this would be impractical for small schools where the proprietor was also the head teacher.

The Best Place to be? Policy, practice and the experiences of residential school placements for disabled children (25) reported on research into the circumstances in which children came to be in a residential special school in four local authorities. It found that most placements funded by LEAs had little input from anyone to monitor care standards and children's welfare. SSDs followed a variety of practices, but very few children received the full protection of the Children Act. Parents received little help in keeping in touch with their children or in attending reviews. The report made recommendations about improving information about numbers of children placed in residential schools, encouraging LEAs and SSDs to take responsibility jointly for protecting and promoting the welfare of disabled children.

The sections on residential placements in the revised *SEN Code of Practice for England* and that for Wales issued in 2001 (39, 40) say the following.

- The LEA and parents should agree the arrangements for the child to keep in contact with the family and any special help needed to maintain home/school contact.

- The LEA *must* tell either the SSD where the family lives or where the school is about the placement. It notes it is good practice to tell both.

- Visits to the school by parents may be helpful.

Ted Cole *et al.* in *Patterns of Provision for Pupils with Behavioural Difficulties in England: A study of government statistics and behaviour support plan data* (46) say 'EBD schools that provide boarding are expensive, difficult to staff and challenging to run effectively. ... A trend away from boarding was therefore to be expected ... From a peak in the mid-1980s there has been a sharp decline in the number of boarders with a decrease in numbers of about 19 per cent between 1994 and 1998. There has also been a move away from seven nightly boarding to young people typically spending only four nights or five nights in the boarding schools or returning home every second weekend'.

DfES's working group on the future role of special schools in *The Report of the Special Schools Working Group* (81) set out a programme of change for this sector. The section on residential special schools said '[they] form an important part of the SEN continuum of provision, but there are a number of issues relating to the quality of the educational and care provision ... which need to be addressed'. It said that the NCSC National Minimum Standards offer an opportunity to make progress, but there was concern among schools about how rigorous the standards were given that they were fairly new. It referred to the NCB's Children's Residential Standards Implementation Project and the need for schools to do some self-evaluation.

DfES in *Removing Barriers to Achievement: the Government's Strategy for SEN* (47) made these key points:

- about 6,200 children are boarders in maintained and non-maintained special schools and 2,800 in approved independent special schools

- nearly all have statements of SEN and many have significant health, social care and mental health needs

- there are concerns about the high cost of such placements, the quality of some provision, patchy monitoring arrangements, and the lack of contact some children have with their families

- DfES wants to 'break down the divide between mainstream and special schools to create a unified system where all schools and their pupils are included within the wider community of schools'

- DfES has already:
  - collected data from 81 local authorities on the number, needs and costs of residential placements; ... in future it will collect this data annually from local authorities
  - carried out a survey of how far LEAs are notifying social services departments about placements, as required under the Children Act
  - worked with LGA and NASS (see below) on developing a contract on the placement of children in non-maintained and independent residential special schools, covering all aspects – from negotiations about fees through to review arrangements with the aim of improving the quality of placements and ensuring a more consistent approach.

DfES proposes to improve use of residential placements by better planning and helping local authorities manage expenditure better through sharing good practice and reinvesting resources in local provision, so children can be educated nearer home.

The National Association of Independent Schools and Non-maintained Special Schools, formed in 1997, has over 100 members – all 70 non-maintained special schools and more than 30 of the independent special schools. It acts, in partnership with other organisations, as a voice for special schools, raising concerns on issues affecting young people with SEN and their families. Its standards include 'Every NASS school will follow legislation and best practice in Child Protection issues and accord them the highest priority'. This includes CRB checks. All member schools have to have a governing body or equivalent. NASS has encouraged the setting up of groups for Heads of Education, Heads of Care, etc., so staff can share ideas and good practice. One of the aims of the model contract mentioned above is to 'improve quality by ensuring and safeguarding high standards of education and care'. It states that 'all' signatories to this Contract agree to adopt and promote values which place children and their parents at the centre of their respective service provision', and 'the Provider will with the Authority … promote the principle of partnership between child, parents, authority and school …'.

OFSTED's *Annual Report for 2001/02* (75) said about its inspection of 30 residential special schools that 'the quality of care is at least good in all but one of the schools inspected. Pupils are safe … Child protection procedures were effective in all but one school. In this school training for staff was unsatisfactory and staff were not aware of how to proceed in the case of any concerns. Many schools have now appointed an independent listener or advocate for their pupils and this has contributed further to their protection'.

'*It doesn't happen to disabled children*': *Child Protection and Disabled Children* (23) says the

following in its chapter on residential special schools.

- There should be an effective framework for protecting disabled children. The relationship between residential special schools and wider child protection is not clear.

- There are barriers preventing social services authorities from protecting disabled children – for example inconsistency and confusion about their 'looked after' status.

- Decisions about placement are often characterised by conflict between parent and local authority and they focus on placement availability rather than child's needs.

- Unclear Government guidance about relationship between placing social services authority and the one where the school is.

- Parents find it difficult to get information about schools and they get little support to help them keep in touch with their child.

Analysis

Dropping the governance clause for independent special schools from the Education Act 2002 is unacceptable. These schools should be required to have a governing body or other type of external oversight. It is not clear what arguments were advanced to show why schools where the proprietor was also the head would find it impractical to have a governing body or equivalent. These schools are now the only institutions accommodating children away from home that do not have to have some sort of external oversight. This may make the children more vulnerable.

It is welcome that NASS draws together non-maintained and independent special schools. This provides a platform for people working in these categories of residential schools to exchange ideas.

These institutions are often geographically isolated and networking possibilities help to reduce a feeling of isolation. It is a pity that there is no equivalent body for maintained residential special schools. SEBDA (the Social, Emotional and Behavioural Difficulties Association, formerly the Association of Workers for Children with Emotional and Behavioural Difficulties), has existed for over 50 years 'to serve the interests of children experiencing difficulties in their social, emotional and behavioural development'. It was not represented on DfES' special schools working group and does not seem to publicise its activities very widely.

The SEN Code of Practice (39, 40) says all the right things about residential placements, but as with many things it does not seem to have been translated into practice.

Notifications under the Children Act

> There should be an SSI inspection on Section 85 of the Children Act 1989, which requires educational establishments to notify local authorities of any child they accommodate for three months or more, as there is a dearth of information about its use.

Government response

- Work to be done to identify the level of notifications, reasons for non-notifications, what is done when a local authority is notified and what better arrangements could be made to safeguard children in England.

- No plans for SSI inspection of Section 85 in Wales.

What happened

Research shows that numbers of children have not been notified under Sections 85 and 86, in relation to disabled children – see Section 5.6 on health settings.

As mentioned above, *Removing Barriers to Achievement* (47) refers to a survey of how far local education authorities are notifying SSDs about children being placed in residential schools out of area, but it does not give any findings.

Analysis

The position is different for children placed in residential schools to that for children in hospital. The SEN Code of Practice for England and that for Wales (39, 40) say 'the LEA *must* inform either the social services department where the child's family lives or the department in the area of the residential school'. While this does not appear to be being done, the fact that it is spelt out in a statutory code of practice makes it easier to force LEAs to comply with the legislation. There appears to be no similar vehicle to force health authorities to do this. It is welcome that DfES has now conducted a survey of LEAs to find out how far they are complying with this duty, but the findings from the survey need to be made public. It should also use the findings to assess the scale of the problem and take any necessary action to ensure compliance with the legislation.

5.5 Prison establishments

What *People Like Us* said

Chapter 5 said that prison is no place for children, particularly unconvicted children, and it is impossible to meet the ordinary needs of children there.

There are considerable problems with bullying, suicide and self-harm. Improving the environment, having more education and leisure provision and a reduction in bullying would help.

Boys aged 15–16 still being remanded to prisons is a serious failure of public policy that should be put right as quickly as possible. Additional secure accommodation should be provided.

The principles of the Children Act in promoting and safeguarding children should be incorporated in penal system regulations and 'A major commitment to welfare as well as containment is needed'.

> Prison Service policy to keep children in
> discrete accommodation is not being
> achieved. The incidence of sexual assaults
> on children in penal settings is unclear and
> research is recommended.

Government response

- Prison Service policy is to keep those aged under 18 separate from other young adults (i.e. 18–20-year-olds) and adults.

- Unconvicted 15- and 16-year-old girls are not held in prison but 17-year-olds held on remand are.

- Plans being drawn up urgently to hold all juveniles separately in dedicated accommodation with significantly enhanced regimes and ensuring this reflects Children Act 1989 principles, regulations and guidance. Plans being developed for three units for juveniles sentenced under Section 53 of the Children and Young Persons Act 1933. Hoped one would be operational in autumn 1998.

- There were four recorded incidents of sexual assault of juveniles in the 12 months to 31 March 1998. Police investigated and no prosecutions resulted. The Prison Service is looking at how research can best be carried out.

Government action

- The Youth Justice Board (YJB) set up September 1998 to monitor the operation of the youth justice system and the provision of youth justice services.

- YJB took on responsibility for commissioning and purchasing places in the juvenile secure estate April 2000.

- Distinct estate introduced for 15–17-year-old boys, April 2000.

- Prison Service Order 4950 (*Regimes for Young Prisoners under 18 years old*) issued 1999 for boys and 2000 for girls. Revised in consultation with DH and reissued in January 2001.

- Three special units for juveniles sentenced under Section 53 of the Children and Young Persons Act 1933 (now Sections 90–92 of the Powers of Criminal Courts (Sentencing) Act 2000) were established at HM Young Offenders Institutions (YOIs) Castington (Oswald Unit), Huntercombe (Patterson Unit) and Warren Hill (Carlford Unit) during 2000/01.

- Discrete units introduced for girls within the Prison Service women's estate.

- Research carried out on '*Sexual Victimisation among 15–17 year old offenders in prison*' RDS Occasional Paper No 65 (2000).

What happened

The Committee on the Rights of the Child, 31st session (50) 'notes with serious concern that the situation of children in conflict with the law has worsened since the consideration of the initial report'. The Committee was concerned that the UK was not in a position to withdraw its reservation to article 37 of the UN Convention on the Rights of the Child relating to children in prison with adults.

Safeguarding Children (4) said 'The 1999–2000 Annual Report [of HM Chief Inspector of Prisons] also identified the most serious concerns about the welfare of girls and young women aged between 15 and 18 years held in custody. There is no specialist provision for them, resulting in their being held in adult prisons alongside adult prisoners'. An inspection of Holloway women's prison had found two 15-year-old girls in the prison at the time of the inspection placed in the ante-natal unit … because managers 'did not know where to put them'.

> Children, particularly those who are disturbed, have special health needs. The NHS should be responsible for the health care of children in penal settings.

Government response

- Report on the organisation and delivery of health care in prisons to be published by end 1998.

Government action

- Prison Health Policy Unit and Task Force established in 2000 to modernise prison health care and establish partnership working between the Prison Service and NHS. The units were jointly accountable to Home Office and DH ministers. Development work over two years included mental health in-reach teams, drug detox programmes, new NVQ in Custodial Care, etc. but no mention of anything related to children and young people.

- Funding responsibility for prison health services in England transferred to DH in April 2003. DH allocating extra resources to improve services, rising to £46 million a year by 2005–06.

- Process of transferring commissioning of services to PCTs started April 2004, to be completed by April 2006.

- Funding for prison service transferred to Welsh Assembly Government on 3 April 2003.

What happened

John Rea Price, Her Majesty's Inspectorate of Prisons (HMIP), February 2003, said this remained a major concern. Young people end up in YOIs, often for months, particularly in the health care unit, simply because there is no NHS adolescent psychiatric provision. Instances have been found of children being received from NHS specialised units because their behaviour has been found too difficult.

Situations such as this put immense strains on prison staff, and these children are often a danger to themselves and others as staffing ratios do not permit an acceptable level of care or oversight.

Barry Goldson's article 'Youth justice' in *YoungMinds* magazine 63, 2003, quoted the HMCIP's thematic review – 'a very significant proportion of young people in custody need help with health care ... adolescents in custody represent a concentration of unhealthy lifestyles, reflecting the need for advice and care related to a range of health issues'. The problem was described as 'even more pressing' in relation to mental health problems. After thematic review, HMCIP said 'over 50 per cent of young prisoners on remand and 30 per cent of sentenced young offenders have a diagnosable mental disorder'. And the BMA – 'patients within prison are among the most needy in the country in relation to their health care needs ... 17 per cent of young offenders were not registered with a GP and generally the young people had a low level of contact with primary health care' (BMA, 2001, *Prison Medicine: A crisis waiting to break*'). It said 'The Prison Service is being consistently starved of adequate funding to meet this clinical and social care agenda ... the prison medical service has been in acute crisis for some time ...'.

A joint YJB/DH review of health needs of juveniles in Prison Service custody has started.

> Boys aged 15 and 16 still being remanded to prison is a serious failure of public policy which should be put right as quickly as possible. Additional public expenditure must be found in order to end the remand of boys to prison establishments.

Government response

- Changes in use of secure estate for juveniles to be made. Plans include discrete secure estate for juveniles within Prison Service accommodation and courts having greater flexibility for remanding the most vulnerable 15- and 16-year-old boys direct to secure accommodation.

Government action
• Juvenile estate established April 2000.

What happened
John Rea Price, HMIP, February 2003, said 15- and 16-year-old boys continued to be remanded to prison establishments. HM Inspectorate of Prisons had expressed concerns at the YJB's failure to specify a care and training regime equivalent to that which it requires for the sentenced. And, although collaboration between Youth Offending Teams (YOTs) and the establishment had significantly improved for the sentenced it has been a problem for the unsentenced, with failure to provide information about vulnerability, social and family circumstances. However, in July 2003 the YJB introduced a system for custody planning comparable with that which works generally well for the sentenced in which YOTs were required to actively participate. In the main it has taken off satisfactorily, although one or two establishments still have been unable to put in place the in-house YOT teams necessary to support the system. (The YJB later confirmed all establishments would have an in-house YOT in place later in the summer.)

The YJB, 2004, say the requirements for information transmission about these matters from YOTs to custodial facilities has always been the same as for sentenced young people. But because remands sometimes happen with little or no YOT involvement, this has been operationally more difficult to achieve.

> **The Department of Health and the Welsh Office should consult LGA and the Prison Service about social services authorities' support to children in penal settings and their families.**

Government response
• Consultation underway about how care of juveniles in prison establishments may best be co-ordinated.

Government action
• *Regimes for Prisoners under 18* require Governors to establish arrangements with Area Child Protection Committees (ACPCs) for dealing with incidents in which a young person has or may have suffered significant harm. *Rethinking Child Imprisonment* (61) says inspectors have expressed concerns about implementation of these new orders.

What happened
This has improved for the sentenced following the creation of YOTs. However, YOTs have been poorly connected with their home area ACPC and the ACPC for the establishment itself have all too often been reluctant to provide the support required – although there are exceptions where there are excellent collaboration between community and prison staff (John Rea Price, HMIP, 2003).

> **The principles of the Children Act 1989 in promoting and safeguarding children should be incorporated in the penal system regulations.**

Government response
• The principles and safeguards in the Children Act 1989 do not expressly apply to children in prison.

• New regime for juveniles will reflect the principles and guidance.

• Prison Service in discussion with Association of Chief Police Officers, ADSS (Association of Directors of Social Services) and LGA about investigation into allegations.

Government action

- Since April 2000 YOIs have been required to develop child protection procedures. Instructions in Annex B to Prison Service Order 4950 (*Regimes for Young Prisoners under 18 years old*) were revised in consultation with the Department of Health and reissued in Jan 2001.

What happened

Safeguarding Children (4) said the following.

- In contrast to the provision of council secure accommodation, the principles and requirements of the Children Act are not automatically applied to YOIs and other prison establishments.

- HMI prisons inspectors have highlighted the very serious risks to the welfare of young people held in some YOIs. Although young people in YOIs are among those at highest risk of serious harm, their safeguarding is not addressed in most areas.

- Few ACPCs had representatives of YOTs on them, and therefore they were not actively addressing the needs of these particularly vulnerable young people. YOTs were working in relative isolation from other services, were not demonstrating a commitment to risk assessment of these young people, and focused upon offending behaviour at the expense of considering welfare needs.

In November 2002 the High Court ruled that children in prison are entitled to the same welfare safeguards as other children. Mr Justice Munby's judgement in the Howard League for Penal Reform Case (82) was that 'human rights law imposes on the Prison Service enforceable obligations ... i) to have regard to the "welfare" principle encapsulated in the UN Convention and the European Charter; and ii) to take effective steps to protect children in Young Offender Institutions from any ill-treatment, whether at the hands of prison staff or of other in-mates, of the type which engages either article 3 or

article 8 of the European Convention' [inhuman or degrading treatment or punishment or which impact adversely or disproportionately on the child's physical or psychological integrity]. It says that HMCIP's *Thematic Review* (83) and *People Like Us* (1) 'had a dramatic effect.' and led to the issue of Prison Service Order 4950 in April 2000. 'These marked a sea-change in the criminal justice system.' 'There can be no doubt that, between them, PSO 4950, the National Standards [for Youth Justice] and Framework for Assessment mark a revolution in official attitudes within the Prison Service to the treatment of children in Young Offender Institutions. The policy which they embody is a revolutionary break with the past, driven in significant measure by the recommendations of Sir David Ramsbotham and Sir William Utting and, I do not doubt, at least in part by a recognition of the imperative need to meet standards mandated since October 2000 by the Human Rights Act 1998.'

He concludes 'There is, however, serious cause for concern as to whether this policy [PSO 4950] is yet being implemented in a satisfactory manner throughout the whole of the Prison Service juvenile estate. The Joint Inspectors' report *Safeguarding Children* (4) and various reports by the Chief Inspector of Prisons of inspections of specific Young Offender Institutions indicate that the State appears to be failing, and in some instances, failing very badly, in its duties to vulnerable and damaged children in Young Offender Institutions. There is material in these reports suggesting that some of these failings may be such as to give rise to actionable breaches of applicable human rights law'.

Keeping Children Safe (17) mentioned the revised Prison Service Order 4950 *Regimes for Prisoners under 18*, 'to take full account of the recent judgement, which found that the Children Act 1989 continues to apply to children in prison, subject to the requirements of their imprisonment'. PSO 4950 is still under revision. The revised version is expected to be issued in Summer 2004. Governors were advised of the implications of the Munby judgment soon after it was delivered.

Analysis

The position of children and young people in prison establishments will be considered in more detail in our companion report *Safeguards for Vulnerable Children*. The main conclusion reached is that this is the most worrying area of all in relation to safeguarding children living away from home. There is ample evidence that children and young people in prison settings are not being safeguarded, although, encouragingly, there are now attempts to improve the situation.

There have been major changes in Government policy and in the criminal justice system as it relates to children and young offenders since the publication of *People Like Us* (1). As part of its efforts to tackle youth crime the Government has introduced the Youth Justice Board, multi-disciplinary Youth Offending Teams, Detention and Training Orders (DTO), Intensive Supervision and Surveillance Programmes, secure training centres, etc.

Far from removing children from prisons, Government policy has led to an increase in the numbers of children in prison despite a reduction in the rate of offending by under-18s. It seemed that the decade-long upward trend in juvenile custody had peaked in 2002. Since October 2002, numbers in custody had fallen by 13 per cent from 3715 under-18s in October 2002 to 2732 in February 2004. However, in April 2004 Rod Morgan, Chair of YJB, said that figures were now beginning to rise due to a steep increase in remands.

Instead of removing boys from prison establishments, as *People Like Us* (1) and others (e.g. *Young Prisoners: A Thematic Review* (83)) recommended, the policy has been to put them in separate establishments from adults and to provide an appropriate regime for them. Extra resources have been provided and a separate Juvenile

Operational Group established for under-18s. However, a number of boys are held on split sites with young offenders (18–21-year-olds), albeit in dedicated juvenile units, rather than in children-only sites and, as the *Child Protection and Safeguards Review 2003. A Review of Safeguards Arrangements for under-18s within the Prison Service Juvenile Estate* (84) acknowledges, it is more difficult to safeguard children in these situations.

The numbers of girls in adult prison establishments has increased and only recently has there been action to provide an appropriate regime comparable with that for boys. The aim to remove all girls aged under 17 from prisons by the end of 2003 was achieved but there is no target to remove under-18-year-olds from prison and the *Child Protection and Safeguards Review 2003* (84) refers to problems of placing them. There were then 100 young women in five establishments and in only one were they completely separated from other young offenders. The plan is to build five new separate units for them.

The Government should remove the UK reservation to Article 37 C of the UN Convention, which says 'Every child deprived of liberty shall be separated from adults unless it is considered in the child's best interest not to do so'.

The new arrangements for commissioning services by the YJB, additional resources and the new Prison Service Order, *Regimes for Prisoners under 18*, has resulted in great improvement. The Children's Rights Alliance for England said there had been 'great, in some cases near miraculous, improvements to Prison Service provision for boys aged 15–17 ' but added that some institutions had been so bad that 'even when improved they still fall short of adequate.' (*Rethinking Child Imprisonment*) (61). And, while there is now an appropriate regime, implementation at local level varies according to a range of factors such as resources, buildings, staff culture and management.

The Howard League for Penal Reform Case judgment (82) was that the Children Act does apply to children in YOIs (and other forms of custody), in the sense that the duties of local authorities are not changed except 'subject to the requirements of imprisonment'. This needs to be reflected in major improvements in the arrangements to safeguard and promote the welfare of children in custody and in more active involvement of local authorities and Local Safeguarding Children Boards.

Remands to prison are a serious problem. The provision in the Criminal Justice Act 1991 to end prison remands for under-17s has not been implemented and some 170 15–16-year-old boys are remanded to prison at any one time. The remand population turns over about 12 times in a year, so the number of boys remanded over the year is around 3000. Moreover, custodial remands and sentences were then only available for over 15-year-olds but have since been extended to 12-year-olds. 17-year-olds on remand in prison are treated as adults for the purposes of remand and bail, in contravention of the UN Convention on the Rights of the Child, and remand to prison is made irrespective of vulnerability. The recent introduction of a system for custody planning is welcome.

The main problems are:

- the numbers of children and young people being remanded to custody and given custodial sentences

- for boys the guidance on the regime is now appropriate but is not adequately implemented – problems of resources (economic and human), culture, attitudes, etc.

- for girls there been less progress in applying an appropriate regime and they are not adequately separated from adults and 18–21-year-olds

- remands in custody have been increasing for boys and girls and 17-year-olds are treated as adults

- the welfare and protection of children has not been a priority for prison establishments – although there are welcome signs that this is now changing though the implementation of PSO 4950 varies

- the health and educational needs of children in prison are inadequately dealt with.

Recommendations

16 The Home Office should undertake a fundamental review of the use and place of custody in society and what the alternatives are, in line with the UN Convention on the Rights of the Child that, i.e. detention of children should be a measure of last resort and for the shortest possible time and that they should be separated from adults – including young adults. It should consider how far existing legislation helps or hinders this.

17 Children in custodial units should have the same rights and access to universal services such as health and education as all other children.

18 It would be helpful if the YJB mounted a 'Quality Protects'-style programme for children and young people in custody with a view to improving the quality of service they receive and improving their life chances.

Other relevant recommendations

3 Safeguards need to be strengthened in private foster care, prisons and health settings. (DfES, DH and HO/Prison Service/YJB)

5 Strategic Health Authorities, Primary Care Trusts and other Health Trusts providing services for children should give priority to looked after children and

(Continued)

children in custody, particularly those with mental health and emotional problems.

6   Local authorities should provide support to young care leavers *and* other vulnerable young people who do not have parental support, including those leaving custody.

5.6 Health settings

What *People Like Us* said

Chapter 5 said health authorities and trusts need robust systems, rigorously enforced and monitored, to keep children safe in hospital, although few children spend long periods as in-patients. Most younger children were in paediatric units with adolescents being in psychiatric units. Child and Adolescent Mental Health Services may be an area of concern that needed robust systems to prevent undesirable people gaining access to children.

It had not been possible to find out the extent to which Section 85 of the Children Act was complied with. This requires health authorities and trusts to notify the relevant local authority when a child has been, or is likely to be, in hospital for three months or more. The local authority then has the duty to take reasonable steps to ensure the child's welfare is being properly safeguarded.

External scrutiny of hospitals' recruitment and selection procedures is important. Existing mechanisms for safeguarding children could be improved to ensure that the recommended checks are being done. This should be pursued with the NHS.

> **SSI should carry out an inspection to obtain information about the operation of Section 85 of the Children Act 1989, which requires health authorities to notify local authorities about a child who has been or is intended to be, in hospital for more than three months.**

Government response

• Thematic review to be carried out and need for further action considered when results available.

• SSI Wales have no plans for an inspection.

What happened

There was no SSI inspection, as this was not thought the most appropriate way of establishing health authority notification of children in hospital for more than three months.

A JRF-funded cross-border study in England and Scotland from October 2000 to December 2002, *Children with Complex Support Needs in Healthcare Settings for Prolonged Periods: Their numbers, characteristics and experiences* (41), found that large numbers of children had spent lengthy periods in hospital. Its main focus was disabled children, it included those aged 0–19 resident in health care settings for more than four weeks but excluded those whose primary diagnosis was psychiatric – as the numbers were very large and because their needs were likely to be very different from those with other conditions and impairments. It said that:

• Over 900 children and young people spent over six months in hospital – a third of these were there for 12 months or more.

• The largest diagnostic group for long-stay patients was 'mental and behavioural problems' (47 per cent) including learning disabilities and those in forensic institutions – 79 per cent were admitted as teenagers.

• At least a quarter admitted as children and young people were discharged as adults.

• In England a group of over 300 children and young people were discharged after an average stay of 10 years.

• It was worrying to find widespread uncertainty regarding the legal status of children who spend prolonged periods in health-care settings.

- There was general agreement that support was less than satisfactory in three areas. These were, first, children with complex support needs from ethnic minority communities, secondly, those at the transition stage between children's and adults services and thirdly, the whole area of consulting children.

The report had three main messages.

- Children's needs should always be treated as paramount.

- Children with impairments or serious medical conditions should receive exactly the same standards of care, treatment and protection as any others.

- Inappropriate and unnecessary admissions of children and young people to health-care or long-stay residential settings should be avoided at all costs, nor should children remain in health-care settings longer than is medically required.

It also drew attention to research evidence from the USA which indicates that more abuse takes place in hospitals than in family homes (Kendrick and Taylor, 2000). A 'culture of secrecy' within residential institutions means that this can go on undetected for years. Kendrick and Taylor identified three types of abuse which may affect children in hospitals – individual abuse (physical or sexual), programme abuse (poor care or treatment) and system abuse (wider failures of child health services to meet children's needs). It concluded there needed to be 'A holistic and integrated approach to the care and protection of children in hospital ... and the NHS must address the particular needs of children when setting care standards'.

The *NSF for Children: Standard for Hospital Services* (10) has a number of weaknesses.

- It includes a section on safeguarding children's welfare and an annex with the draft standard on child protection (from *Getting the Right Start: NSF for Children. Emerging Findings* (13)) but the annex is weak – for example it refers only to police checks and whistle-blowing in the bullet on recruiting and managing staff in a manner which safeguards children.

- The section on disabled children has no reference to their vulnerability to abuse.

- It describes the general duty of the local authority to promote and safeguard the welfare of children in their area but does not mention the hospital's duty to notify the local authority under Section 85 of Children Act 1989 if a child was in hospital for three months.

- It just says it covers 'links with' CAMHS but does not seem to apply to it directly.

The *Advisory Report Proposing Changes to Regulations and Minimum Standards* (19) covered a number of important safeguarding issues, including:

- children in hospices should have the same level of protection as elsewhere – e.g. child protection, statutory notifications and consultations with children/young people – current standards focus too much on clinical aspects

- all independent hospital regulations should be amended to ensure they meet 'welfare, rights and safety needs'.

The lack of safeguards for children in hospices is a major issue. These vulnerable children need the same level of protection. Only independent hospitals are regulated at the moment and they will be the responsibility of the new Commission for Health Care Improvement (CHAI) not the Commission for Social Care Improvement.

A draft report on *Disabled Children in Residential Placements*, which was discussed at an invited seminar in May 2003, said 'as it appears that Sections 85 and 86 are not widely implemented, there will be no overview of the welfare of children living away from home who are not looked after. Children with SEN statements should have their educational progress reviewed annually and residential schools are subject to more stringent inspection under the Care Standards Act. Despite these safeguards, there are enduring concerns about the welfare of disabled children placed in residential settings, especially those placed at some distance from home for up to 52 weeks a year where contact with family diminishes'.

The final version of the report (38), which was put on DH website in May 2004, did not include this. It summarised the situation as:

- current available data on admissions into health-care settings does not identify disabled children as a group for whom data is collected

- in the last three years 2,200 children have spent over six months in hospital

- the most common reason for admission of children that spend long periods in hospital is categorised as 'mental and behavioural disorders'

- 245 of these children apparently spent more than five years in hospital.

It said that children appear to spend long periods in hospital and there are concerns about protection.

> **Psychiatric units should ensure their systems are robust and prevent visits by undesirable people.**

Government response

- Forthcoming report by Health Advisory Service 2000 on in-patient mental health units in Wales to be considered.

Government action

- The report by the Health Advisory Service 2000 on units in Wales is incorporated into the CAMHS Strategy and Carlile Report (44) recommendations.

- Guidance published on protocols for welfare and protection of children visiting high security hospitals. *Directions Governing Visits by Children to Special Hospitals (Ashworth, Broadmoor and Rampton)* July 1999 (HSC 1999/160) (84) with linked guidance to local authorities (LAC(99) 23).

Analysis

The recommended work on health authority notification to local authorities of children in hospital for three months has not been carried out yet it appears from recent research (Kirsten Stalker *et al.* (41)) that significant numbers of children and young people *do* spend long periods in hospital.

Hospitals do not appear to be notifying local authorities about these children and this failure to comply with Section 85 of the Children Act 1989 means that there is no overview of the welfare of children living away from home who are not looked after. The failure to mention the duty of the hospital to notify the local authority under Section 85 of the Children Act 1989 if a child was in hospital for three months in the *Standard for Hospital Services* (10) is a major omission. How is the local authority to fulfil its duty if it has no knowledge of children who are in hospital for long periods of time? DH should ensure that hospitals comply with their duty under the Children Act to notify local authorities when a child is in hospital for three months. As Kirsten Stalker (41) recommended, the inspection and monitoring of children's wards should be improved, with the same expectation about rights and facilities accorded to looked after children.

Kirsten Stalker's research (41) covered disabled children aged 0–19 years living in health-care settings for more than four weeks but excluded those whose primary diagnosis was psychiatric because the numbers were very large. Therefore there is likely to be another group of children and young people in this category in health-care settings for significant periods. Research should be commissioned to establish the situation regarding this group of vulnerable children.

There should be the same care for the education and general life chances of children who spend long periods in hospital as for those living in other places away from home. Educational provision may need strengthening for those who spend some months in health settings. This also seems to be the case with transition to independent living and/or adult services.

We are unclear about the arrangements for safeguarding and protecting children in psychiatric units, although shortage of CAMHS in-patient provision leads to children and young people being admitted to adult provision. This is clearly unsuitable and should be brought to an end as soon as possible. The need for major improvements in CAMHS is discussed in Section 4.2 on health, education and transition to independent living and on right to treatment.

People Like Us (1) was concerned about whether CAMHS units had sufficiently robust systems to prevent undesirable people gaining access to children in them. Action has been taken in relation to visits by children to 'high secure hospitals' (formerly called 'special hospitals') (84) but this study has not found action to prevent visits to psychiatric units by undesirable people or of any action taken to protect children in psychiatric units.

The *Choosing with Care* (11) recommendations on recruitment and selection procedure checks for staff

dealing with children and young people in health-care settings have been implemented. The alert letter system for doctors and dentists was extended to nurses, midwives, health visitors and Professions Ancillary to Medicine (PAMs) in 2002. However, *Safeguarding Children* (4) said 'There were serious concerns about the arrangements to check health service staff who have unsupervised access to children'. In particular, paediatricians in post for many years and GPs had not had the necessary checks. *People Like Us* (1) recommended that health services ensure that recent guidance is followed for all staff and suggested some external scrutiny of hospitals' recruitment and selection procedures. This does not appear to have happened. This is very worrying, particularly given the number of staff, including agency staff, who may have access to children when they are in hospital.

The standard of protection for children and young people needs to be the same whatever setting they are in living away from home. It seems this is not true of all health settings – those in hospices, according to the NCSC, do not have the same level of protection, although they are certainly vulnerable children. The same standards and regulation should apply to children in all hospitals, not just independent ones. Where children spend significant periods in health settings the standards should cover their general welfare and protection and not be overly dominated by clinical matters.

The NSF draft standard on child protection is intended to apply to all settings but is weak in a number of respects.

This amounts to a catalogue of concerns about the situation of children in health settings. Safeguards seem less developed for health settings than elsewhere in a number of respects. This is disappointing as the significant policy developments to improve the quality of services for children and the safeguards for them since *People Like Us* (1) were largely led by DH. It seems that the health side of the department has been less focused on this than the social care side. This is a matter of some concern since responsibility for children in hospital and for CAMHS remains with DH rather than DfES.

Recommendations

19 DH should ensure that priority is given to safeguarding children in all health settings including hospices and CAMHS and other psychiatric units which admit children and young people and that the safeguards provided are consistent with arrangements in other settings where children live away from home.

(Continued)

20 DH should collect and analyse statistics on children in hospital for more than a month. It should fund research to identify the needs of these children, particularly those with a psychiatric diagnosis. This should include broader educational and welfare needs as well as child protection arrangements.

21 Children in health settings should, as elsewhere, be informed and consulted about decisions affecting their everyday lives and have access to independent advocacy and an accessible complaints procedure. (DH and health authorities)

6 Parents

What *People Like Us* said

Chapter 6 made three Principal Recommendations about parents, one on their duties and responsibilities and the other two on the information they need to help them fulfil these when their children are living away from home.

6.1 Parental rights and responsibilities

> **Principal Recommendation 9. Government should define parental rights and responsibilities in legislation.**

Government response

- *Rejected.* No intention to define parental rights and responsibilities in legislation.

- Home Secretary's Family Group to consider as part of work on family policy.

Government action

- The Government's principal statement on family policy – *Supporting Families* was published in 1998 by the Home Office.

- Task Force established and then a Ministerial Group on the Family (now the Active Communities and Family Issues Committee).

- National Family and Parenting Institute established (whose original sponsors included six Government departments).

- Plans for a sequel to *Supporting Families* were dropped, despite a Council of Europe recommendation calling for member states to produce 'coherent and integrated family policies'.

What happened

Two studies published in March 2003 confirmed the need for Government action to define parental rights and responsibilities.

The NSPCC *Review of Legislation Relating to Children in Family Proceedings Consultation Draft* (21) obtained responses to a questionnaire on the Children Act from a wide range of professionals. These suggested it would be helpful to clarify the role of parents and their rights and duties in permanency planning meetings, in reviews, in relation to their right to use Section 26 complaints procedures and in Adoption Panel meetings. It said 'A considerable number of local authority respondents feel there is still too much emphasis on parental rights, rather than responsibility'.

The National Family and Parenting Institute published a study by Clem Henricson, *Government and Parenting: Is there a case for a parents' code?* (86). The study demonstrated 'a deficit in clear messages and commonly recognised obligations and entitlements … of parenthood and highlighted that the Government had given high priority to parenting in its social cohesion and criminal justice agendas but pointed to ambiguities in other policy areas. It argued for a regular policy review and a national debate on whether there should be an official statement of parents' rights and responsibilities. This could be in legislation or outside it – as guidance or as information about the current position'. A Code would be helpful to parents and the agencies working with them and should aim to provide clarity and 'transparency about the sorts of issues that will be taken into consideration in depriving a parent of their social parenting responsibilities; have potential for enhancing the social significance of parenting and deal with parents rights – though the interests of the child would ultimately remain paramount'.

At the launch seminar for *Government and Parenting* (86) in March 2003 Beverley Hughes, then Minister of State at the Home Office, announced that the Home Secretary had agreed to a wide-ranging review of family policy across Government. The possibility of a code would be considered as part of it.

Analysis

The need for action to define parental rights and responsibilities has been affirmed by subsequent work since the *People Like Us* (1) recommendation was rejected. It is good that the Government has now agreed to a wide-ranging review of family policy.

6.2 Information for parents and others

> **Principal Recommendation 10. All organisations caring for children away from home should provide parents with all relevant information about their arrangements for safeguarding children before a placement is made.**

> **Principal Recommendation 11. Government should sponsor a programme to inform parents and relevant staff of the risks to the welfare of children living away from home and ways of reducing them.**

Government response
- Detailed implementation plans will be developed in time for an information campaign at the beginning of 1999.

- DfEE are working to encourage independent schools and ISIS to include information on welfare arrangements in their brochures.

Government action
- Standards 1, 2 and 3 of the National Minimum Standards for Boarding Schools require schools to do this – making a statement of their boarding principles and practice (including welfare and support arrangements) available to parents, boarders and staff.

- The Independent Schools Council's Information Service (ISCIS) guide to parents choosing an independent school was amended to include a section on safeguards in 2000.

What happened
In relation to schools, DfES said that the Government already sponsors and supports the Boarding Schools' Association's Professional Development and Publications Programme, which includes advice to parents on supporting their children as boarders. There are two DfES-sponsored publications *Choosing a Boarding School* (78) and *Parenting the Boarder* (87). The National Assembly for Wales said the National Minimum Standards will require schools to publish information for parents and children on their purpose, standards of care and safeguards for children.

In response to the Victoria Climbie enquiry (16), in May 2003, six Government departments issued a booklet *What to do if you are worried a child is being abused* (12) addressed to people working directly with children and families. It explains their role in safeguarding children.

However, there seems to have been no central public information campaign to tell the parents of children living away from home, or parents generally, about the risks to the welfare of children and what can be done to reduce them. The campaigns warning them of the dangers of internet use are much more specific.

Individual organisations have taken some action about the need for information – for example Kidscape has produced publications for the carers of young children, supported by Sure Start and the Home Office and a leaflet *Protecting children from paedophiles. Advice and information for parents*, sponsored by Marks and Spencer. And NSPCC produce a range of leaflets for parents and children.

The *Stop it Now! Together We Can Prevent Child Sexual Abuse* project, supported by an alliance of organisations – Barnardo's, ChildLine, the Lucy

Faithfull Foundation, NCH, NOTA, NSPCC and West Midlands Police, with representatives of government and statutory agencies, was launched in September 2002. It is based on local campaigns and aims to increase knowledge of child abuse and its signs and to work with abusers and their families to change behaviour. There is a national helpline for those who are abusing/fear they might abuse and for others who suspect abuse. This is based on a public health education model with emphasis on education and early intervention. Leaflets include 'Child's Play?' – with advice to parents and others on how to recognise signs that a child is being abused and when a child is abusing others and encourage them to take early action – and 'What we all need to know to protect our children'.

The NCSC and NCB are producing children's, parents' and staff guides to the minimum standards for children's homes. NCB will publish these but people will need to pay for them. Copies will also be on the Children's Rights Director's website.

In the meantime, others have called for information for parents and children – the Committee on the Rights of the Child, 2002, recommendation 38d) (50) was 'to carry out large scale public education campaigns and programmes (including through schools) on reducing child death and child abuse with information on the role of statutory and other services in protecting children'.

NCH's ten-point plan for radical reform in *Protecting Children from Risk: NCH's View* (88) has this as point 4: that the Government should tell the public what they need to know about child protection and clarify their rights and responsibilities in this respect. It should take proactive steps to inform parents about the real risks to their children and what they can do to help minimise them ... in partnership with children's and family's organisations. There should be an ongoing, high profile public education campaign aimed at parents and families, which should action the following.

- Acknowledge that abuse is perpetrated most often by men and a significant amount (probably a third) by young people under 18, but abuse by women is probably under-reported so may be more prevalent than we yet know.

- Explain the correlation between domestic violence and child abuse – domestic violence is the biggest predictor of child abuse that we currently know.

- Explain that it is futile to worry unduly about where a convicted child abuser is living, as for every one of these there may be dozens who are unconvicted and unknown to any agency, who may exploit our lack of vigilance if we allow them to. A key challenge is to ensure these people can't succeed.

- Admit that child abuse can never be eliminated entirely and say 'police checks' are necessary but never sufficient for the effective safeguarding of children.

- Be based on the understanding that a central part of child protection is giving children the information and confidence they need to help protect themselves, without frightening them: parents should be given guidance on how they can equip their children in this way.

Multi-agency Public Protection Panels (MAPPPs) have been introduced to monitor sex offenders in their area, assess risk levels and advise communities on how they can protect their children. The NSPCC think panels should make information more readily available to the public. 'MAPPPs must now be vigorous in bringing their reports to the attention of the public, so that they know how to recognise and report suspicious activity and know who to contact to voice their concerns' (*Children's Friend*, November 2002).

Analysis

Action has been taken to increase the information and guidance available to people working with children and families – e.g. the recent leaflet *'What to do if you are worried a child is being abused'* (12) – and this needs to be continually reinforced through training.

There have been a number of useful leaflets produced by organisations such as Kidscape, NCPCC and the Stop it Now! Campaign but much still needs to be done to increase public awareness of the risks to children. Little seems to have been done centrally to tell parents about the risks to children when they are away from home, what measures they should expect to be put in place and the questions they might ask about these.

There does now seem to be more general awareness of sexual abuse issues – although this is still focused too much on stranger abuse rather than abuse by those who are trusted or within families. However, the awareness of what can be done to minimise risks is limited. There has been too much concentration on police checks and too little on other measures that can and should be taken. Police checks are very important but by no means sufficient in themselves, particularly given the low rate of convictions for sexual offences against children. Parents should know what other procedures are followed in order to protect their children, such as the other checks recommended in *Choosing with Care* (11). They should have a good understanding about the safeguarding arrangements and be encouraged to ask questions. It would be helpful if the Government funded information programmes for parents to inform them of the risks to children and the range of measures that can be taken to safeguard them to enable them to ask the right questions of organisations responsible for settings in which their children may live away from home. These would need to be repeated regularly.

There are now more sources of information for young people – such as young people's centres and NSPCC's 'There4me' website – a virtual young people's centre. And there is evidence that young people are now making use of these sources. Before *People Like Us* (1) most NSPCC referrals were from adults but contacts by children and young people have been increasing. They now account for about a quarter of contacts. The willingness of young people to obtain information and help at an earlier stage must be encouraged and more information and ready sources of guidance should be provided for all ages of children and young people so that they can recognise abusive behaviour and know where to go for help.

The production of children's, parents' and staff guides to National Minimum Standards, being produced by NCSC and NCB is welcome but it is unfortunate that people will have to pay for them.

7 Abuse and abusers

What *People Like Us* said

Chapter 9 discussed the threat from persistent sexual abusers and measures to deter them. It considered child pornography, child prostitution and bullying.

Persistent sexual abusers are the scourge of childhood. Their numbers are difficult to estimate. Each one who adopts a lifetime career will amass hundreds of victims, some of whom will become abusers. They are largely, but not exclusively, men. They establish themselves as trusted friends, colleagues or employees. Exposure may be a matter of chance, often after many years of abuse. They seek out situations in which their preferred kind of children are accessible. Children living away from home are vulnerable, some exceptionally so. Some settings are particularly vulnerable to abusers, as staff or volunteers.

Programmes for sex offenders are impressive, but too much should not be expected of treatment. Sexual abuse of children is highly addictive but control, containment and coping can be enhanced. Treatment may reduce the number of children assaulted.

Child pornography involves the serious abuse of children. Its strong link with paedophiles means detection is important to prevent further abuse and provide useful information on abusers and their networks.

Child prostitution should be treated as a child protection issue.

The term 'bullying' is often used to describe activities that are more sinister than this description suggests. It covers physical violence, racial and sexual harassment, sexual exploitation, using threats to obtain money or property, and psychological torture. It is extremely destructive and one of the main problems that worry children. It needs to be tackled in all institutional contexts.

7.1 Abusers

> An inter-departmental review of treatment (of persistent sexual abusers) to develop proposals for its co-operation and development is recommended. It is important that it covers adolescent abusers.

Government response
- More needs to be done.

- Home Office and DH taking forward recommendation by HM Inspector of Probation that youth justice services should include treatment to ensure sexual offending by adolescents is properly addressed through assessment, intervention and relapse prevention services.

- Probation Service delivering many programmes to sex offenders under their supervision.

- Home Office and Prison Service evaluating outcomes of sex offender treatment programmes and will decide on further action.

Government action
- Review of residential treatment for sex offenders by the National Probation Service announced in July 2002 (on the day the Wolvercote Clinic closed).

What happened

Donald Findlater, Deputy Director, Lucy Faithfull Foundation (LFF) (July 2003) said the closure of the Wolvercote Clinic in July 2002, after 7 years, illustrated the fear and misinformation about the problem of sexual abuse, abusers and their management within communities. The Wolvercote Clinic operated a four-week residential assessment and a year-long treatment programme, more intensive than any other in the UK. It accepted men assessed as high risk or high deviance. Out of 305 men assessed and treated, the clinic is aware of only a handful who have been reconvicted of subsequent sex offences.

The National Probation Service is the main provider of community programmes. There are three accredited sex offender treatment programmes with each probation area running one of them. Twenty-seven prisons have sex offender treatment programmes. A few health services run programmes as does the NSPCC, with the probation service.

However, the need is far greater than the provision. There are about 4,500 sex offenders in prison and a target of 900 places on sex offender programmes.

Sheila Brotherston reported that LFF had developed a pilot programme run for women at HMP Styal in collaboration with seconded probation staff. The pressure on resources is such that the group work programme no longer runs – it was difficult to have enough time for the whole programme. This was more a problem of resources, the logistics could be managed if running the programme was a priority within the female estate. Women who needed treatment were scattered throughout the prison system.

The Female Outreach Service funded by the National Probation Directorate and provided by LFF provides access to assessment and intervention for female sex offenders supervised by the Probation Service in the community. The project also works with women serving sentences for sexual offences. The work of the project is based on the group programme piloted at HMP Styal but is delivered as individual work. The assessment and intervention processes are supported by the use of psychometrics developed by Richard Beckett, Consultant Clinical Forensic Psychologist.

LFF have also collaborated with the AIM Project in Greater Manchester in researching the prevalence of young women who come to the attention of statutory agencies in the Greater Manchester area as a consequence of their sexually

harmful behaviour. The initial findings of this study indicate that the needs of these girls and young women are frequently overlooked.

Working Together (69), says that young abusers are likely to be children in need and may need protection but should also be held responsible for abusive behaviour. There should be a co-ordinated approach by relevant agencies in which dual assessments are carried out which address not only the criminal activity but also the protection needs of the child.

The first 'Stop it Now! UK & Ireland' project, launched in Surrey in September 2002, provides a preventative approach to child sexual abuse through providing information and advice aimed at people who abuse, people who are at risk of abuse and family and friends of abusers, motivating them to seek help. Key messages have been developed for abusers and potential abusers, for friends and family of abusers and for parents or carers of young people with sexually worrying behaviour. These groups represent more than 80 per cent of over 1000 calls to the helpline in less than two years.

At the Stop it Now! conference in March 2003, Hilary Eldridge, Director of the Lucy Faithfull Foundation, quoted Lucy Faithfull – 'Changing offenders is the best way of protecting children'. She said we can be proud of the programmes for convicted adult male offenders in this country, but provision is patchy for young people and women and for all abusers who fall outside the criminal justice system. There is clear evidence that appropriate treatment based on good assessment does reduce re-offending but it is available only to a fraction of abusers. What is missing is a service for the majority and a more sensitive way of accessing services for perpetrators and for all those affected by abuse. We need services for young people and adults who are at the early stages of offending to prevent abusive behaviours developing. For children and young people who abuse the need is far greater than the provision. An inter-agency approach is vital to ensure clear routes for referral through assessment and treatment to move on. Children and young people should be assessed *both* as an abuser and as someone with his/her own child protection needs. Under-18s commit a third of offences against children. Often abuse is by an older sibling.

In '*I think I might need some more help with this problem …'. Responding to children and young people who display sexually harmful behaviour* (89) Elizabeth Lovell says 'Research suggests that juveniles commit at least a quarter of all sexual offences, therefore any effort to lower the level of child sexual abuse must address the problem of children and young people who display sexually harmful behaviour ... While there has been some progress over the last ten years, the lack of a joined-up, strategic approach by government has resulted in poor co-ordination and inadequate service provision'. Detailed recommendations for action are made.

In an article in *Community Care* 17–23 October 2002, Elizabeth Lovell says the following.

- The Criminal Justice and Public Order Act 1994, the Sex Offenders Act 1997 and the Crime and Disorder Act 1998 have resulted in a move away from a child welfare approach to a criminal justice approach.

- DH and HO have issued limited guidance but from different starting points and DfES has issued no national guidance for schools and teachers.

- Funding is not co-ordinated across departments ... there has been no agreed overall approach. As a result there is an inconsistent response to children and young people at the local level, with different systems and policies operating in different areas.

- A coherent response to lower the level of child sexual abuse and to help stop these children developing their behaviour into adulthood is needed.

In 2003 John Rea Price, HMIP, said there were no accredited sex offender treatment programmes in the under-18 prison estate. Units such as Carlford at Warren Hill were trialling approaches, but almost without exception young people have to wait until they are transferred into the 18–21 estate to go on programmes such as that provided at Swinfen Hall. The LFF is currently piloting an assessment and intervention service for young people between the ages of 15 and 21 convicted of sexual offences whose needs fall outside existing provision.

In May 2004 LFF reported that there were two programmes in the 18–21 estate at Young Offender Institutions Swinfen Hall and Aylesbury. The piloting of an assessment and intervention service for young people between the ages of 15 and 18 years within the Juvenile Estate was being funded by the Youth Justice Board until March 2005.

The LFF has also been funded by the Public Protection Unit within the National Probation Directorate to provide a national outreach service for young people between the ages of 18 and 21 convicted of sexual offences whose needs remain unmet.

The LFF is also delivering an assessment and treatment intervention at the Carlford Unit for nine/ten boys convicted of sex offences. From April 2004, LFF began supporting staff at Wetherby to provide assessments for up to ten boys, mostly from the local catchment area and started providing psychology and probation staff at YOI Castington, including staff from the Oswald Unit, with consultancy and training. This work is being funded by the YJB who have allocated £400,000 for this work in 2004–05.

The Home Office Juvenile Offenders Group and the YJB set up a cross-Departmental Working Group, with DH and DfES, in response to a recommendation in the 2001 report on Dominic McKilligan,[1] that the Government should develop a national strategy for young people who sexually abuse. It has been looking at how outcomes for young people who sexually abuse can be improved. The aim is to develop tools to identify high risk recidivists early on and provide targeted interventions to reduce the risk of further sexual and violent offending. They are also looking to develop prevention services for young people who start to display sexually harmful behaviour, before they offend. A consultation event with key practitioners took place in October 2003 which helped to identify priorities for research and service development. The Juvenile Group within the Prison Service, Young Offenders Unit and YJB are working on the development of treatment services for young offenders in custody and aim to roll out a pilot from March 2005.

More recently an Inter-Departmental Ministerial Group has been established and will promote and co-ordinate cross-Government action to tackle sex offending.

Analysis

Lack of available treatment for sex offenders against children is a major issue.

It is encouraging that action is now being taken to address the problem of young people who sexually abuse others. However, given the scale of the problem of sexual abuse of children, treatment arrangements/provision seem unlikely to be anywhere near sufficient. Significant increases in treatment programmes are needed for:

- adult male offenders against children, including for those found guilty in relation to child abuse images

- adult female offenders

- children and young people of both sexes.

Donald Findlater, LFF, says that, while the majority of child sexual abuse is committed by adult males, as much as one-third is committed by other children and young people and between 5 and 20 per cent by adult females. There is an urgent need for identification and intervention with these categories of offenders.

There is clearly a long way to go before the problem of young abusers is properly addressed. It is vital that treatment of young offenders starts at a very early stage to prevent them entering on a career of abuse in which possibly hundreds of other children may be abused – some of whom may then go on to become abusers themselves. They may often need treatment facilities separate from other children, and help and some degree of supervision into adulthood. All staff working with children and foster carers should receive training to help them recognise warning signs that a child or young person may be being abused or abusing others.

There is little research in the UK into re-offending or re-conviction rates of young people who abuse following treatment this should be rectified.

Specialist fostering schemes for young people with sexually harmful behaviours, such as Barnardo's Genesis Service in the northeast, demonstrate good practice and should be further developed.

The YJB/Prison Service should give priority to introducing treatment programmes for young sex offenders in YOIs so treatment can start as soon as the young person is admitted to custody. There should be arrangements for continued supervision and treatment in the community after release.

There should be considerably more help and treatment for those who have been abused. This is necessary both in its own right and to help reduce

---

1 A young person who sexually abused and killed a child.

the likelihood of some of them going on to abuse others. The NHS should provide or arrange services for those who have been abused. These need to be available when the individual is ready.

Help and counselling should be available for those who recognise they are at risk of offending. Consideration also needs to be given to how to deal with those who are offenders who may be prepared to accept help but who have not been convicted. Stop It Now! provides a useful model for engagement with such individuals and other adults in their lives with the clear aim of preventing future abuse.

The issue of abusers is discussed in more detail in our companion report *Safeguard for Vulnerable Children*.

Recommendations

22 The Government should fund a major expansion of treatment for those who abuse children – men, women and young abusers. Priority should be given to providing early treatment for both male and female young abusers. (Home Office and DH)

23 The Government should fund a national expansion of preventative schemes, on the lines of Stop it Now!, to provide information and advice for all adults, but especially for those who are abusing children, or fear that they may, and for those who suspect others may be abusing or being abused. (Home Office to take lead responsibility)

7.2 Child abuse images (child pornography)

There is some recognition of the importance of discovering pornography and pursuing the leads that it provides but resources allocated to this are relatively small. The police and HM Customs and Excise should dedicate more resources to this and build up their expertise so more pornographers are identified and prosecuted and more of their customers are identified and put on centrally held lists of paedophile suspects.

There should be a ban on the export of child pornography as well as its import; the Customs Consolidation Act should be amended to cover 'signals' so that the internet is covered.

Government response

- High priority given to this.

- HM Customs and Excise (HM C&E) set up network of Paedophile Intelligence Liaison Officers and a National Intelligence Co-ordinator appointed in 1997.

- Deployment of police resources a matter for individual Chief Officers of Police. Combating child pornography, particularly via internet, a challenge.

- Strategic implications for law enforcement of internet-related crime under consideration.

- Options for legislation on export being considered.

- Legal advice that 'signals' cannot be covered by the Customs Consolidation Act, other means to cover internet being considered.

Government action

- DfES published 'Superhighway Safety Guidance', 1999.

- Under the Criminal Justice and Court Services Act 2000 maximum penalties for taking and possessing indecent photographs of children were increased from January 2001 – the former from three years to ten years imprisonment; the latter from six months to five years.

- £25 million over three years from April 2001 for policing 'high tech' crime.

- Regulation of Investigatory Powers Act 2000 helps with investigation of child pornographers who misuse the internet, e.g. by requiring them to give passwords to data stored on computer.

- Support for the Internet Watch foundation and the development of its hotline for reporting child pornography.

- Importation included in offences entailing registration under the Sex Offender Act 1997 and added to schedule of Serious Arrestable Offences in Police and Criminal Evidence Act 1984 through the Criminal Justice and Police Act 2001.

- Established a Task Force on Child Protection on the Internet, March 2001.

- £1.5 million public awareness campaign between December 2001 and Spring 2002 and in January 2003.

- *Working Together* (69) deals with pornography and the internet.

What happened

Export prohibition is now considered unlikely: domestic legislation already prohibits possession; an export ban would be vulnerable to challenge from other EU Member States with less stringent criteria. Possession can be prosecuted under the Criminal Justice Act and intent to distribute under the Protection of Children Act 1978.

HM Customs and Excise have used intelligence for enforcement work in close co-operation with other agencies. Its focus is on identifying persons who are charged, summonsed or accept a police caution for offences which would render them liable on conviction to register under the Sex Offender Act 1997. Action on child pornography is no longer (2003) a priority in the HM C&E Service Delivery Agreement on which a target is guaranteed to ministers – but detection is still a departmental objective. The onus has now shifted to the police to follow up information provided by HMC&E. An operational protocol formalising the primacy of the police in investigation of material, detected at import, that might indicate a risk of child abuse was introduced on 1 April 2003 and reviewed in September 2003.

Due to changes in digital technology, its accessibility and relative inexpensiveness, a big shift has occurred since *People Like Us* (1) from paper and video tape almost entirely to web-based images and video; images are shared internationally to a greater extent than previously imagined. Postal material is now reduced – to mainly 'collectors' of material.

The Home Office says recent police operations show resources are being allocated to the problem and even technically sophisticated paedophiles are being investigated and prosecuted. However, these investigations can be resource intensive; many suspects have amassed large volumes of material, which need to be analysed for intelligence on victims and other suspects, in parallel with ensuring the safety of any children at immediate direct risk from the suspect.

Allocation of operational resources is a matter for individual Chief Constables, but they are supported centrally by the National Crime Squad (including the National High Tech Crime Unit) and the National Criminal Intelligence Service. In addition, the Association of Chief Police Officers (ACPO) have developed a revised strategy for tackling child abuse online.

The name of a paedophile, convicted of a possession or distribution offence, is automatically added to the sex offenders register.

The *National Plan for Safeguarding Children from Commercial Sexual Exploitation* (63) said 'The Internet has become a significant tool in the distribution of child pornography'. Other dangers to children are chat rooms and 'grooming'. New laws on internet chat room grooming and other online activities related to child safety and on child abuse images are included in the Sexual Offences Act 2003 which came into force in May 2004.

Operation Ore was launched to deal with people in the UK who had paid for pictures of child abuse on US websites. Some 7,000 individuals were involved, including teachers, police officers and other professionals. In all, 95 per cent of those identified were previously unknown to police. The length of time taken to deal with these people illustrates that resources for this important area of work are grossly inadequate.

In December 2003 the LFF called for an alternative approach for selected cases on the undertaking that they surrender their computer hard drives, undergo a comprehensive risk assessment and participate in appropriate therapeutic intervention to manage and reduce their risk of both harming children and of viewing further child pornography. A police caution and the full sharing of information within child and public protection agencies were crucial components of the approach, which also speculated on the possibility of the offender contributing towards the costs of his assessment and treatment as well as the cost of educative work with immediate family members. The intention is to speed up the process and reduce the risk that more children will be harmed.

At the Stop it Now! conference in March 2003, Carole Howlett, Deputy Assistant Commissioner of the Metropolitan Police, said Operation Ore had been 'a wake-up call' for the police and a National Law Enforcement Strategy was being created consisting of:

- a national Strategic Experts Group

- a national tasking and co-ordinating group – for risk assessment and prioritisation

- a national practitioners group – learning about best practice, evaluating software and training needs.

In *Child Abuse, Child Pornography and the Internet* (89) John Carr concludes that 'the arrival of the Internet almost certainly has led to an increase in sexual offending against children and to the exposure of children to a range of other undesirable influences which are abusive in character or may become so'. He refers to *People Like Us* (1) on its use to 'normalise' behaviour. There is no hard data on the scale of problem but there has been an enormous expansion since *People Like Us* (1). The Report also warns of the dangers of new mobile phone technology which will 'bring the internet to the streets'. This will facilitate the distribution of abusive images of children and make it even more difficult to trace.

In October 2003, the *Independent* reported an NSPCC research report which found more than 20,000 images of child pornography were posted on the internet every week. Distributing these was a 'commercial, globalised cottage industry'. Monitoring the internet for six weeks found 14,000 images. Twenty children were estimated to have been abused for the first time and 1,000 images of each child created. Another study in the review found younger children being abused. In recent pictures about half were between 9 and 12 and the rest are younger. The number of boys is increasing.

Just one click (91) said the number of children online had increased dramatically in the past three years with the biggest increase in the UK. It made a number of recommendations for action which should form a national strategy involving all those organisations, both statutory and voluntary, charged with safeguarding children as well as internet service and mobile phone providers.

Analysis

People Like Us (1) raised concerns about the use of the internet in the serious abuse of children and urged more resources be devoted to its detection. Since 1998 the use of the internet to acquire and spread abusive images of children has emerged as a major problem – on a scale unsuspected hitherto. This major and increasing problem affects all children whether living at home or away from home. And the internet is now also used for grooming and meeting children. This is a new phenomenon since *People Like Us* (1) was published. Developments in mobile phone technology pose another serious new threat.

Experts believe that accessing child abuse images is likely to lead to an increase in child abuse, partly through feeding and developing a sexual interest in children and partly through the sharing of views and information with like-minded individuals across the world which may reinforce and encourage the behaviour. It may well encourage those who have not previously actually abused a child to do so. The prospect of financial gain from creating and selling the images will draw in others, including criminal networks. Operation Ore showed the extent of the profit to be made from just one website. A proportion of those who are abused as a result may well go on to abuse others. This very serious threat needs to be tackled urgently.

Grooming via the internet is also a serious issue which needs to be addressed by all concerned. Creating a new offence to cover this is very welcome. Information is needed for children and parents. It is vital that children living away from parental supervision are also protected. Foster carers, staff in children's homes and residential and independent schools need to be aware of the risks and how they can be reduced. Government information campaigns and training should provide staff responsible for children living away from home as well as parents with information

about the dangers of the internet and how they can be reduced.

7.3 Child prostitution

Child prostitution should be dealt with as a child protection issue, and there should be a review of the legislation to ensure … adequate means of deterring and punishing those who exploit young people in this way.

All agencies should work together to ensure that there is a coherent policy for dealing with child prostitution from a child protection perspective. Area Child Protection Committees should take an active interest in (child prostitution) in their area and social services should ensure that … staff [are] trained in how to deal with child prostitution. Those dealing with child prostitution on police forces should know about child protection, or work closely with those who do.

Government response
- Area Child Protection Committees (ACPCs) to be encouraged to develop protocols in new *Working Together* guidance.
- Home Office/DH preparing new guidance to police and social services on how to deal with children in prostitution.
- Law relating to sexual offences to be reviewed, including the offences and penalties that apply to those who exploit child prostitutes.

Government action
- *Working Together* (69) deals with children involved in prostitution.
- *Safeguarding Children in Prostitution – Supplementary Guidance to Working Together to*

Safeguard Children (92) – guidance for agencies working with children.

- *National Plan for Safeguarding Children from Commercial Sexual Exploitation* (63), September 2001.

- The Children Bill which will reform children's services as set out in the *Every Child Matters* (7) Green Paper (introduced to Parliament February 2004).

What happened

Child protection and agencies working together

The key message of these documents is that those under 18 who engage in prostitution are almost invariably victims and must be treated as such. Another key message is that wherever possible those who abuse children through prostitution or seek to exploit them as prostitutes should be dealt with under the criminal justice system.

The purpose of *Safeguarding Children Involved in Prostitution* (92) was to get all agencies and professionals to work together in recognising the problem; treat the child involved primarily as a victim of abuse; safeguard children and promote their welfare; work together to prevent abuse and provide children with opportunities and strategies to exit from prostitution; investigate and prosecute those who coerce, exploit and abuse children through prostitution.

The *National Plan for Safeguarding Children from Commercial Sexual Exploitation* (63) was prepared by a Steering Group of representatives from Government, relevant professional organisations and a representative group of voluntary organisations in the UK. The plan is to be 'reviewed annually and updated regularly'. The first key area for future action is to ensure that *Safeguarding Children Involved in Prostitution – Supplementary Guidance to Working Together to Safeguard Children* (92) is properly implemented. DH commissioned a study of this in June 2001. The second priority area

for action is to raise awareness about safe use of the internet. The Government announced a Task Force on Child Protection on the Internet in March 2001 – to report on progress to Home Secretary in summer 2001. It lists key areas for review including children in the public care and children who go missing but not very young children or disabled children. Other areas include 'increasing knowledge of the profile and offending patterns of adults involved in the sexual exploitation of children and identifying what types of intervention are effective'.

The report of the review of *Safeguarding Children Involved in Prostitution* (92) was published on DH ACPC website in June 2002. It is quite hard-hitting and contains vital information for ACPCs, many of which are still grappling with how best to safeguard children involved in prostitution. Findings include:

- 90 per cent of ACPCs in England now have protocols for dealing with children involved in prostitution

- 76 per cent of all ACPCs in England reported children involved in prostitution in their areas

- 5 per cent of ACPCs simply do not know whether or not children are involved in prostitution in their areas.

The report contains examples of good practice and lots of networking opportunities. It records some of the problems encountered in implementing the guidance. It is careful to acknowledge that the guidance is still new.

Safeguarding Children (4) said 'Very few areas had investigated the extent of sexual exploitation of children and young people, and many agencies denied that child prostitution was a problem in their areas. This was a denial of a serious issue that ACPCs in most areas needed to address'.

State of Children's Rights in England (60) welcomed the 2001 National Plan for safeguarding children from sexual exploitation but was concerned that trafficking for sexual exploitation or other exploitation is still a problem and that children who are sexually exploited are still criminalised by law.

It's someone taking a part of you. A study of young women and sexual exploitation (51) says that, following the 2000 DH guidelines on children involved in prostitution, police data on young people convicted of offences related to prostitution have dropped. However, estimates from project work suggests that up to 5,000 young people are involved in prostitution in the UK at any one time. A key theme is 'the need for a focused inter-agency strategy on supporting young people vulnerable to entry to sexual exploitation and prostitution'. This includes the need for:

- a common, shared, understanding of what constitutes sexual exploitation so that consistent data on prevalence can be collected

- fast-track, targeted work to support young people at the start of their runaway 'careers'

- co-ordinated inter-agency work on overlapping causes and effects between drug and alcohol misuse and vulnerability to exploitation

- an expansion of the scope of current legislation to protect young people from abuse and to press charges against those abusing them.

The British Asssociation for Adoption and Fostering says foster carers also need training on this problem, but often do not have access to it.

Her Majesty's Inspectorate of Prisons has been concerned at the lack of interest in ACPCs in prison establishments. Child protection procedures to cover disclosures, which can be made at any age, should actually exist for prison establishments, particularly in the female estate.

In December 2000 the Home Office awarded £850,000 from the Crime Reduction Programme (CRP) to 11 multi-agency projects (the CRP projects) to assess what works in reducing the number of young people and women involved in prostitution, reducing crime and disorder associated with street-based prostitution and to find out which interventions helped women to exit prostitution.

Through the Children Bill the Government plans to require local authorities to establish Local Safeguarding Children Boards (LSCBs). The overall objective of LSCBs, which will replace the ACPCs, will be to co-ordinate the work of key local agencies in relation to safeguarding children. It is likely that their functions will be wider than those of ACPCs, including a greater focus on safeguarding and the prevention of harm more generally and a responsibility for strategic planning in relation to safeguarding children. LSCBs will need to ensure that there are mechanisms in place for addressing the needs of vulnerable children in their local area, including those involved in prostitution.

On the reform in the law

Government action

The consultation document *Setting the Boundaries: Reforming the Law on Sex Offences* (93), issued in July 2000, recommended new offences to tackle the problem of pimping. Separate offences would cover the exploitation of children and adults to set an unambiguous standard that sexual exploitation of children is wrong.

Protecting the Public (15) set out proposals to reform sexual offences and set out the Government's commitment to carrying out a separate review of prostitution. This review would consider amending the law so that children abused through prostitution are not criminalised.

The Sexual Offences Act 2003 introduced new offences which will protect all children up to the age of 18 from prostitution and pornography. The new offence of paying for sex with a child will for the first time criminalise the buyer specifically in an attempt to tackle demand.

The new offences include:

- paying for the sexual services of a child – carrying a maximum penalty of life when under 13, 14 years when aged 13–15, and 7 years when aged 16 or 17

- causing or inciting a child into prostitution or pornography; arranging or facilitating child prostitution or pornography; and controlling a child prostitute or a child involved in pornography – all carrying a maximum penalty of 14 years.

What happened

The Report of the State of Children's Rights in England (60) said 'children sexually exploited are still criminalized by law' and recommended a study on the scope, causes and background of child prostitution be carried out; legislation should be reviewed not to criminalise children who are sexually exploited and adequate resources (human and financial) be allocated to policies and programmes in this area.

It's someone taking a part of you. A study of young women and sexual exploitation (51) described the difficulty in prosecuting those who exploit young people without putting them at risk while the case is being investigated. Without the young women being able or prepared to collaborate in providing evidence and pressing charges, it has been difficult for cases against abusers to be made. It refers to some attempts in the Netherlands to address these problems – where prosecution of the abuser does not have to rely on a complaint being made by the young persons themselves. The Dutch legislation says minors (under 18 years) cannot be criminalised for offences relating to prostitution and abolishes the 'complaint requirement' for sexual acts involving children under 16. It is hoped this will enable child prostitution and sex tourism to be tackled more effectively. The study welcomes the proposals in *Protecting the Public* (15) for specific offences relating to sexual exploitation of children but says 'While this

is welcomed and encouraged, the question of how credible evidence is gathered to bring a case against an alleged offender, without placing the child at further risk, remains in need of consideration'..

Tink Palmer, Principal Policy and Practice Officer (Child Sexual Exploitation) (Barnardo's), March 2004 confirmed that, to date, young women under 16 years of age can still be prosecuted under the Street Offences Act 1959 and, if found guilty of soliciting, can still be termed common prostitutes and have their names placed on the sex offenders register. However, the Home Secretary will be publishing a Consultation Document on Prostitution and it is hoped that this anomaly will be rectified. Proactive policing was needed but this would not happen when child protection was not included in the four priorities in the National Policing Plan (2003–2006). (The Met, for example had included it as a fifth priority). Her book *Just one Click* (91) recommended that child protection should be a UK national policing priority. Resources were needed.

Analysis

It has been accepted that abuse of children through prostitution is a child protection issue and guidance reflects this. The recent changes in the law on sexual offences in relation to the commercial exploitation of the child are welcome and it is hoped these will be fully and effectively implemented.

However, the Review was also concerned about the way children involved in prostitution were treated as the law does not distinguish according to age and children are still criminalised. It is regretted that the Government has not yet amended the existing law so that child prostitution is not dealt with as a criminal offence for the child, but encouraging that it seems now to have plans to do so.

While there has been some very useful policy work in this area over the past few years and some progress in integrating services on the ground, there still seems to be a worrying level of denial and/or ignorance about the scale and nature of the problem at the local level. This needs to be addressed. It can be very difficult to extract a child from prostitution once they have been drawn in and preventative strategies are needed as well as programmes to work with those who are involved. Local Safeguarding Children Boards will need to ensure that there are mechanisms in place for addressing the needs of vulnerable children in their local area, including those being abused through prostitution.

Recommendation

24 Local authorities all need to have active prevention and rescue strategies in relation to children being abused through prostitution in their area. Local Safeguarding Children Boards should ensure the needs of these children are addressed.

7.4 Bullying, racial abuse and sexual harassment

To combat bullying, managers of children's homes should set and monitor standards of acceptable conduct, including the conduct of staff to residents. Organisations ... should implement effective anti-bullying strategies.

The Prison Service should take the management action needed to implement anti-bullying strategies consistently in all establishments in which children aged under 18 are detained.

Bodies with responsibilities for children living away from home should possess effective policies for preventing and

(Continued)

confronting all forms of racial harassment and ensure managers enforce them. No adult with responsibilities for children living away from home should 'not notice' it or assume nothing can be done.

Sexual harassment should be regarded as seriously as racial harassment and appropriate sanctions and training applied to perpetrators.

Government response

- Revised *Working Together* will discuss building on good practice and work in schools.

- New Youth Justice Board to advise on standards and monitor them.

- Staff training being given to change culture of establishments with juveniles.

- Education being provided for juveniles.

Government action

- Bullying covered in *Working Together* and National Minimum Standards.

- Racial harassment covered in *Working Together* and National Minimum Standard 18 for Boarding Schools.

- Welsh Assembly Government issued guidance to social services departments (SSDs) to ensure consideration is given to issues specific to black and ethnic minority children when planning services. Needs of black and ethnic minority children addressed in Framework for Assessment of Children in Need. Assembly is developing proposals for supplementary guidance on child protection issues around black and ethnic minority children.

- Sexual harassment was dealt with in Minimum Standard 18 for Boarding Schools.

What happened

Bullying continues to be a major problem. Prison establishments have anti-bullying strategies of varying effectiveness. HM Inspectorate considers that the normal living unit at 60 places is far too large and that 40 is a maximum for safety.

On Young Offender Institutions (YOIs), *Safeguarding Children* (4) says ' there were very serious levels of bullying and assault in many of these institutions and in one establishment the regime itself was such that fears of safety and of bullying put most of the population of young people at risk of harm. In one YOI there were over 700 reported incidents of injuries to young people over an 8 month period'. It also says 'Yet we found that there were very few referrals under the local child protection procedures being made to social services ... and could not be confident of the response to safeguard these young people'. 'In contrast to the provision of council secure accommodation, the principles and requirements of the Children Act are not automatically applied to YOIs and other prison establishments.' 'The major threat to young people is not from staff: where there were concerns about staff behaviour, these were generally responded to promptly. There was, however, a high level of violence between young people.'

The Home Office/YJB say that data on the number of incidents of bullying is not collected centrally. However, there are centrally held figures on the numbers of assaults. The great majority of assaults are comparatively minor, and may include, for example, one trainee simply pushing another trainee in the course of a fight. Where an injury is sustained requiring medical treatment, the assault is recorded as 'serious'. It should be noted that the level of *serious* assaults is very low, from April 2003 to March 2004 only 1.1 per cent of all assaults were recorded as serious within the dedicated juvenile establishments.

A new Prison Service Order on Violence Reduction was introduced from April 2004, and includes juvenile establishments.

Barry Goldson, in *Young Minds Magazine,* 2003, says it has long been known that bullying is endemic in prisons. This is now officially recognised with many formal attempts being made [to improve things] through anti-bullying strategies and 'a more sensitised awareness of child protection'. While staff are keen to emphasise the efforts being made there are doubts about effectiveness because of the many forms bullying can take (including verbal abuse and 'discipline' which is really an abuse of power). 'Bullying is ... extremely difficult to identify, it may be transmitted by no more than a look-in-the-eye, and besides staff–child ratios are so stretched within prisons that supervision is slight. Moreover bullying is contagious. It is entrenched deep within the fabric of prison life and its survival-of-the-fittest cultures. It is of little surprise that within this context, children's health deteriorates and their vulnerabilities are often compounded and exposed.'

The National Working Group on Child Protection and Disability, in its response to *Every Child Matters* (7) says that although DfES's pack *Bullying: Don't suffer in silence* highlights bullying of disabled children, there is concern that implementation has not been very effective. It recommends that DfES evaluates this.

Policy in prisons is set out in policy documents, Prison Service Orders and the joint Prison Service and Commission for Racial Equality document *Implementing Race Equality in Prisons.* The Prison Service Diversity and Equality Group are looking to develop race relations training for all prisoners including an adaptation for trainees.

HMIP say nearly all prisons have race relations co-ordinators and committees but that effectiveness varies. Establishments which are geographically remote have great problems in recruiting staff from ethnic minorities.

In December 2003 the Director General of the Prison Service, Phil Wheatley, was reported (*Independent* 17 December) as expressing 'shock and horror' over a catalogue of racial abuse and prejudice in jails, catalogued in a report by the Commission for Racial Equality.

In *The State of Children's Rights in England* (60) CRAE says 'Although children's rights to enjoy their own culture, religion and language is promoted by social services legislation, there is no equivalent protection in education, health or juvenile justice legislation'. It welcomes the Race Relations (Amendment) Act 2000, which places a duty on public authorities to tackle discrimination and promote equality of opportunity and good relations between persons of different racial groups, but says that active monitoring by the Commission for Racial Equality and individual inspectorates and regulatory bodies will be crucial, and that accessible information must be disseminated to children and parents to ensure they know about the new provisions and ways in which they can challenge discrimination. The UN Committee on the Rights of the Child (50) recommended that the State party should 'take measures and adequate mechanisms and structures to prevent bullying and other forms of violence in schools and include children in the development and implementation of these strategies'.

The SSI report *Excellence not Excuses. Inspection of Services for Ethnic Minority Children and Families* (93) found the following.

- Most councils did not have strategies in place to deliver appropriate services to ethnic minorities ... families were often offered services that were not appropriate to their needs.

- While most authorities had anti-racist and equal opportunities policies and strategies, there was little evidence that they had been implemented.

- In some instances the safety of ethnic minority children was being compromised because physical and sexual abuse had not been identified and properly dealt with as a child protection issue.

- There was little evidence that care planning took a lifelong view of the situation of ethnic minority looked after children. Although there was a general recognition of the need to find placements to meet their needs holistically, it was often difficult to do so in practice. Strategies for recruiting black foster carers did not always recognise the changing characteristics of this group of children. The placement needs of mixed race children were often the hardest to meet. The health and educational needs of ethnic minority children were in the main addressed, although there were gaps in child and adolescent mental health services and psychological support in most councils.

- Black children with disabilities were a group for whom there was 'little provision for their various needs'.

- Children in various authorities had complained of racial and verbal abuse. Children in residential homes, away from their communities, told us about being subjected to racial abuse. This was mainly labelled as 'bullying' by staff perhaps because residential staff found it easier to resolve.

- Consultation with ethnic minority groups was poor.

Analysis

Bullying is recognised as an important problem that needs to be tackled. It remains a major concern to young people and needs to be systematically and continuously addressed, particularly in prison establishments where young people are at their most vulnerable and least well supported, and in relation to disabled children. It is not clear from the evidence gathered that sufficient attention is being paid to this.

Racial abuse is a real problem but is not apparently always recognised as such or dealt with adequately. Whilst prisons have race relations co-ordinators and committees, their effectiveness varies and race remains a serious issue in prison establishments, particularly the geographically remote ones where recruiting staff from ethnic minorities is difficult.

The same appears true in relation to sexual harassment.

8 People who work with children

8.1 Choosing the right people

What *People Like Us* said

Chapter 13 said 15 recommendations in *Choosing with Care* (11) – the Warner Report – on defining the job, advertising the post, application forms, selection methodology, references and final interviews represent good personnel practice to be expected of all employers providing services for children living away from home.

> **Principal Recommendation 12. All organisations in which children live away from home should apply the recommendations of *Choosing with Care* ... in selecting and recruiting staff and volunteers with substantial unsupervised access to children.**

Government response

- Will be enforced in social services and adopted in other settings.

- Social Services – part of Quality Protects programme – monitoring, auditing and quality assurance will help deliver. Inclusion of care leavers on panels to be recommended. Code of Practice on foster care commissioned.

- NHS recent guidelines on recruitment practices (HSC (98)64). Alert letter system about doctors and dentists to be extended to nurses, midwives, health visitors and PAMs. Further guidance in 1998 requiring NHS to review, by April 1999, recruitment processes for those working with children admitted to hospital. DH Consultancy Index to be extended to include NHS staff.

- Education – will extend DH Consultancy Index checks to potential employees in all boarding schools.

- Prison Service – Youth Justice Board will advise on standards and monitor whether they are met and ensure effective checks are made for all staff working with young people in secure establishments.

Government action

- Covered in *Working Together*.

- DH produced *Towards Safer Care* (2000) – training pack on recruitment and selection for councils (95).

- Covered in National Minimum Standards.

- HSC 1998/212 *Children's Safeguards Review: Choosing with Care* (November 1998). Trusts and health authorities were required to implement by 31 March 1999. The alert letter system for doctors and dentists was extended to nurses, midwives, health visitors and PAMs in 2002. The new system will apply to all regulated professions.

- DfES's Circular DfES/0278/2002 gives guidance on pre-appointment checks to be made on all people who will have contact with children and young persons; explains the role of the Criminal Records Bureau and the circumstances under which people may be reported to the Secretary of State.

- Boarding Schools Association's Boarding Briefing Paper Number 1 *Safer Staff Recruitment* (published 1999 and revised Summer 2002).

- Wales. Achieved in social care settings. Also included in the Carlile Report (44) as recommendation 84. Further guidance to be published by National Health Service Directorate.

- Prison Service Order (PSO) 8100 sets out recruitment and selection procedures to ensure staff working with children are carefully vetted and CRB checked. PSO 4950 (*Regimes for Under 18 year Olds*) also refers to appropriate selection and recruitment for juveniles.

What happened

Developing Quality to Protect Children (58) found that a particular area of concern was staff recruitment. This was not robust enough to ensure adequate safeguards. Fourteen councils had serious weaknesses in their recruitment processes to safeguard children. Foster carer recruitment was more consistent and better documented.

Safeguarding Children (4) said all councils had developed policies and procedures to check the suitability of staff working with children in line with the requirements of the Warner Report (11) and other Government regulations and guidance. The implementation of such procedures is, however, inconsistent and variable. Shortcomings in the systems for recruitment of both staff and foster carers included:

- inconsistent recording of checks being carried out with DH Consultancy Index/ PoCA List

- not obtaining two separate references for new employees

- not recording examinations of proof of identity or qualifications

- staff starting work and carers taking placements before all necessary checks had been completed

- poor systems for tracking and recording the outcomes of checks

- variable interpretations between police forces on the implications of the Data Protection Act on the release of information.

Checking of residential staff was better than that of fieldwork staff and largely Warner compliant. In the report of the SSI Inspection of Foster Care Services, *Fostering for the Future* (96) it found some councils had closer scrutiny of staff employed in children's homes than those who had other substantial access to children.

Safeguarding Children (4) reported serious concerns about arrangements to check health service staff who have unsupervised access to children. In particular, paediatricians in post for many years and GPs had not had the necessary checks. It recommended 'health services ensure that recent guidance is followed for all staff'.

It says OFSTED inspection of independent schools identified frequent changes of staff, both teaching and care staff, which had a destabilising effect on the children. There were also a number of examples of checks being carried out on staff after their appointment and taking up post. (As happened with Ian Huntley in the Soham case.) Checks on host families accommodating young people (including those under 16 years) were not always undertaken. At provisionally registered schools there were examples of children being placed on a bed and breakfast basis with adults who had not been vetted.

The remit of HMIP does not include recruitment and selection procedures and HMIP have found it difficult to establish whether Prison Service screening matches *Choosing with Care* (11) requirements. It is suspected not, particularly for staff transferred from adult establishments or working on mixed age sites (particularly in the female estate).

Retrospective checks on staff where these have not been done routinely at point of entry in the past is an issue. Jeremy Whittle, Juvenile Group, Prison Service, May 2003, said recruitment checks were not made on prison staff working with children in the past, but they were now made on new entrants. The CRB was now saying that it could do retrospective checks on batches of existing staff. Kerry Cleary, NSPCC, August 2003 said retrospective checks can now be done but more advice needs to be given about the implications for an employment contract. People cannot be forced to have a CRB check in non-statutory regulated positions if their contract does not say that they have to have one. It would be helpful to have more guidance from the CRB and the Government on how to do this and legislation on who should have compulsory checks. The NSPCC are planning to do retrospective checks but need to look at the contract issue and the huge increase in costs to £33 for an enhanced check.

In relation to checks on prison staff, Kerry Cleary said (May 2004) that, whilst CRB checks are being made on new entrants to the prison service, prison officers are recruited generically, not specifically to work with young people, and it is not clear whether the section on the CRB form to ask for checks against List 99 and PoCA is always ticked so they are checked against these lists too, nor do the current processes look at suitability to work with children. NSPCC recommend that the YJB need to review their recruitment processes and base them on the Warner recommendations.

The NSPCC have used Warner (11) as it is comprehensive on recruitment and shows best practice. But it does not cover the 'how'; in particular how to conduct a preliminary interview looking at attitudes and motives but in such a way as not to lead to discriminatory practice against individuals by the use of inappropriate questioning and probing. The NSPCC have developed 'value-based interviewing' to do that. Other organisations have tried their approach and then shied away a little because they fear the legal consequences of getting it wrong. There needs to be a Government-funded or led initiative which invests time and money in developing good processes for doing this work in the context of current employment legislation so that practice takes account of this.

The Commission for Health Improvement reported in March 2004 that criminal record checks in NHS Wales were inconsistent. Although most organisations checked new staff, not all rechecked permanent staff or checked temporary staff or volunteers. Also many staff had not been trained in child protection, and record-keeping systems needed improvement.

> Inspection is effective in identifying poor personnel practice and OFSTED and HM's Inspectorate of Prisons should cover recruitment and selection procedures in their inspections as a matter of course.

Government response
- Consideration being given to whether practicable in education inspections.
- Legislation would be needed to allow HMICP to do so in establishments holding under-18s but may comment in inspections as matter of routine.

What happened
OFSTED inspections cover verification of police checks on staff.

HMIP's statutory remit is to report on treatment of, and conditions for, prisoners. The Inspectorate reports the outcomes it sees. It is constrained in its capacity to comment on the management (including personnel) processes that it might think are causing problems. However, it does in an indirect way frequently press points on recruitment and training.

Analysis

The need to comply with the *Choosing with Care* (11) arrangements has been generally accepted and enshrined in policy documents, although in some cases more definitive guidance, e.g. the Code of Practice on Foster Care (68) have been undermined by the omission of some important checks and enquiries in the Foster Care Minimum Standards.

However, *Safeguarding Children* (4) showed there is no room for complacency, as the implementation of these procedures is inconsistent and variable and they are applied more rigorously in some settings than others:

- they are applied better in respect of residential staff than for fieldwork staff

- some staff in the educational field are checked after taking up post

- the arrangements for checking health staff give rise to 'serious concerns'

- some prison staff have not been checked.

And carrying out timely checks has been severely hampered by the initial problems encountered by the Criminal Records Bureau.

The Soham case illustrated the problem with implementation of the procedures – the school accepted references that Huntley brought to the interview and did not follow them up or check them out, contrary to DfES guidance.

Whilst there is quite widespread acceptance of the need to apply *Choosing with Care* (11) principles, there are some practical difficulties as follows.

- Organisations may not have any training in recruitment and therefore do not have the skills and knowledge to implement the Warner recommendations.

- They may understand the importance of looking at the attitudes and motivation of applicants for work involving children but have little guidance on *how* to do this.

- There is uncertainty about how to do this in a way which does not lead to discriminatory practice against individuals and legal reprisals. There should be Government-led or funded work on good processes to be followed which comply with existing employment legislation.

- The CRB is not well understood by organisations and the training it gives is minimal. It should provide guidance, or a toolkit, to assist employers in checking ID and identifying forgeries.

- There are difficulties in carrying out retrospective checks and advice is needed on how to do this which takes account of contractual issues.

- It is thought that the Social Services Inspectorate is the only inspectorate to have examination of personnel files and recruitment processes as a standard part of its inspection programme. All inspectorates dealing with children living away from home should have this.

It would be helpful if DfES/DWP could provide guidance on the processes that can be followed in checking applicants which comply with existing employment legislation and on retrospective checks of staff already in post.

NSPCC have developed a recruitment audit tool against which they audit themselves annually. It covers all the relevant legislation, CRB code of practice, government guidance from reports such as Warner (11), Safe From Harm, Utting (1), and best practice from organisations such as the Chartered Institute of Personnel and Development. This good practice should be adopted by other organisations and be carried out on an annual basis.

> **Recommendation**
> 25 All inspectorates dealing with children living away from home should have the remit to cover the recruitment, assessment and selection of staff and should routinely cover and report on these arrangements.

8.2 Sources of background information

What *People Like Us* said

Chapter 14's analysis of sources of background information about individuals considered unsuitable to work with children concludes that criminal record checks, List 99 and the Consultancy

Index are all helpful in preventing such people working with children but that their administration can be improved.

> **The delays in processing criminal record checks are wholly unacceptable and must be addressed by the Home Secretary.**
>
> **Whatever system is chosen for criminal record checks it should adopt the principle of comprehensive coverage and minimum delays. It should serve as a one-stop shop for employers, so that they can ask for a criminal record check, a List 99 check and a Consultancy Index check at the same time.**
>
> **Use should be made of soft information, including charges as well as convictions, in the checking arrangements for potential employees.**

Government response

- Will take two years to put arrangements in place but when Criminal Records Agency (CRA) [later called the Criminal Records Bureau] is established should be possible to avoid long delays.

- Work undertaken to extend role of CRA to include List 99 and Consultancy Index but extension would require primary legislation.

Government action

- Criminal Records Bureau should have been established by April 2001 but was not operational until March 2002 – 11 months late. It provides a one-stop shop.

- The information released by the police for an 'enhanced check' includes 'soft information' as well as convictions.

- The Protection of Children Act 1999 created reciprocity between DH (the Consultancy Index) and DfES systems (List 99).

- The Criminal Justice and Court Services Act 2000 introduced arrangements to disqualify people from working with children.

What happened

CRB enables employers to make more thorough recruitment checks against records held by the police, DH and DfES. Its early days were dogged by problems and delays. The backlog of cases built up as a result caused major staffing problems for children's homes and schools. In August 2002 DH had to scrap the deadline for registering managers and providers of children's and older people's homes, since CRB delays meant only half the 20,000 providers and managers had been able to register with NCSC by the 1 August deadline. DfES had to advise schools employing new staff to revert to 'List 99' checks. CRB targets were missed and had to be relaxed – in September 2002 the target time for enhanced disclosures was doubled from three to six weeks. The Home Secretary admitted that CRB performance had been 'unacceptable' and an independent review was set up to examine why it was operating so slowly.

Things did improve during 2003 but in July the charges were more than doubled, with no consultation with employers and after the budget was set for most organisations – so they had to choose between checks or cuts in services. There were further increases in April 2004 (announced in December 2003).

The accuracy and consistency of the data have caused problems. There have been disputes about wrong identity and therefore incorrect information being given. In one case the NSPCC had two CRB checks done on someone within 12 months and had no information on the first check and a raft of old soft data on the second. Information from the local police forces on the enhanced check is inconsistent, some give no information, some very focused information, and some information that was irrelevant. It can be hard to make a fair assessment of the importance since it is not possible to contact the police directly about the information provided, and the CRB staff are not trained and do not have access to more in-depth explanations.

Ample evidence of the importance of soft information was provided in the wake of the conviction of Ian Huntley in December 2003 for the murder of two young girls. Had the number of previous allegations against him been brought together, he would not have been appointed as a school caretaker. The Home Secretary immediately announced an inquiry by Sir Michael Bichard to establish why the information had not been brought together. Subsequently it transpired that problems included:

- failure to bring together 'soft' information about allegations of rape and indecent assault when subsequent allegations arose

- inconsistency in how long soft information was kept, by local police forces (some held this only for a month or so)

- significant delays in recording convictions on the national police computer, thus undermining CRB checks. Some forces only recorded 5 per cent of the convictions in the target time of seven days and the average time was 35 days.

Failure to keep and use soft information was justified by reference to the Data Protection Act despite the fact that the ACPO 1995 Code of Practice for data protection says 'In cases where a sexual offence is alleged, but the subject is acquitted or the case is discontinued because of a lack of corroboration or allegation of consent by the victim, the details may be retained for a period of five years upon the authorisation of an officer not below the rank of superintendent and will be reviewed again at the end of the retention period'. In such cases retention can be authorised if the following criteria are met.

- The circumstances of the case would give cause for concern if the subject were to apply for employment involving substantial access to vulnerable persons.

- The facts of the case show that the involvement of the subject in an unlawful act is such that information can be graded A1.

- The decision to retain the information can be defended on public interest grounds.

There are also many situations not covered by the legislation, so children are not protected.

- Information is not available on people who have abused their own children and are on a social services list of people suspected of abuse or who had abused but this had not led to police involvement.

- List 99 and PoCA list checks talk about abuse in a work setting, but what about people who commit domestic violence or abuse at home? This may or may not come out on a CRB check if the police were involved. Checks against records held by social services departments would plug this gap.

- There are many roles in which people can get access to children without having to be CRB checked, e.g. people who manage databases of children's information, people who speak to children on the phone, people who work for a children's charity and can get access to children and their information. These posts do not fall within the definition of 'Regulated Position' for the purposes of the Criminal Justice and Court Services Act; however, under this Act the Secretary of State has the power to amend the definition of Regulated Position.

CRB checks are limited to those with the greatest access to children and the most visible in terms of their activities with children, not those who can be grooming children through other less visible means.

There are other problems about how CRB operates as follows.

- CRB will have the power to place sanctions on organisations which do not follow its code of practice. However, organisations receive no training on what they should be doing and make mistakes.

- The legal definitions of who can have a CRB check, and whether it should be enhanced or standard, are very general and unhelpful. Organisations have to interpret them, but requesting a check when not entitled to do so is a criminal offence. More training and guidance are needed on this.

> **Department of Health and the Department for Education and Employment should examine their procedures to ensure that information about such people can be considered for inclusion in the Index.**
>
> **More should be done to publicise the Index, so that all employers working with children in any setting use it both to check names against it and refer appropriate people.**

Government response
- Consultancy Index undergoing review and these issues will be considered.

- Legislation will be sought to put it on a statutory basis. Once on the statute books employers, including local authorities, will have to consult and refer names to it. Inclusion in the Index is a bar to employment in relevant fields.

Government action
- Protection of Children Act (PoCA) 1999 requires child care organisations to check against the Protection of Children Act List and the relevant part of List 99 and not employ anyone in a child care capacity who is on it.

- DfES regulations make it a requirement for employers in the education sector to report dismissals for misconduct, or resignations where dismissal might have been appropriate if the person had not resigned.

What happened
PoCA requires child care organisations to both check and refer names to the Secretary of State for consideration of inclusion on PoCA List – this includes dismissal on grounds of misconduct; resignations or retirements in circumstances where dismissal would have been considered; where the person has been transferred to a non-child care position or has been suspended. However, for 'other organisations' there is no *duty* to do so, they *may* check and refer for those in regulated positions.

Barbara Starns, child care and protection co-ordinator for East Riding, Yorkshire (*Community Care*, 19 Dec–8 Jan 2003) discussed the problems with the PoCA list including the following.

- Voluntary groups who work with children (scouts, sports, etc.) may be unaware of the need to check prospective staff, nor does the law require them to. ('Child care organisations' are defined as those providing accommodation, social or health care services or the supervision of children.)

- Child care organisations in the voluntary sector seem less clear about their responsibility and the process of referral for inclusion in the list.

- Criteria for the list are unclear and professionals have difficulty deciding on referral. Many think they should do this when employee is prosecuted for an offence against a child whilst the Act goes much wider – dismissal, suspension or moving a person on grounds of misconduct which harmed or placed a child at risk of harm.

- Definition of 'harm' may not include new internet offences and may lead to employers not referring some people. Similar problem will arise with new 'grooming' offence.

- Most fundamental problem is that referral is entirely the responsibility of employer who may not recognise the need to refer.

- Some professionals who work with children are self-employed, e.g. GPs, with no employer to refer. Significant omission.

- There may be a conflict of interest – there have been instances where abuse was not reported to protect the reputation of the institution or cover the lack of procedures within the organisation.

NSPCC agree more needs to be done about publicising the PoCA list and the process for making a referral. There is a lack of awareness that consideration of referral should be a standard part of the final stages of a disciplinary. The guidance for employers on using the list and making a referral is helpful but not well known.

Donald Findlater, LFF, July 2003, said there was a long way to go to raise public awareness of the risks. There was still much work to be done with professionals – church organisations, for example were still reluctant to move people against whom allegations had been made away from work with children. He suggested there should be a 'finding of fact' in the same way as in Family Court proceedings, where the burden of proof was not sufficient for a criminal conviction. This would help in situations where the employing organisation does not have all the information available to the police on which to base a judgement.

Analysis

The Protection of Children Act 1999 placed the Consultancy Index on to a statutory footing, introduced an appeals mechanism and required

child care organisations not to employ a person who was included in the PoCA List or List 99. It also amended section 218 of the Education Reform Act 1988 to enable DfES to identify people who are put on List 99 because they are not fit and proper persons to work with children.

However, the PoCA list and List 99 still operate as two separate lists and problems remain in ensuring the right people are referred and employers make full use of the lists. NSPCC say there is a real lack of awareness of organisations about what the lists are for and how to refer people, so people are not referred as often as they should be. There is also concern about the threshold for admission. In its experience it is very difficult to get people referred onto the lists and there is no guidance as to what criteria they have failed on – even when they have been investigated and dismissed.

There should be more publicity about the list and the process of making a referral so that all human resources departments know that referral should be considered as a standard part of the final stages of a disciplinary case. Consideration should be given to whether the PoCA list should be broadened to cover other people, such as those on social service lists of people suspected of abuse or who had abused rather than limiting it to people in the work setting, and whether it should be mandatory for any organisation to refer staff or volunteers to the list.

The establishment of the CRB has been fraught with dificulty and delays. These are gradually being resolved but some problems still need to be addressed as follows.

- Checks must be available for *all* situations in which children are vulnerable. Solutions need to be found to the difficulties facing voluntary organisations and community bodies in obtaining checks, or these sectors will simply become targets for determined abusers.

- There are many situations not covered by the legislation where people can get access to children but this is not clear from their job titles – for example people working for a children's charity or who speak to children on the phone. These people should also be checked.

- Enhanced checks include 'soft information' and it is necessary to ensure accuracy, consistency and clarity in this, as employers cannot query information at source. There should be guidance to local police forces on the need to record accurately information that may have a bearing on child safety and the need to provide this for enhanced checks. This should include evidence from police involvement in possible abuse or violence in the home. It is hoped that the Bichard Inquiry[1] which followed the conviction of Ian Huntley will lead to the improvements that are obviously needed.

- The CRB will have power to place sanctions on organisations not following its code of practice, but the legal definitions of who can have a CRB check and whether it should be enhanced or standard are considered very general and unhelpful. Organisations have to try to interpret them and wrongly requesting a check is a criminal offence. This power should, therefore, be accompanied by training and guidance for organisations so they are not penalised for genuine mistakes.

CRB checks are only as good as the information provided by police forces. If information is out of date they can be seriously misleading and place children at risk. All police forces should have effective systems for:

- retaining and linking information about allegations of rape and other sexual offences, particularly where children are involved

- entering criminal records information into the national computer within the target times.

The importance of keeping and making use of 'soft' information as recommended by *People Like Us* (1) is repeated and the proposal to keep a national police database on this is strongly supported.

Whilst police checks are important in preventing unsuitable people working with children and deterring those who have been convicted of a relevant offence they are nowhere near sufficient. There is a danger that they will be seen as *the* means of safeguarding children whereas they are just one element in this. There are many more abusers without convictions than there are with them. Rigorous checking of other information such as life histories, references and probing interviewing is also needed.

It is hoped that the Bichard Inquiry will make recommendations on how children can be better protected against unsuitable people and that these will be implemented speedily.

Recommendations

26 DfES should review the scope of the Protection of Children Act List to see whether it should be widened to cover other sources of information and consider whether it should be made mandatory for organisations to refer staff and volunteers to the list. It should publicise the list and the process of making a referral.

27 The Home Office should review the coverage of CRB checks and ensure they are available for *all* situations in which children are vulnerable.

(Continued)

---

1 The Bichard Inquiry Report June 2004 was published after this report was completed. Its recommendations are supported.

28 The Home Office/ACPO should issue guidance to all police forces to ensure they have effective systems for recording and retaining 'soft' information and ensure that target times for entering criminal record information into the national computer are met.

8.3 Dealing with unsuitable people

What *People Like Us* said

Chapter 15 has two Principal Recommendations – one on legal protection for sharing information and the other on whistle-blowing.

On whistle-blowing it said cultural change must be led from the top, policies of openness and promptness should be adopted in dealing with complaints about staff that affect children. Codes of conduct should include a duty to report any behaviour by staff, managers, volunteers or others which may harm children and should offer confidentiality for the initial reports and protect a complainant making a report in good faith against any subsequent disadvantage.

Information sharing

Principal Recommendation 13. Government should examine the need to strengthen the legal protection of agencies communicating information about the suitability of individuals to work with children.

There should be a review of legislation – the Data Protection Act, law on defamation, employment protection legislation and judicial review – to establish whether a protocol could be developed to legitimise exchange of information between parties with a proper interest in protecting children.

Government response

Positive steps being taken to reduce confusion over legal position on sharing of information including:

- issuing guidance on disclosure of information in relation to sex offenders;

- ensuring organisations can share information for the purposes of the Crime and Disorder Act 1998;

- producing a Code of Practice on use of information in Criminal Records Certificates.

A Home Office-led inter-departmental group is looking at this and additional safeguards to prevent unsuitable people working with children.

Government action

- Criminal Justice and Courts Services Act 2000 (enacted January 2001) covered identification and banning of unsuitable people from working with children; created a new criminal offence which the 'unsuitable person' would commit if they worked with children; provided a new definition of 'working with children'; and created a 'one-stop shop' through the CRB to provide information on people deemed unsuitable to work with children.

- Covered in *Working Together* and Appendix 4 on Data Protection Act. Refers to *Draft Guidance on the Disclosure of Information about Sex Offenders who may present a risk to Children and Vulnerable Adults* (Home Office, July 1999).

What happened

Safeguarding Children (4) says 'The HMIC [Her Majesty's Inspectorate of Constabulary] report on Child Protection identified concerns about the reluctance of some agencies to pass on information about suspicions of possible child abuse or children thought to be at risk of harm. Social workers, probation officers and prison staff were found to be comfortable with passing on information, but teachers, medical staff and youth workers often felt inhibited by their lack of understanding of confidentiality, a lack of clarity of expectations and fears of jeopardising relationships with parents or young people. They recommended clear protocols for sharing information and making referrals be drawn up with each agency'.

Safeguarding Children (4) pointed to the difficulties the probation service was having with the ACPC agenda and said all areas were having difficulties in making effective links between the work of the ACPC and MAPPAs, the local arrangements in respect of adults who present a risk of significant harm to other people, and specifically to children. 'We found that the local MAPPA had been developed quite independently from the local safeguarding arrangements and that formal links had not been established.'

The Children Act Report 2002 (29) summarised this – '*Safeguarding Children* (4) found that many staff from all agencies were confused about their responsibilities and duties to share information about child welfare concerns and were not confident that other agencies shared information with them. Formal agreements between agencies about how and when information should be shared were few'.

Complex Child Abuse Investigations: Inter-agency Issues (97) said that work is currently underway in the context of a wider project on disclosure to develop a national protocol on disclosure from social services in child abuse cases.

Learning from Past Experience: A Review of Serious Case Reviews (98) put 'inadequate sharing of information' top of a list of 'concerns expressed most often in reports'. It says 'the linked issues of the ineffective sharing of information, poor inter-agency working and inconsistent recording reflects fears among some professionals about litigation arising from breaches of data protection law'. Inadequate sharing of information was an intra-agency issue too. It says 'There is no insurmountable legal barrier to prevent the lawful and justifiable disclosure of "confidential",

"personal" and "sensitive" information between agencies and professionals for the protection of children or the detection or prevention of serious crime. However such sharing of information is best managed under arrangements or protocols which should be agreed between local agencies. The Data Protection Checklist (see Appendix Four of *Working Together to Safeguard Children* (69)) helps to identify the issues that should be considered when drawing up such a protocol'. It goes on to say that 'All those working in child protection should have a basic understanding of the legal principles underpinning information sharing'.

The problem of when agencies could and should share information also featured strongly in the report of the Victoria Climbie Inquiry (16). Recommendation 16, for implementation within two years, said 'The Government should issue guidance on the Data Protection Act 1998, the Human Rights Act 1998, and common law rules on confidentiality. The Government should issue guidance as and when these impact on the sharing of information between professional groups in circumstances where there are concerns about the welfare of children and families'.

Roger Morgan, Children's Rights Director, May 2003, said it was very important to have clear guidance from the centre. It should be based on an expectation that information should ordinarily be shared whenever required in order to contribute to safeguarding the child (i.e. the general 'welfare' principle). At the moment agencies sought legal advice locally and this varies.

NSPCC highlighted a number of concerns.

- Organisations who use high profile people from the business world or celebrities should have a way of checking a database or with the police as to whether someone should be engaged with children.

- The inability to talk direct to the police in more depth after receiving a CRB disclosure means that organisations have to assess the relevance of criminal convictions without professional advice. More guidance and support are needed.

- The portability of information from CRB is clearly laid out in the guidance but there are concerns about accepting disclosures from employment agencies and how long past checks should be accepted. (The guidance is three months.)

- Information is limited on those who have worked abroad.

- References are now becoming harder to get in any detail due to new legislation around slander and the ability of people to sue employers for inaccurate references. This means very little quality information is written down and references have to be followed up with phone calls. Exemptions in the legislation for the sharing of this sort of information should be granted.

Analysis

As the Laming Report (16) and the *Review of Serious Case Reviews* (98) show, the appropriate sharing of information remains a major problem. Despite some efforts to clarify the position, the balancing act needed to decide when the interests of protecting a child override the legal rights of the individual remains extremely difficult. Five years after the publication of *People Like Us* (1) it was necessary for Lord Laming (16) to make a very similar recommendation. If the current legislation is too complicated to give staff the clear guidance they need, then the law should be changed to ensure that information that may be important in protecting a child can be passed on. It should cover information both about the child and about the people who may be a risk to them, whether this is a parent, member of staff or volunteer.

The recent focus has been on sharing information between agencies about the child, rather than about people who may be a risk to children. The latter is equally important and needs to be addressed.

Keeping Children Safe (17) said that 'new or very recent guidance' will cover 'Overarching, high-level, Government guidance on the current legal framework for the sharing of personal data, which will cover issues of administrative and common law, and the relevant parts of the Data Protection Act 1998 and the Human Rights Act 1998/ European Convention on Human Rights'. But does this/will this cover information on individuals who may be a risk to children?

It would be helpful if the Government issued clear guidance on information sharing, covering both information about children who may be at risk *and* people who may pose a risk to children. If the Data Protection Act is unduly restrictive, it should be amended.

Whistle-blowing

> **Principal Recommendation 14. All organisations accommodating children should instruct staff to raise legitimate concerns about the conduct of colleagues or managers and protect them against victimisation.**
>
> **There is a need for urgent advice to staff about professionals who abuse [children with disabilities], including what to do if they suspect a colleague.**

Government response

- Governing bodies of all organisations responsible for the care of children and young people to be reminded they should have procedures so that staff can raise concerns outside their normal line management and to inform staff of procedures for making complaints.

Government action

- Public Interest Disclosure Act 1998 provides protection against victimisation for persons who in good faith raise concerns about a wide variety of malpractices both within the organisation and externally, in the public interest.

- Care Standards Act requires each provider to establish clear whistle blowing procedures.

- Covered by appropriate National Minimum Standards.

- Some regulations, e.g. Children's Homes Regulations 2001, provide a legal duty to report concerns.

- Included in the 'basic safeguards' in *Working Together*.

- The Education Act 2002 made it mandatory for independent and non-maintained schools to have complaints procedures in line with these guidelines.

- PSO 4950, *Regimes for Under 18 Year Olds*, deals with this for Prison Service staff.

- Welsh Assembly Government reminded governing bodies of all organisations responsible for care of children that they should have procedures to enable staff to raise concerns outside normal line management structures. Guidance on 'whistle-blowing' issued to local authorities in Wales. This has also been addressed by a number of Carlile recommendations covering clinical governance and human resources.

What happened

Safeguarding Children (4) said 'All services took allegations about staff seriously, and arranged for their investigation by someone independent from that service. The approach was generally robust, but we found weaknesses in the way allegations were recorded and in the final stages of decision-making and resolution of the issues'.

Learning the Lessons (33) said the Department for the Environment, Transport and the Regions (DETR) and LGA were discussing whistle-blowing in the context of the Local Government Bill, which included provisions to establish a statutory code of conduct for employees that would form part of their terms and conditions of employment.

HMIP said it was beginning to see a change of culture in some prison establishments with staff being prepared to report assaults by colleagues. But it can cause very difficult dynamics.

NSPCC is reviewing its whistle-blowing policy, which is very rarely used. The issues are around fear that no action will be taken and what will happen to the whistle-blower. A new harassment policy has recently been introduced and there are the same concerns about that. Organisations need to drive it from the top and change the culture to a more open one so that the policy works.

Community Care, 16–22 October 2003, said that Public Concern At Work's report on calls to its whistle-blower's helpline found calls by staff in the care sector have increased threefold over the past decade. A change in the law now means that workers in social care can now take concerns direct to the NCSC or the General Social Care Council (GSCC). Previously they had to report worries to someone in their organisation.

Analysis

Measures have been taken to protect whistle-blowers (Public Interest Disclosure Act 1998) and ensure procedures are in place (Care Standards Act) but how well are the procedures known, understood and, most important of all, used? It seems, from the use of the Public Concern at Work helpline that people are becoming more willing to report concerns now that they can do so outside their own organisation. *Safeguarding Children* (4) found weaknesses in the way allegations were dealt with. The conclusion seems to be that there have been attempts to put procedures in place and to recognise the legitimacy of whistle-blowing, although it is doubtful that this has made it much easier for staff to come forward.

8.4 Training

What *People Like Us* said

Chapter 12 said that training is likely to be useful if carers work to clear objectives, have a coherent view of what they are trying to achieve and believe in what they are doing. The content of training courses at all levels of qualification must support these requirements, as must the way the institution is managed.

> **CCETSW should specify the content of child care training on courses which lead to qualifications by defining the content of a curriculum of learning, in addition to describing the competencies and standards which must be demonstrated.**

Government response

- National Training Organisation for the Personal Social Services (TOPSS) should help engage employers in addressing deficiencies in quality and quantity of training.

- Draft curriculum guidance commissioned for new Post Qualifying award in childcare (PQCCA). Intended to fund development of curriculum guidance at six or eight centres of excellence and start courses in January 2000. Will inform review of Diploma for Social Work in 1999.

- Review of regulatory functions of CCETSW underway for benefit of General Social Services Council which will be created when legislative time allows.

Government action

- A new three-year degree level professional qualification in social work introduced in England from September 2003, based on a prescribed curriculum.

- A new non-means-tested bursary introduced in September 2003. Social work students receive at least £3,000 a year in living and travelling expenses and £1,075 in tuition fees.

What happened

The prescribed curriculum for the social work degree comprises:

- Department of Health requirements for entry to social work courses and teaching, learning and assessment

- National Occupational Standards for Social Workers developed by the TOPSS which specifies what employers require social workers to be able to do on entering the workforce

- Quality Assurance Agency (QAA) Benchmarking Statement for Social Work specifies outcome requirements for the degree level academic award.

Students will learn and be assessed on, among other things: working in partnerships, information sharing across professional disciplines, communication skills with adults and children and those with particular communication needs, human growth, development, mental health and disability. One of the major changes is that students will now complete a minimum of 200 days learning in practice settings. To secure an increase in the quantity and quality of practice learning opportunities a Practice Learning Task Force was established in autumn 2002.

Fiona Waddington, Practice Learning Task Force for Social Work Training, TOPSS, England, said the new degree would include placements in police, criminal justice system, housing departments, schools and colleges as well as traditional social care settings.

BAAF says the PQCCA does not address Family Placement issues. Agencies are having difficulty in funding and releasing staff to go on PQCCA courses. It is unrealistic to plan to create an adequately trained workforce via this route. The location of PQCCA courses exclusively in universities needs reviewing. More scope for an independent route to the Award would be helpful. Many staff and managers in social work agencies remain generally ignorant about PQCCA, TOPSS and the GSCC.

In addition, it does not appear that training addresses the needs of staff working with disturbed children who have complex emotional problems. Training could, and should, provide staff with confidence about how to use physical intervention safely but it does not do this. The necessity to get the basics right, the practical things, should be in the ethos of the establishment and repetition is needed because of staff turnover.

Keeping Children Safe (17) says the Government is seeking to fill the gaps in training programmes to ensure that 'all workers have an appropriate level of training in safeguarding children'. Apart from the new three-year social work degree course and the PQCCA, DfES is considering what child protection training is needed by teachers; from 2003 child protection will be an explicit part of police probationer training. Also professional bodies have been asked to review training needs, including inter-agency training.

Hilary Searing (*Community Care*, March 2003), said training courses do not prepare social work students adequately for their child protection role, for example, they lack confidence in determining whether there is enough evidence to justify further investigation.

Department for Education and Employment and Department of Health should jointly review and explore the scope for a common approach to developing training opportunities for carers in schools and homes in relation to NVQs and DipSW qualifications.

Department of Health and the Department for Education and Employment should commission the production of further training materials designed for the in-service training of carers without professional qualifications in schools and homes.

Government response

- Scope for joint training and a common approach to be considered, recognising the two workforces are not identical and have some divergent needs.

- DH to consult employers on new material and how provided and DfEE to discuss needs of workers in schools.

What happened

TOPSS' induction package for all social care staff, including those in residential child care, will supplement DH initiative which is providing funding to train all residential child care staff in England to NVQ level 3 in 'Caring for children and young people'. TOPSS is also developing a training programme for managers in residential childcare. First students began new PQ training in childcare in January 2000. There is a DH target for 7,000 staff to be trained for the award by 2006 with 10 per cent being from residential child care.

DfES gives annual funding to the Boarding Schools Associations for appropriate professional training.

The Secretary of State for Health announced to the October 2002 Annual Social Services Conference that he was asking the GSCC, training organisations and local government to work with Central Government to develop new types of social care professionals, because a combination of skills is needed to deliver modern effective services which meet individual needs.

There is DfES funding for the York Group to produce INSET training package for boarding staff on child protection issues.

> Department of Health and the Home Office should jointly explore the potential for developing guidance and training materials designed to heighten awareness of childcare professionals about the profiles and methods of perpetrators of child abuse.

Government response

- Training Support Programme to fund a project in 1998/99 and 1999/2000 with a view to introducing training materials by end 1999.

What happened

Working Together (69) says 'staff and foster carers are trained in all aspects of safeguarding children; alert to children's vulnerabilities and risks of harm; and knowledgeable about how to implement child protection procedures'.

Under the Quality Protects programme DH produced the *Towards Safer Care* (95) package of materials for local councillors.

Tink Palmer of Barnardo's says that all those involved in child protection work need to have the right tools and skills for all the tasks they might be called upon to perform – including presenting evidence in court. (Apart from police for whom this was a standard part of training.) There is often some resistance to this. Training should be seamless, covering all stages of child protection including recording information provided by the child that was relevant to a possible court case, giving evidence in court, etc. It should be based on the skills that practitioners need to empower and enable them to do all the tasks required. This should include medical staff, nurses, etc. and would be needed for caring staff, such as foster carers, where necessary.

Analysis

There have been a number of developments for social services training since *People Like Us* (1) – TOPSS, new PQ award in child care (PQCCA); new three-year degree level professional qualification in social work, etc. How far these will go in addressing needs in this area is unclear. BAAF say there are difficulties with the PQCCA, which does not address family placement issues. The Advisory Group for this study was concerned that training should get the basics right – and be constantly renewed because of staff turnover. Nor is training always as effective as it should be. There is a need for skilled trainers and time out for training.

Little progress seems to have been made on a common approach for carers in schools and homes. The most important development in this area is the Secretary of State for Health's October 2002 announcement that the GSCC, training organisations and local government have been asked to work with Central Government to develop new types of social care professionals since a combination of skills is needed to deliver modern effective services which meet individual needs.

There has recently been welcome recognition, particularly in the wake of the Victoria Climbie report (16), of the need for all professionals who deal with children to have training in child protection. All organisations and agencies employing staff to work with children should ensure they are aware of the signs that a child may be being abused, how to deal with any disclosure, how and when to involve specialist staff who can undertake joint enquiries with the police, and that they may need to give evidence in court. This should include the medical and nursing professions and carers, such as foster carers where necessary. They should also be aware of normal child development at different ages so that they are able to recognise divergences from this.

9 Maintaining standards: inspection

What *People Like Us* said

Chapter 17 dealt with management, monitoring, inspection and enforcement. It said the following.

- Both internal and external management must be continually vigilant in safeguarding the welfare of the children for whom they are responsible.

- Monitoring by management is necessary and proper resources should be devoted to it. Governing bodies or their equivalents should require annual reports on safeguards.

- External monitoring is also needed and inspection is the main source of this locally.

Chapter 16 also considered inspection, as part of central government responsibilities.

> The Social Services Inspectorate should continue to undertake inspections to monitor arrangements for safeguarding children living away from home and the Department of Health to keep the resourcing of the Inspectorate under review.
>
> The Secretary of State should take action to ensure that local authorities carry out inspections at the required frequency.
>
> SSI should continue its oversight of local inspection units on behalf of the Secretary of State in order to achieve consistently high standards nationally.

Government response

- SSI to continue to monitor and resourcing to be carefully considered.

- National Priorities Guidance has made this a priority for all inspection work of both local authorities and health authorities.

- Quality Protects will cover their concerns and directions be issued where not the case.

- Social Services White Paper will cover plans for regulatory arrangements and central monitoring. SSI will continue its oversight until new legislation is in place.

Government action

- Inspection work transferred to the National Care Standards Commission in April 2002. NCSC is responsible for the regulation and inspection of children's homes, fostering services, boarding schools, residential special schools and Further Education (FE) colleges accommodating students under 18. NCSC Children's Rights Director is responsible for ensuring registration and inspection are carried out effectively.

- Commission for Social Care Inspection replaced NCSC from April 2004.

- Commission for Health Inspection (CHI) replaced by Commission for Health Audit and Inspection (CHAI) from April 2004.

What happened

There was interruption of the pattern of inspections of residential services in the handover from local authority inspection services and NCSC. In an article in the 1–7 May 2003 edition of *Community Care*, John Burton said that for six months of 2002, inspection was virtually non-existent. Inspections under the NCSC were the first in many homes for nine months or more.

The NCSC had some teething problems. It had 400,000 care services in England to register and inspect. By end January 2003 it had carried out 84 per cent of necessary inspections but this varied between regions, with the South East Office only completing 69 per cent (*Community Care*, 27 March–2 April 2003). NCSC figures show that at the end of January 2003 only 35 per cent of inspection reports had been completed. Overall, 22,203 inspections had been carried out. The annual conference report of the National Association of Inspection and Regulation Officers, whilst acknowledging the

NCSC's positive impact on the sector, made 13 recommendations in relation to training, the need to reduce unnecessary bureaucracy, address problems with IT systems and provide better training to promote consistency.

Further disruption may result from the merger of NCSC and SSI in April 2004 into the Commission for Social Care Inspection and replacement of CHI by CHAI. There may also be changes in other key inspectorates – OFSTED will have substantial new responsibilities and changes to HMI Prisons and Probation Inspectorates are under consideration.

Lord Laming (16) recommended that 'As part of their work, the government inspectorates should inspect both the quality of the services delivered, and also the effectiveness of the inter-agency arrangements for the provision of services to children and families'. *Every Child Matters* (7) responded by saying that an integrated inspection framework for children's services would be created with OFSTED taking the lead and bringing together joint inspection teams. It will ensure that services are judged on how well they work together.

Modernising Social Services (3) made a commitment, following *People Like Us* (1), that the Chief Inspector of the SSI would, with other relevant inspectorates, conduct a review and report every three years on how well children are being safeguarded. *Safeguarding Children: A Joint Chief Inspectors' Report on Arrangements to Safeguard Children* (4) is the first of these. There are some omissions in its coverage; it does not cover the most vulnerable children – those living away from home, or disabled children – nor does it include the work of the National Care Standards Commission (established April 2002). The Report says the NCSC will be covered in subsequent reports. It identifies groups of young people who 'present particular challenges to services that safeguard children' and recommends that particular attention be given to them in future inspection work. These are:

- unaccompanied asylum seekers
- children with special needs in residential special schools
- children of travellers' families
- children who change address frequently
- children looked after placed outside their home local authority area
- children with disabilities
- children in residential care.

Keeping Children Safe (17) said that the next triennial joint Chief Inspectors' Children's Safeguards Report, due to be published in late 2005, will cover the arrangements to safeguard children living in the community, living away from home and those involved in the justice system.

A steering committee has been set up to plan the next joint Chief Inspectors' report in 2005. Eight inspectorates are involved – SSI/NCSC/CSCI; CHI/CHAI; HMI Constabulary; HMI Probation; HMI Prisons; HMI Magistrates Courts Services; HMI Crown Prosecution Services and OFSTED. There will be more emphasis on joint work and on child protection. In future all inspectorates will be able to report on this. One particular focus of the work is on children living away from home and, for the first time, all the inspectorates will be using common safeguarding standards. The work will also cover circumstances in which children live away from home but in situations not covered by regulation, such as the armed services and sport and recreation. This is very welcome. Other helpful developments are the intention to pay particular attention to the views of children and young people and to ensure that inspection work covers disabled children and provides specific comment on services for them. It is not yet clear whether the 2005 report will be the last joint report on safeguarding or whether these will be continued after the joint inspection framework with OFSTED in the lead is established.

Analysis

It seems that there has been something of a hiatus in inspection activity whilst waiting for the NCSC to be set up and then some further delay in the NCSC getting to grips with its work programme. There will, no doubt, be further disruption with the change to the Commission for Social Care Inspection and CHAI in 2004 and then again with the establishment of the 'joint inspection framework' in 2005. Other inspectorates are also undergoing change.

This degree of constant change is worrying and there are real dangers that inspection work will suffer and unsatisfactory services go untackled for longer than they should. The overall direction of change is, however, welcome and there should be benefits from more joint working, especially if combined with priority being accorded to child protection arrangements.

Safeguarding Children (4) is an extremely helpful and illuminating document, and the timing of its production was very useful for this study. It is unfortunate that it did not cover children living away from home but welcome that the next joint Chief Inspectors' Children's Safeguards Report in 2005 will do so, including disabled children in residential special schools, in hospital settings for more than 30 days and in out of authority placements, those involved in the criminal justice system and in unregulated settings.

It is important that the triennial safeguarding children reports continue after the establishment of the joint inspection framework in 2005 and cover those groups of children who are particularly vulnerable but still being marginalised and neglected. These include:

- very young children
- children with mental health problems
- children with emotional and behavioural difficulties
- children in hospices.

As part of the commitment that all inspectorates cover child protection, they should all routinely cover and report on the arrangements for recruiting, assessing and selecting staff to ensure consistency in all areas in preventing unsuitable people from working with children and young people.

CSCI should also monitor whether the 'more proactive' approach to the notification of private fostering arrangements is having the desired effect.

Recommendations

25 All inspectorates dealing with children living away from home should have the remit to cover the recruitment, assessment and selection of staff and should routinely cover and report on the arrangements for these procedures.

29 The triennial safeguarding children reports should continue after the establishment of the joint inspection framework in 2005 and should cover those groups of children who are particularly vulnerable and neglected. The necessary inspection work should be programmed well in advance. (All inspectorates)

10 Criminal justice

What *People Like Us* said

Chapter 20 said the criminal justice system does not deter offenders or secure convictions of those who are guilty. Its failings are most marked in relation to those who are most vulnerable – the very young and the disabled. The process itself is damaging to children. Action is needed to make it more effective: the reliability of systems of notification of sex offenders depends heavily on guilty people being convicted.

Suggestions are made for increasing the proportion of cases that go to trial and for making the process less damaging for the children involved.

Principal Recommendation 20. Government should implement the remaining recommendations of the Advisory Group on Video Evidence (The Pigot Report) and undertake a comprehensive review of arrangements for prosecuting sexual offenders against children.

10.1 Assisting children to give evidence

Action should be taken to make the process of the justice system less damaging for children by: greater use of video recording and television links; judges and barristers who specialise in work with children; preparation of the child via the child witness pack and programmes such as the NSPCC's Witness Support Project; minimise the time it takes cases to come to court and making careful arrangements for child witnesses.

The Memorandum of Guidance for interviewing children should be reviewed; there should be flexibility in allowing evidence in a form suited to the age of the

(Continued)

---

child and the child should be helped to communicate if necessary.

The Crown Prosecution Service (CPS) should issue a code of practice on pre-trial therapy as soon as possible.

Government response

- Range of action being taken to improve effectiveness of procedures and afford greater protection to children.

- Government announcement shortly on recommendations of Working Group on Vulnerable and Intimidated Witnesses in *Speaking up for Justice* to improve way such witnesses, including children, are dealt with in the criminal justice system including implementation of outstanding Pigot recommendations (pre-trial cross-examination and use of an intermediary), greater use of CCTV and training.

- Steering Group on Child Evidence to monitor and improve child evidence provisions, including preparation of child witnesses, fast-tracking of cases, guidance on pre-trial therapy, consider relevant information or research and act on a number of procedural issues raised in the report.

- Consultation on a draft code of practice on pre-trial therapy planned by the end of 1997 and guidance thereafter.

Government action

- The Youth Justice and Criminal Evidence Act 1999 enables the court to take one or more of a range of special measures available to assist child witnesses under 17 years old to give their best evidence in criminal proceedings. The measures include use of a screen round the witness box; use of TV link; video-recorded statements admitted as evidence in chief; use of communication aids; removal of formal court dress; clearing the public gallery in sex offence cases and those involving intimidation. It provides for examination of a witness to be conducted through an intermediary approved by the courts to assist vulnerable witnesses who have communication difficulties. The majority of measures to be implemented in the Crown Court during 2001–2002.

- *The Memorandum of Good Practice on Video Recorded Interviews with Child Witnesses for Criminal Proceedings* (1992) was replaced by *Achieving Best Evidence in Criminal Proceedings: Guidance for Vulnerable or Intimidated Witnesses, including Children* (99) (HO, LCD, CPS, DH, NAW, January 2002).

- *Provision of Therapy for Child Witnesses Prior to a Criminal Trial: Practice Guidance* published 2001 (HO, CPS and DH). The Foreword says 'the Government, in its response to Sir William Utting's report *People Like Us*, said it was determined to ensure that children and other vulnerable witnesses should be able to give their best evidence in criminal proceedings with the minimum of distress'.

What happened

The Report of the 31st session of the Committee on the Rights of the Child (50) made very similar recommendations – 'establish effective procedures and mechanisms to receive, monitor and investigate and prosecute instances of abuse, ill-treatment and neglect, ensuring the abused child is not victimised in legal proceedings and that his/her privacy is protected'. And 'record in the British Crime Survey all crimes committed against children'. (The Children's Rights Alliance in England, CRAE, say this was promised by the Government but under-16s are still not included.)

In relation to video interviews, *Safeguarding Children* (4) said the following.

- Police officers lead the interview in almost all cases, with social workers in a supporting role. Where police were not from specialist teams, there was greater concern about the quality of video evidence. The CPS expressed concern about the quality of video evidence in most areas.

- CPS areas should ensure child abuse cases are given preferential treatment in the review process; that intervals between the key stages of the prosecution process are the minimum … that high standards of timeliness are achieved and that child abuse cases are dealt with by lawyers and caseworkers of appropriate experience.

- Child witnesses should be afforded as much protection as may be necessary to enable them to give their evidence in a way that both maintains the quality of that evidence and minimises the trauma suffered by the child.

There are evidently particular problems in the video recording of children in prison establishments.

Implementation of the Youth Justice and Criminal Evidence Act 1999 has been phased in over time 'to reduce the burden on the various agencies involved'. *Achieving Best Evidence in Criminal Proceedings: Guidance for Vulnerable or Intimidated Witnesses, including Children* (99) is a comprehensive package of guidance covering arrangements for child witnesses involving sexual offences and the special measures that can be requested for them. These were due to be implemented in July 2002; however, it was a year or so late for all 78 Crown Courts and by the end of February 2004 only about half of the 200 Magistrates Courts were expected to have live links suites. Witness satisfaction is being monitored and an interim report went to ministers in October 2003. On the basis of the positive results in this report, a timetable for further implementation was announced in December 2003, which aimed to complete this process by the end of 2005. The final report of the research will be published in summer 2004. The provision for examination of a witness to be conducted through an intermediary approved by the courts to assist vulnerable witnesses with profound communication difficulties is being piloted. A register of 45 trained intermediaries has been established and the pilot went live in Merseyside in February 2004. The scheme will be extended to five other areas by late summer. The scheme will be evaluated and results available in 12–18 months time.

In 'It doesn't happen to disabled children' (23) the National Working Party on Child Protection and Disability said that support for disabled/vulnerable witnesses is variable throughout the UK; there have been delays in piloting initiatives and there are important limitations to these developments. And in its response to Every Child Matters (7), the Working Party welcomed the new measures but said that they do not address all the barriers experienced by disabled children.

Judges are to have one day's training before taking a case with child witnesses. This is not mandatory. Young children are thought to 'present a challenge'.

Tink Palmer, Barnardo's, October 2003, said there are still a number of issues to be resolved about who can support the child at different stages of the process. The Bar is now less adversarial although there is a lack of consistency and there are still exceptions. What is needed is far greater understanding of child development and how children of different ages can tell their stories.

Guidance on pre-trial therapy, which is couched in terms of therapy being a right for the child, has helped a lot since implementation but it is not widely used. The Guidance recommends that relevant agencies in each CPS area draw up a protocol for pre-trial therapy. Although this provision has been available since February 2001,

there is no national overview of how it has been implemented. There needs to be an evaluation of the extent to which protocols have been put in place and any outstanding issues addressed.

The intention to improve the arrangements for child witnesses was reaffirmed in Every Child Matters (7) which says 'the Government is taking a range of measures to protect children and young people who suffer as victims: support for young victims and witnesses going through the criminal justice system, including the early assessment of their needs and the provision of support and information, as well as improvements in the provision of special measures, such as separate entrances to court buildings and facilities for giving evidence via video link'.

Analysis

There has been a good deal of work to improve arrangements for child witnesses, including implementation of the remaining Pigot recommendations, although much remains to be done to ensure the arrangements in Government guidance are properly resourced and implemented in all areas. The delay in implementation is unfortunate and leads to an uneven application of justice and reduction of stress for the children and young people involved. Particular attention should be given to arrangements for disabled and very young children. Criminal justice and disabled children will be discussed in our companion report Safeguards for Vulnerable Children.

More training on child development should be provided in the criminal justice system.

Work is still needed to improve the judiciary's understanding about child development and how children of different ages can be expected to recount their stories. There should be more than one day's training on this and it should be mandatory, with judges not being eligible to hear cases involving child witnesses unless they have received this. There should also be more support and guidance for non-abusive carers of children who are witnesses – on how to handle disclosures, etc.

It would help if all those involved in the child protection system were to receive training to provide them with the skills needed to deal with all stages of the process, including giving evidence in court.

The Home Office should ensure the new arrangements for vulnerable witnesses are better resourced to ensure that they are fully and consistently implemented in all areas.

The new arrangements both for vulnerable witnesses *and* for pre-trial therapy need to be monitored and evaluated so that lessons are learned and further improvements made in the light of experience. There are still a number of issues that need to be resolved around who can support the child at different stages of the process. It is argued that an intermediary who interviews a child with the police in the video interview should not then support the child in court. This is extremely unhelpful as what the child needs is consistency. There needs to be a clear rationale which is open to discussion.

Recommendation

30 The Home Office should commission research to establish the best methods of dealing with child witnesses. This will inform debate and policy making so that fewer children are harmed by the process of giving evidence and more perpetrators can be brought to justice. Particular attention should be given to arrangements in relation to very young children and those who are disabled.

10.2 Prosecuting sex offenders

The severance of cases should only be allowed if requested by the prosecution.

The Review recommends a proposal for modifying the balance of probability and suggests that the Home Office investigate it further.

Information should be kept, monitored and published on charges and their outcomes in relation to offences against children.

Government response
- Not right to change standard of proof in one type of case where witness happened to be a child. Might breach obligations under Article 6 of ECHR.

- Law Commission reviewing the admissibility of evidence of previous misconduct – due to report early 1999.

- Government to consider the wider prosecution issues in the light of research.

Government action
- In January 1999 the Government commissioned a national review of sex offences in England and Wales – to review sex offences and 'provide coherent and clear sex offences which protect individuals, particularly children and the more vulnerable, from abuse and exploitation; enable abusers to be appropriately punished and be fair and non-discriminatory in accordance with the ECHRA 1998'.

- Recommendations were published in *Setting the Boundaries* (93) in July 2000.

What happened
Protecting the Public (15) sets out proposals for new offences against children as follows.

- Adult sexual activity with a child – where adult is over 18 and child under 16. Ten years maximum where no contact and 14 years where contact.

- Sexual activity between minors – 5 years maximum.

- Sexual grooming – maximum 5 years.

- Familial sexual abuse of a child – wide definition of family, including fostering and quasi-marital relationships – maximum 14 years.

- Abuse of a position of trust – prohibits sexual activity between those over 18 who are looking after children under 18 in a range of settings, including prisons – maximum 5 years.

And three new offences aimed at protecting vulnerable people:

- sexual activity with a person who did not, by reason of learning disability or mental disorder at that time, have the capacity to consent – maximum life

- obtaining sexual activity by inducement, threat or deception with a person who has a learning disability or mental disorder – maximum life

- breach of a relationship of care – maximum 7 years.

In relation to the admissibility of evidence of previous misconduct, the White Paper, *Justice for All* (100) proposes judges should decide on the relevance of previous convictions, or acquittals, and the court be allowed to know if they are considered relevant unless it would have 'a disproportionate effect'. Safeguards would be set out in legislation. Examples given include a GP accused of assaulting a patient who had been accused and acquitted on two previous occasions.

On 15 October 2002, the *Independent* reported that the Law Commission of England and Wales had proposed sex offenders be tried a second time for any linked offences to stop them escaping full punishment for their crimes. This follows a change of the law in 1997 which stopped judges taking account of related criminal activity not proven in court. Ministers will consider the proposal that a defendant could be sent before a judge to be tried on all other related offences. It recommended a two-stage trial 'where there are allegations of "repetitious offending"'. The first stage would take place before a judge and jury in the normal way, if convicted on one or more counts there would be a second stage in which the defendant would be tried by a judge alone.

Whilst there has been much Government action to strengthen arrangements for dealing with sex offenders, Barnardo's estimate at the Stop it Now! conference, March 2003, was that if children do tell and are heard, only 5 per cent of disclosures will result in convictions.

As far as the effectiveness of the criminal justice service in bringing prosecutions against perpetrators of abuse against children is concerned, the picture is not at all encouraging. There has continued to be a steep rise in recorded offences and a reduction in the proportion of convictions. Figures provided by the Home Office show that, since *People Like Us* (1):

- the percentage of convictions of gross indecency has more than halved (from 42 per cent to 19 per cent) whilst recorded offences with children have more than doubled between 1985 and 2001

- convictions for indecent assault on a female have reduced from 19 per cent to 11 per cent

- and, whilst there has been more than a fourfold increase in recorded offences of rape, convictions have dropped from 23 per cent to less than 7 per cent.

There has been little change between 1996 and 2000 in the percentage of convictions for rape where the victim was under 16, and indecent assault on a male but the percentage has fallen for indecent assault on a female, from 66 per cent to 60 per cent.

The Home Office researched the low and falling rate of conviction in rape cases (*A Question of evidence? Investigating and prosecuting rape in the 1990s* (101)). Of 500 incidents studied, only 6 per cent of the cases originally recorded by the police as rape resulted in convictions for rape. Those involving particularly young or particularly old complainants were most likely to be proceeded with.

There is countervailing pressure to making the criminal justice system more effective in securing convictions. Some feel innocent people are being convicted. An organisation – Falsely Accused Carers and Teachers – has been established which objects to the way in which police have handled allegations of institutional abuse. In November 2002, *Community Care* reported that in the past five years 34 of the 43 police forces in England and Wales have been involved in investigations of historical abuse in children's homes and other institutions. But between 1997 and 2000 the Crown Prosecution Service rejected 79 per cent of cases of institutional abuse referred by the police. A High Court libel ruling cited poor investigative methods in clearing two former nursery nurses of allegations of sexual abuse made by an independent review team. The Home Affairs Committee looked into this and produced the report – *The Conduct of Investigations into Past Cases of Abuse in Children's Homes. Fourth Report of Session 2001–2002* (102). The Committee rejected a ban on 'trawling' but recommendations urge greater care in methods of 'trawling' for evidence, taking witness statements, etc.

In January 2004 a review of 120 cases of historical abuse that had led to convictions was announced and one former care worker was released on appeal.

The Home Affairs Select Committee report (102) reaches a different view on 'similar fact evidence' and severance of cases to *People Like Us* (1). It recommends 'that the law of similar fact evidence is reformed to require a "striking similarity" in historical child abuse cases. We suggest that the law of severance is also reformed, to introduce a presumption in favour of severance in cases where the similar allegations are inadmissible on a similar fact basis'. On severance it said 'In multi-complainant cases, the defendant may also apply for the indictment to be severed, so that each allegation can be tried separately. We are informed, however, that the law of severance has developed along similar lines to the law on similar fact evidence. Just as it has become easier for the prosecution to admit similar allegations as evidence in one trial, we understand that it has become more difficult for the defendant successfully to apply to sever the allegations into separate trials'.

Analysis

The changes in the law concerning sexual offences against children in the Sexual Offences Act 2003 are welcome and it is hoped that they will be implemented effectively and lead to more convictions of abusers.

We reiterate support for the current arrangements on the severance of cases which are in line with *People Like Us* (1) recommendations and oppose the recommendations of the Home Affairs Committee on severance and similar fact evidence.

It is clear from the extremely low rate of convictions for child sexual abuse that there has been no progress in bringing perpetrators to justice. This allows perpetrators to continue abusing children and undermines efforts to prevent them obtaining work with children.

It is certainly a matter of great concern for people to be wrongly accused of abuse and suffer considerable disruption to their career and personal life while this is investigated and proceedings brought, but it is essential that all allegations are thoroughly investigated. Whilst only a small fraction of cases result in a conviction this is most unlikely to be because a majority of cases are malicious or false. It is undoubtedly because of a combination of factors including:

- the very private nature of sexual abuse, with invariably no other witnesses

- the word of a child against an adult

- the additional difficulties where the child is very young, or has communication difficulties or has a learning disability

- the high burden of proof in criminal cases – of beyond reasonable doubt – which is extremely difficult to achieve in these circumstances.

It seems that Government has done a great deal in this field, including the following.

- The Youth Justice and Criminal Evidence Act 1999 (enables range of measures to be made available to assist child witnesses under 17 years).

- Practice guidance on provision of therapy for child witnesses prior to a criminal trial.

- *Justice for All* (100) proposal that judges should decide on the relevance of previous convictions or acquittals.

- A national review of sex offences in England and Wales to 'provide coherent and clear sex offences which protect individuals, particularly children and the more vulnerable, from abuse and exploitation; enables abusers to be appropriately punished and be fair and non-discriminatory in accordance with the ECHRA 1998'. Recommendations were set out in the consultation paper *Setting the Boundaries* (93).

- *Achieving Best Evidence: Guidance for Vulnerable or Intimidated Witnesses, including children* (99) and Home Office Circular 06/ 2002 on its implementation.

- *Protecting the Public* (15) set out the action taken to build on and improve the arrangements to protect the public from sex offenders, including funding the new VISOR database (violent and sex offender register); new offences against children and three new offences to protect vulnerable people.

- The Sex Offences Act 2003.

There has, thus, been good progress in improving the legislation and guidance in this area. Progress had been made, although there is still a lot more to be done.

Whilst this looks good on paper, it is less clear what the practical effect has been. In some areas people have been more effective in ensuring that the new arrangements are in place than in others.

It appears that:

- the system is no better at bringing abusers to justice, securing convictions and deterring offenders

- there seems to be no evidence as yet that the system is any better in protecting the very vulnerable – although implementation of the *Vulnerable Witness* (98) guidance may help to bring more cases to court in due course

- whilst some progress has been made in making court processes less traumatic for children, implementation of the new arrangements is uneven and under-resourced

- those involved in the criminal justice system, particularly judges, need to have greater understanding of child development.

Recommendations

31 The Home Office should commission research to find out why so many allegations of offences against children are not pursued with/have a low rate of conviction and to suggest how conviction rates can be improved. The age and any disabilities the child has should be covered in the analysis.

32 The Home office should break down statistics on the age of offenders by sex as well as age so that any trend in the conviction of females for sexual offences can be monitored.

References

1   Utting, Sir William (1997) *People Like Us: The Report of the Review of Safeguards for Children Living Away from Home.* London: The Stationery Office

2   *The Government's Response to the Children's Safeguards Review* (November 1998). Cm 4105. London: The Stationery Office

3   Department of Health (1998) *Modernising Social Services.* London: Department of Health

4   Department of Health (2002) *Safeguarding Children: A Joint Chief Inspectors' Report on Arrangements to Safeguard Children.* London: Department of Health

5   Welsh Office (1999) *Building for the Future: A White Paper for Wales.* Cardiff: National Assembly for Wales

6   Department of Health (2001) *Shifting the Balance of Power within the NHS: Securing Delivery.* London: Department of Health

7   Department for Education and Skills (2003) *Every Child Matters.* Cm 5860. London: The Stationery Office

8   National Assembly for Wales (2000) *Children and Young People: A Framework for Partnership Consultation Document.* Cardiff: Welsh Assembly Government

9   Welsh Assembly Government (2004) *Children and Young People: Rights to Action.* Cardiff: Welsh Assembly Government

10   Department of Health (2003) *National Service Framework for Children: Standard for Hospital Services.* London: Department of Health

11   Department of Health (1992) *Choosing with Care – The Report of the Committee of Inquiry into the Selection, Development and Management of Staff in Children's Homes.* London: The Stationery Office

12   Department of Health (2003) *What to Do if You're Worried a Child Is Being Abused.* London: Department of Health. HSC 2003/7: LAC (2003)11

13   Department of Health (2003) *Getting the Right Start: National Service Framework for Children: Emerging Findings.* London: Department of Health

14   Her Majesty's Inspector of Probation (2003) *Safeguarding Children: Findings on the National Probation Service Role from Three Inspection Reports.* London: Home Office

15   Home Office (2002) *Protecting the Public: Strengthening Protection against Sex Offenders and Reforming the Law on Sex Offences.* Cm5668. London: The Stationery Office

16   Lord Laming (2003) *The Victoria Climbie Report.* Cm 5730. London: The Stationery Office

17   Department for Education and Skills, Department of Health, Home Office (2003) *Keeping Children Safe: The Government's Response to The Victoria Climbie Inquiry Report and the Joint Inspectors' Report Safeguarding Children.* Cm 5861. London: The Stationery Office

18   Department of Health (2000) *Lost in Care, Report of the tribunal of inquiry into the abuse of children in care in the former county council areas of Gwynedd and Clwyd since 1974.* London: HC Sessions 1999–00 201

19   National Care Standards Commission (2003) *The Advisory Report Proposing Changes to Regulations and National Minimum Standards.* Newcastle: National Care Standards Commission

20   Timms, Judith E., Thorburn, June (2003) *Your Shout! A Survey of the Views of 706 Children and Young People in the Public Care.* London: NSPCC

21 NSPCC (2003) *NSPCC Review of Legislation Relating to Children in Family Proceedings: Consultation Draft*, London: NSPCC

22 Department of Health (1995) *Looking after Children: Good Parenting Good Outcomes. Training Guide*. London: The Stationery Office

23 NSPCC (2003) *'It doesn't happen to disabled children' – Child Protection and Disabled Children: Report of the National Working Group on Child Protection and Disability*. London: NSPCC

24 Department of Health (2002) *Modern Social Services: A Commitment to Reform. The 11th Annual Report of the Chief Inspector of Social Services 2001–2002*. London: Department of Health

25 Abbott, David, Morris, Jenny, Ward, Linda (2001) *The best place to be? Policy, practice and the experiences of residential school placements for disabled children*. York: Joseph Rowntree Foundation

26 Department of Health (2002) *Delivering Quality Children's Services: Inspection of Children's Services*. London: Department of Health CI (2002) 19

27 Social Exclusion Unit (2002) *A Better Education for Children in Care*. London: Social Exclusion Unit

28 Department of Health (2001) *Transforming Children's Services: An Evaluation of Local Responses to the Quality Protects Programme Year 3*. London: Department of Health

29 Department for Education and Skills (2003) *The Children Act Report 2002*. London: Department for Education and Skills

30 The Roberts Centre (2002) *A Review of the Children (Leaving Care) Act 2000: A Report of a Seminar on 26 November 2002*. London

31 Department of Health (2000) *The Children Act Report 1995–1999*. London: Department of Health

32 Department of Health (2001) *Valuing People: A New Strategy for Learning Disability for the 21st Century*. Cm 5086. London: The Stationery Office

33 Department of Health (2000) *Learning the Lessons: The Government's Response to Lost in Care: The Report of the Tribunal of Inquiry into the abuse of children in care in the former County Council areas of Gwynedd and Clwyd since 1974*. Cm 4776. The Stationery Office

34 Department of Health (2000) *Assessing Children in Need and their Families: Practice Guidance*. London: Department of Health

35 Department of Health (2000) *The Children Act Report 2000*. London: Department of Health

36 Department of Health (2001) *The Children Act Report 2001*. London: Department of Health

37 Department of Health (2003) *Modern Social Services – A Commitment to the Future: The 12th Annual Report of the Chief Inspector of Social Services 2002–2003*. London: Social Services Inspectorate

38 Department for Education and Skills, Department of Health (2004) *Disabled Children in Residential Placements*. Quality Protects Website

39 Department for Education and Skills (2001) *Special Educational Needs: Code of Practice*. DfES Publications

40 National Assembly for Wales (2002) *Special Educational Needs: Code of Practice*. Cardiff: Welsh Assembly Government

41 Stalker, Kirsten, Carpenter, John, Phillips, Rena, Connors, Clare, MacDonald, Charlotte, Eyre, Janet with Noyes, Jane, Chaplin, Stephen, Place, Michael (2003) *Care and Treatment? Supporting Children with Complex Needs in Healthcare Settings.* Brighton: Pavilion Publishing

42 Office for Standards in Education (1999) *Effective Education for Pupils with Emotional and Behavioural Difficulties, Principles into Practice Series.* London: Office of Her Majesty's Inspectorate of Schools

43 Department of Health (2000) *Framework for the Assessment of Children in Need and their Families.* London: Department of Health

44 Welsh Assembly Government (2002) *Too Serious a Thing: The Review of Safeguards for Children and Young People Treated and Cared for by the NHS in Wales. The Carlile Review.* Cardiff: Welsh Assembly Government

45 Daniels, Harry and Cole, Ted (2002) *The development of provision for young people with emotional and behavioural difficulties: an activity analysis, Oxford Review of Education,* Vol. 28, Nos 2 and 3, pp. 311–29. Oxford: Carfax Publishing

46 Cole, Ted, Daniels, Harry and Visser, John (2003) *Patterns of provision for pupils with behavioural difficulties in England: a study of government statistics and behaviour support plan data, Oxford Review of Education,* Vol. 29, No. 2, pp. 187–205. Oxford: Carfax Publishing

47 Department for Education and Skills (2004) *Removing Barriers to Achievement: The Government's Strategy for SEN.* London: Department for Education and Skills

48 Kidscape (2000) *Protecting your children, Keeping young children safe.* London: Kidscape

49 Home Office (2000) *Feeling Happy Feeling Safe: A Safety Guide for Young Children.* London: Home Office

50 United Nations (2002) *The Report of the 31st Session of the Committee on the Rights of the Child.* United Nations

51 Pearce, Jenny with Williams, Mary and Galvin, Cristina (2002) *It's someone taking a part of you: A study on young women and sexual exploitation.* School of Social Sciences: Middlesex University

52 Social Exclusion Unit (2002) *Young Runaways.* London: Social Exclusion Unit

53 The Children's Society (1999) *Still Running.* London: The Children's Society

54 Department of Health (1999) *Children Missing from Care and from Home – A Guide to Good Practice.* London: Department of Health

55 The Children's Society (2004) *Thrown Away.* London: The Children's Society

56 Welsh Assembly Government (2002) *Annual Report and Accounts of the Children's Commissioner for Wales.* Cardiff: Welsh Assembly Government

57 NCH (2002) *Factfile 2002–03: Facts and Figures about Children in the UK.* London: NCH

58 Department of Health (2001) *Developing Quality to Protect Children – Inspection of Children's Services.* London: Social Services Inspectorate

59 National Care Standards Commission (2003) *Children's Views on Complaints and Advocacy: Report of the Children's Rights Director.* Newcastle: National Care Standards Commission

60 Children's Rights Alliance (2002) *State of Children's Rights in England: A Report on the Implementation of the Convention on the Rights of the Child in England.* London: The Children's Rights Alliance for England

61 Children's Rights Alliance (2002) *Rethinking Child Imprisonment: A Report on Young Offender Institutions*. London: Children's Rights Alliance for England

62 Department of Health (2002) *Improvement, Expansion and Reform: The Next 3 Years Priorities and Planning Framework 2003–2006*. London: Department of Health

63 Department of Health, Home Office, National Assembly for Wales, Scottish Executive, Northern Ireland Office (2001) *National Plan for Safeguarding Children from Commercial Sexual Exploitation*. London: Department of Health

64 Welsh Assembly Government (2000) *Practice Guide to Investigate Allegations of Abuse against a Professional or Carer in relation to Children Looked After*. Cardiff: Welsh Assembly Government

65 Department of Health (2000) *Listening to People: A Consultation on Improving Social Services Complaints Procedures*. London: Department of Health

66 House of Commons (1998) *Second Report of the Health Select Committee: Children Looked After by Local Authorities*. London: HC 391-1

67 Training Organisation for Personal Social Services (TOPSS) UK Partnership (2003) *National Occupational Standards for Managers in Residential Child Care*. Leeds: TOPSS

68 Department of Health (1999) *Code of Practice on the Recruitment, Assessment, Approval, Training, Management and Support of Foster Carers*. London: Department of Health

69 Department of Health, Home Office, Department for Education and Employment [now Department for Education and Skills] (1999) *Working Together to Safeguard Children: A Guide to Inter-agency Working to Safeguard and Promote the Welfare of Children*. London: Department of Health

70 Department of Health (2002) *By Private Arrangement: Inspection of Arrangements for Supervising Children in Private Foster Care*. London: Department of Health

71 Social Care Institute of Excellence (2003) *Effectiveness of Childminding Registration and its Implications for Private Fostering*. London: Social Care Institute of Excellence

72 National Care Standards Commission (2003) *Protecting People Improving Lives: Annual Report and Accounts 2003*. Newcastle: National Care Standards Commission

73 Office for Standards in Education (2001) *Inspecting Independent Schools: A Framework for use by Her Majesty's Inspectors of Schools*. London: Office of Her Majesty's Chief Inspector of Schools

74 Office for Standards in Education (2003) *Handbook for Inspecting Special Schools and Pupil Referral Units*. London: Office of Her Majesty's Inspectorate of Schools

75 Office for Standards in Education (2003) *Annual Report of Her Majesty's Chief Inspector of Schools: Standards and Quality in Education 2001/02*. London: Office of Her Majesty's Inspectorate of Schools

76 Independent Schools Inspectorate (2001) *All Round Education in ISC [Independent Schools Council] Schools – A Digest of Reports 2000–1*. London

77 Office for Standards in Education (2000, 2002, 2003) *Independent Schools Council Inspections 1999, 2000/01, 2001/02*. London: Office of Her Majesty's Inspectorate of Schools

78 Holgate, Tim (2000) *Choosing a Boarding School: A Guide for Parents*. London: Boarding Schools Association

79 Morris, Jenny (2003) *The Right Place?* York: Joseph Rowntree Foundation

80 Department for Education and Employment (2000) *Proposals for the Placement of Children with Statements of SEN in Independent Schools.* London: Department for Education and Skills

81 Department for Education and Skills (2003) *The Report of the Special Schools Working Group.* London: Department for Education and Skills

82 Mr Justice Munby (2002) *Judgment by Mr Justice Munby on the application from the Howard League for Penal Reform 27 November 2002.* Neutral Citation Number [2002] EWHC 2497 (Admin)

83 Home Office (1997) *Young Prisoners: A Thematic Review by Her Majesty's Chief Inspector of Prisons for England and Wales.* London: Home Office

84 Her Majesty's Prison Service and Youth Justice Board (2003) *Child Protection and Safeguards Review: A Review of Safeguards Arrangements for under-18s within the Prison Service Juvenile Estate.* London: Her Majesty's Prison Service and Youth Justice Board

85 Department of Health (1999) *Directions Governing Visits by Children to Special Hospitals (Ashworth, Broadmoor and Rampton).* London: Department of Health HSC 199/160, LAC (99) 23

86 Henricson, Clem (2003) *Government and Parenting: Is There a Case for a Parents' Code?* London: National Family and Parenting Institute

87 Purves, Libby (2002) *Parenting the Boarder.* London: Boarding Schools Association

88 NCH (2003) *Protecting Children from Risk: NCH's View.* London: NCH

89 Lovell, Elizabeth (2002) *'I think I might need some more help with this problem —'. Responding to Children and Young People Who Display Sexually Harmful Behaviour.* London: NSPCC

90 Carr, John (2004) *Child Abuse, Child Pornography and the Internet.* London: NCH

91 Palmer, Tink and Stacey, Lisa. *Just One Click. Sexual Abuse of Children and Young People through the Internet and Mobile Phone Technology.* London: Barnardo's

92 Department of Health, Home Office, Department for Education and Employment [now Department for Education and Skills], National Assembly for Wales (2000) *Safeguarding Children involved in Prostitution: Supplementary Guidance to Working Together to Safeguard Children.* London: Department of Health

93 Home Office (2000) *Setting the Boundaries: A Consultation Paper.* London: Home Office

94 Social Services Inspectorate (2002) *Excellence not Excuses: Inspection of Services for Ethnic Minority Children and Families.* London: Department of Health

95 Quality Protects (2000) *Towards Safer Care: A Councillor's Briefing Pack.* London: Department of Health

96 Social Services Inspectorate (2002) *Fostering for the Future: An Inspection of Foster Care Services.* London: Department of Health

97 Home Office and Department of Health (2002) *Complex Child Abuse Investigations: Inter-agency Issues – Guidance.* London: Department of Health

98 Department of Health (2002) *Learning from Past Experience: A Review of Serious Case Reviews.* London: Department of Health

99 Home Office, Lord Chancellor's Department, Crown Prosecution Service, Department of Health, National Assembly for Wales (2002) *Achieving Best Evidence in Criminal Proceedings: Guidance for Vulnerable Witnesses or Intimidated Witnesses including Children.* London: Home Office

100 The Secretary of State for the Home
Department, the Lord Chancellor, the Attorney
General (2002) *Justice for All*. Cm 5563. London:
The Stationery Office

101 Harris, Jessica and Grace, Sharon (1999) *A
Question of Evidence? Investigating and
Prosecuting Rape in the 1990s*. London: Home
Office Research Study No. 196

102 House of Commons Home Affairs Select
Committee (2002) *The Conduct of Investigations
into Past Cases of Abuse in Children's Homes.
Fourth Report of Session 2001–2002*. London

Appendix 1

Action on recommendations in *People Like Us* not covered in the report

Recommendation	Government response	Action/current position
3.38 Authorities and agencies should review their policies on family placements to ensure they take account of the dangers of peer abuse	Will be part of Quality Protects (QP) and National Standards and Code of Practice on foster care	Not covered in the National Standards. Government has not required authorities and agencies to review their policies on family placements
3.42 Authorities should carry out an audit of their long-standing carers	Should be part of regular reviews and concerns addressed in annual reviews. Will be covered in National Standards for Foster Care	Not covered in the National Standards. Government has not required authorities and agencies to undertake an audit of long-standing foster carers. Some local authorities have asked the Fostering Network for help with the audit. It is likely, therefore that the situation varies in different localities
3.47 LAs should assess any special or additional needs for the support of single foster parents and children placed with them and consider whether to provide the child with an Independent Visitor	Should already be considered. QP should ensure that all children entitled to an Independent Visitor receive them. National Standards and Code of Practice will address	The Fostering Network is not aware of special support being provided for single carers
3.48 Children in foster care should be given information to help them protect themselves. Social workers should arrange this and discuss it with the child on his/her own	Government to work with other agencies (including schools and the voluntary sector) to provide better information and ensuring they know how to contact outside help to raise concerns	National Standards say 'The child's social worker ensures that she or he is taught appropriate self-care and self-protection skills'
3.49 Children should be given age-appropriate sex education and have access to help and counselling	As 3.48	Code of Practice (68) says 'The child's social worker should agree with the carer how age-appropriate sex and relationship education should be provided. This should be set in the wider context of independence, self-care/protection skills and relationships. He or she should also be responsible for providing information on appropriate behaviour, in relation to both themselves and others'

(Continued)

Recommendation	Government response	Action/current position
4.52-53 DH and DfEE statistics on number of schools also required to register as children's homes are markedly different. The two departments should look into the effect of the Children Act 1989 definition and take steps to make the regulatory framework simpler and more effective	Current legislation on definition of schools subject to dual registration as children's homes to be reviewed, simplified and clarified. More detail to be announced in 1999	The Care Standards Act requires all schools which accommodate or arrange accommodation for any child for more than 295 days a year, or intends to do so, to register with the NCSC as a children's home
5.19 A number of babies live in prison. Child protection procedures are needed in two prisons that lack them	Agreed. All the mother and baby units in women's prisons now have written child protection procedures in place	In 2004 there are four mother and baby units (MBU) operating and two new ones due to open in a few months. These will raise the number of places for a child and its mother to 90. In addition, the new prisons at Ashford and Peterborough will also have units. They are due to open in June 2004 and early in 2005, respectively

The day to day management of the MBUs is for the individual prisons but there is now a central operational policy control which monitors the national position on places and also assesses and, if need be, manages difficult cases, particularly any that may involve a separation. The central policy control also advises on the appropriate standards expected. This includes the child protection policies for the establishments which are currently being reviewed |
| 7.9 The Review believes that SSDs must give full weight to the child protection aspects of investigations when abuse is alleged in residential settings and foster care | To be covered in Code of Practice on foster care and new 'Working Together' guidance, Spring 1999. WO Practice guide being produced by end 1998 | Leaflet prepared by the HO *et al. Caring for young people and the vulnerable? Guidance for preventing abuse of trust* sets out guidance on model principles which recommends that all organisations involved with caring for young people or |

(Continued)

Recommendation	Government response	Action/current position
		vulnerable adults should have codes of conduct to protect against sexual activity within relationships of trust
		BAAF: Most local authorities now have clear procedures for dealing with allegations of abuse in foster care, and it is our impression that these are working satisfactorily. Many authorities, recognising the dilemmas for the support worker of the carer, have made arrangements for independent support of carers whilst allegations are being investigated. Agencies also recognise that automatically to move a child from an established placement in such circumstances can itself be abusive
8.26 There should be greater interchange between disability and child protection services and clarity about who is responsible for child protection procedures when a child is disabled	ACPCs should ensure local inter-agency child protection policies and procedures address needs of children with disabilities. Responsibility of each agency to follow own agreed procedures	*Working Together* (69) deals with role of ACPC in safeguarding disabled children
10.6 The right to corporal punishment should be removed from those boarding schools that still use it	Legislation to do so comes into force in September 1999	Done
10.17 A new organisation for children who are or have been in care is needed which should be supported from statutory as well as charitable sources	First Key to take forward project to establish a group to be funded from Section 64 over next three years WO supports Voices from Care	DH funded A National Voice for three years to March 2003 with the organisation mentored by First Key. Grant renewed in 2003 with the Prince's Trust as host, after First Key closed in June 2003 Voices From Care continues to be core funded by the Welsh Assembly Government

(Continued)

Recommendation	Government response	Action/current position
10.30 Training materials, such as those produced by Kidscape, should be used as soon as possible to introduce children living way from home to what is 'appropriate' physical and sexual conduct	Government to work with other agencies on this and to ensure they know who to contact to raise concerns	Kidscape material recommended in Code of Practice
11.28 DH, DfEE and HO should consider commissioning a study which surveys issues of control across all settings for which these departments have policy responsibility with a view to publishing a handbook of guidance and standards for managers and practitioners	Departments considering how to take this forward in light of Comprehensive Spending Review outcome and current guidance and practice	*Learning the Lessons* (33) said 'We recognise that there is currently no accredited method of restraint and that there is a need for further guidance in this area. Under the Care Standards Bill there is a power to make regulations the DfEE are currently conducting a consultation exercise on restraint in special schools'
		The YJB is supporting a project by the Children's Residential Care Unit at NCB to highlight the range of practice in the use of control, restraint and physical intervention with children living away from home and the issues for both carers and children. It will report on the particular dilemmas within the secure estate
16.19 The LGA should undertake, together with BASW, a study of the role of the field social worker in relation to children looked after	Government to work with LGA and BASW who have begun a study, with view to guidance	BASW report published 2003. *Be my social worker: the role of the child's social worker:* Keith Bilton, Venture Press Publishing
16.26 The Review supports the need for a Strategic Plan in Wales for services for children in need	Will be developed in wider context of children's strategy	National Assembly for Wales says this has been achieved through a range of actions including: Children First objectives and targets for improving services and outcomes for children in need in National Priorities Guidance for Health and Social Services. Framework for

(Continued)

Recommendation	Government response	Action/current position
		Assessment of Children in Need (43) (2001). New national collection of expenditure returns for children and families services. Councillors given information on the performance of their own and other authorities. Extra resources through specific grant and Revenue Support Grant Settlement for 2000–01
17.41 The Government should examine the need to strengthen the privilege of information communicated to registering authorities about the people and places they are responsible for registering	Thought being given to how to do this	*Safeguarding Children* (4) said 'All areas were struggling to respond to unconvicted people who present a high risk of harm to the public, including children ... This is currently being addressed by the Home Office Dangerous Offender Steering Group'
18.11 In complex [child protection] cases, where practicable, investigations should be carried out by staff who have specialised in such work and are not employed by the authority under investigation	Revised *'Working Together'* to set out principles for investigating complicated child abuse, whatever the setting. The issue of specialist teams to be considered in that context and response to this recommendation made then	Welsh Assembly – Guidance on conduct of abuse investigations out to consultation July 2002. Proposes establishment of specialist joint police/social services team
18.21 Telephone helplines and counselling should be accessible to children living away from home, and should receive financial support from statutory and charitable sources	A number of helplines already funded, including ChildLine's dedicated helpline for Children in Care	In *State of Children's Rights in England* (60), CRAE says access to private telephones and to private mail are seriously restricted in juvenile justice settings, and there is need for national research on progress in ensuring the privacy rights of disabled children in residential care
19.6 Departments of State should respond to the recommendations of reports they have commissioned	Fully responding to this report and intend to respond to others	Full response in *Government's Response to the Children's Safeguards Review* (2) and to other major reports such as *Lost in Care* (18)

Appendix 2

Bibliography

Audit Commission (2004) *Services for Disabled Children: A Review of Services for Disabled Children and their Families*. London: Audit Commission

Audit Commission (2004) *Youth Justice 2004. A Review of the Reformed Youth Justice System*. London: Audit Commission

Biehal, N. Mitchell, F. and Wade, J. (2003) *Lost from View: Missing Persons in the UK*. Bristol: Policy Press

Bilton, Keith (2003) *Be My Social Worker: The Role of the Child's Social Worker*. London: Venture Press Publishing

Boyd, Robert (1999–2000) *Running a School Boarding House: A Legal Guide for Housemasters and Housemistresses*. London: Boarding Schools Association

Department for Education and Employment and Department of Health (2000) *Education of Young People in Public Care: Guidance*. London: DfES

Department for Education and Employment and Department of Health (2001) *Education Protects: Implementing Joint Guidance on the Education of Children and Young People in Public Care*. London: DfES

Department of Health (1998) *Quality Protects Programme: Transforming Children's Services*. London: Department of Health LAC (98) 28

Department of Health (1999) *The Government's Objectives Children's for Social Services*. London: Department of Health

Department of Health (1999) *The Quality Protects Programme 2000/01: Transforming Children's Services*. London: Department of Health LAC (99) 33

Department of Health (1999) *Mapping Quality in Children's Services: An Evaluation of Local Responses to the Quality Protects Programme*. London: Department of Health

Department of Health (2000) *The Protection of Children Act 1999: A Practical Guide for All Organisations Working with Children*. London: Department of Health

Department of Health (2000) *The Quality Protects Programme: Transforming Children's Services 2000/01 – The District Council's Role*. London: Department of Health LAC (2000) 15

Department of Health (2000) *The Quality Protects Programme: Transforming Children's Services 2001–2002*. London: Department of Health LAC (2000) 22

Department of Health (2000) *Tracking Progress in Children's Services: An Evaluation of Local Responses to the Quality Protects Programme Year 2*. London: Department of Health

Department of Health (2001) *The Quality Protects Programme: Transforming Children's Services 2002–03*. London: Department of Health LAC (2001) 28

Department of Health (2001) *Child and Adolescent Mental Health Services – Everybody's Business: Strategy Document*. London: Department of Health

Department of Health (2001) *Guidance on the Education of Children Looked After by Local Authorities*. London: Department of Health

Department of Health (2001) *Children (Leaving Care) Act 2000: Guidance*. London: Department of Health

Department of Health (2002) *Friends and Family Care (Kinship Care) Current Policy Framework, Issues and Options – Discussion paper*. London: Department of Health

Department of Health (2003) *Guidance on Accommodating Children in Need and their Families*. London: Department of Health LAC (2003) 13

Department of Health, Department for Education and Skills (2002) *Guidance for Restrictive Physical Interventions: How to Provide Safe Service for People with Learning Disabilities and Autistic Spectrum Disorder*. London: Department of Health, Department for Education and Skills

Department of Health, Welsh Office (1999) *Mental Health Act 1983: Code of Practice*. London: Department of Health

Elliott, Michele (ed) (1997) *'What Survivors Tell Us'* in *Female Sexual Abuse of Children*. New York: The Guilford Press

HM Treasury (2002) *Children at Risk Cross-cutting Review*. London: HM Treasury

Heiney, Rose (2003) *Being a Boarder*. London: Boarding Schools Association

Hibbert, Pam (2002) *Voices and Choice: Young People Participating in Inspections. Learning from the Listening and Responding Component of SSI Inspections of LA Children's Services*. London: Save the Children, First Key, SSI, NCB, Barnardo's

Holgate, Tim (2001) *Good Practice in Boarding Schools*. London: Boarding Schools Association

Home Office (2003) *Youth Justice – The Next Steps. Companion Document to Every Child Matters*. London: Home Office

Home Office, Crown Prosecution Service, Department of Health (2001) *Provision of Therapy for Child Witnesses Prior to a Criminal Trial: Practice Guidance*. London: Home Office

Home Office, Crown Prosecution Service, Department of Health (2001) *Child Witnesses Pre-Trial Therapy: Practice Guidance*. London: Home Office

Howard League for Penal Reform (the) (2002) *Children in Prison. Barred Rights: An Independent Submission to the UN Committee on the Rights of the Child*. London: The Howard League of Penal Reform

Independent Schools Inspectorate (2001) *Report on the Performance of the ISI 2000–2001*. London: ISI

Local Government Association, NHS Confederation, Association of Directors of Social Services (2002) *Serving Children Well – A New Vision for Children's Services*. London: Local Government Association, The Chameleon Press Ltd

Lowe, Marian and Murch, Mervyn (2002) *The Plan for the Child. Adoption or Long-Term Fostering*. London: BAAF

Mainey, Amanda (2003) *Better Than You Think. Staff Morale, Qualifications and Retention in Residential Child Care*. London: National Children's Bureau

McGurk, Barry J., Forde, Robert and Barnes, Ann (2000) *Sexual Victimisation among 15–17-year-old Offenders in Prisons*. London: Home Office RDS Occasional Paper No. 65

Morris, Jenny (2000) *Having Someone Who Cares. Barriers to Change in the Public Care of Children*. York: Joseph Rowntree Foundation

Myhill, Andy and Allen, Jonathan (2002) *Rape and Sexual Assault of Women: The Extent and Nature of the Problem. Findings from the British Crime Survey*. London: Home Office Research Study 237

National Probation Directorate (2002) *The Treatment and Risk Management of Sexual Offenders in Custody and in the Community*. London: National Probation Directorate

Philpot, Terry (2001) *A Very Private Practice. An Investigation into Private Fostering*. London: BAAF

Polat, Filiz and Farrell, Peter (2002) 'What Was it Like for You? Former Pupils' Reflections on their Placement in a Residential School for Pupils with Emotional and Behavioural Difficulties'. *Emotional and Behavioural Difficulties*, Vol. 7, No. 2, ed Paul Cooper. London: Sage Publications

Sellick, Clive and Connolly, Jo (2001) *National Survey of Independent Fostering Agencies*. Norwich: University of East Anglia

Social Exclusion Unit (2002) *Reducing Re-offending by Ex-prisoners. Summary of SEU Report*. London: Social Exclusion Unit

Sullivan, Joe (2003) *Comparative study of demographic data relating to intra and extra-familial child sex abusers and professional perpetrators*, unpublished report, Lucy Faithfull Foundation

Welsh Assembly Government (2002) *A Statistical Focus on Children in Wales: Statistical Bulletin*. Cardiff: Welsh Assembly Government

Welsh Assembly Government (2003) *Response of the Welsh Assembly Government to the Annual Report of the Children's Commissioner for Wales 2001–2002*. Cardiff: Welsh Assembly Government

Who Cares Trust (2001) *In the Know – Quality Protects*. London: Department of Health

Appendix 3

Glossary

Bichard Inquiry	Inquiry under Sir Michael Bichard set up on 18 December 2003 by the Home Secretary to look into the way the police handled intelligence about Ian Huntley's past
Children's Services Grant	Ring-fenced monies awarded to local authorities for Quality Protects, Choice Protects, Adoption Support and Children Leaving Care
Children's Trusts	These can be set up under powers in the Health Act 1999. They bring together local authority education and children's social services, some children's health services and Connexions
Choice Protects	A review of fostering and placement services for looked after children set up in March 2002
DH Consultancy Index	List formerly maintained by DH of people considered unsuitable to work with children. Superseded by the PoCA list – see below
Integrated Children's System	Multi-agency and integrated approach to delivery of services to children and families announced in 2000 and now being piloted in four local council areas in England and Wales
List 99	List of people barred or restricted from working in schools, now maintained by the CRB
LSCBs	Local Safeguarding Children Boards. Subject to the Children Bill now going through Parliament receiving Royal Assent, these will replace ACPCs
National Minimum Standards	Documents issued by the NCSC (see below) to accompany statutory regulations governing regulation of children's homes, schools with boarding provision and fostering services
PoCA List	List set up under Protection of Children Act 1999 with the names of people considered unsuitable to work with children
Quality Protects	Programme launched in 1998 as part of the Government's response to *People Like Us* (1) to improve children's services especially for children in the public care
Stop it Now!	Campaign aimed at preventing child sexual abuse, led by the Lucy Faithfull Foundation
Sure Start	Government programme set up in 1998 to improve facilities for families with children aged under five living in disadvantaged areas

Appendix 4

Acronyms

ACPC	Area Child Protection Committee
ACPO	Association of Chief Police Officers
ADSS	Association of Directors of Social Services
AEGIS	Association for the Education and Guardianship of International Students
BAAF	British Association for Adoption and Fostering
BMA	British Medical Association
BSA	Boarding Schools Association
CAFCASS	Children and Family Court Advisory and Support Service
CDC	Council for Disabled Children
CAMHS	Child and Adolescent Mental Health Services
CHAI	Commission for Health Audit and Inspection – now called the Healthcare Commission
CHI	Commission for Health Inspection
CISS	Chief Inspector of Social Services
CPS	Crown Prosecution Service
CRAE	Children's Rights Alliance in England
CRB	Criminal Records Bureau
CRP	Crime Reduction Programme
CSCI	Commission for Social Care Inspection
CSIW	Care Standards Inspectorate for Wales
CYPU	Children and Young People's Unit
DfES	Department for Education and Skills
DH	Department of Health
DTO	Detention and Training Order
DWP	Department for Work and Pensions
ECHRA	European Convention on Human Rights Act – the Human Rights Act 1998
EBD	Emotional and behavioural difficulties
GSCC	General Social Care Council
HMC&E	Her Majesty's Customs and Excise
HMIP	Her Majesty's Inspectorate of Prisons
HMIC	Her Majesty's Inspectorate of Constabulary
HMICP	Her Majesty's Inspectorate of the Crown Prosecution Service
HO	Home Office
ICS	Integrated Children's System
IFAs	Independent fostering agencies
ISC	Independent Schools Council
ISI	Independent Schools Inspectorate
ISCIS	Independent Schools Council Information Service
LAC	Looked after children
LASCH	Local authority secure children's homes
LASSA	Local Authority Social Services Act 1970
LEA	Local Education Authority

LFF	Lucy Faithfull Foundation
LGA	Local Government Association
MAPs	Management Action Plans
MAPPA	Multi-agency Public Protection Arrangements
MAPPPs	Multi-agency Public Protection Panels
MOD	Ministry of Defence
NASS	National Association of Independent Schools and Non-maintained Special Schools
NCB	National Children's Bureau
NCSC	National Care Standards Commission
NPG	National Priorities Guidance
NPS	National Probation Service
NSF	National Service Framework
NVQ	National Vocational Qualification
OFSTED	Office for Standards in Education
PAF	Performance Assessment Framework
PAMs	Professions Ancillary to Medicine
PCT	Primary Care Trust
PLASC	Pupil Level Annual Schools Census
PoCA	Protection of Children Act
PQCCA	Post Qualifying Award in Child Care
PSO	Prison Service Order
SCE	Services children's education
SCIE	Social Care Institute of Excellence
SEN	Special educational needs
SEU	Social Exclusion Unit based in the Cabinet Office
SSDs	Social Services Departments
SSI	Social Services Inspectorate
TOPSS	Training Organisation for Personal Social Services
WLGA	Welsh Local Government Association
WO	Welsh Office
YJB	Youth Justice Board
YOIs	Young Offender Institutions
YOTs	Youth Offending Teams